PREFACE

Password is a series of multiple choice question books on business and accountancy topics. If you are studying for an examination, or would just like to test your knowledge on one of these topics, Password books have two special features which are designed to help you.

1 They contain about 300 multiple choice questions, with answers provided later in the book. You can get an objective idea of your strengths and weaknesses, and whether your standard is as high as you would like it to be.

2 We explain most solutions in some detail, to show why one answer is correct and the others are wrong. Our comments should help you to learn from any mistakes you have made, and to improve your understanding of the subject.

Objective testing is an increasingly popular method of examination. An answer is right or wrong, and there are no 'grey areas' or 'in-between answers' that are half-right or arguably correct. Multiple choice questions (MCQs) are the form of objective testing that is now most widely used. Professional bodies that have adopted MCQs for some examination papers include the Institute of Chartered Accountants in England and Wales, the Institute of Chartered Accountants of Scotland and the Chartered Institute of Management Accountants.

MCQs offer much more than exam practice, though. They test your knowledge and understanding. And they help with learning.

- The brevity of the questions, and having to select a correct answer from four choices (A, B, C or D), makes them convenient to use. You can do some on your journey to or from work or college on the train or the bus.

- We know from experience that many people like MCQs, find them fun and enjoy the opportunity to mark their own answers exactly.

- Being short, MCQs are able collectively to cover every aspect of a topic area. They make you realise what you know and what you don't.

If you're looking for the fun and challenge of self-testing, or preparing for an examination - not just a multiple choice exam - Password is designed to help you. You can check your own standard, monitor your progress, spot your own weaknesses, and learn things that you hadn't picked up from your text-book or study manual. Most important, Password books allow you to find out for yourself how good you are at a topic, and how much better you want to be.

Good luck!

Brian Coyle
May 1990

PASSWORD. MULTIPLE CHOICE

HOW TO USE THIS BOOK

The scope of financial management

Financial management is concerned with the management of the finances of an organisation.

More specifically, it is about

- setting financial objectives for the organisation. With companies, the main objective of the organisation is a financial one, and might be expressed as the aim of improving or maximising the wealth of ordinary shareholders

- trying to ensure that these financial objectives are achieved.

Business organisations need to invest funds in order to achieve a financial return, and the funds for investment have to be obtained from somewhere. Financial managers must therefore:

- help to identify worthwhile investments for achieving a financial return. Investments might be 'internal' or 'external': external investments might involve mergers and takeovers. Disinvestment (for example, demergers) will occasionally be appropriate

- ensure that funds are available to finance these investments, from a suitable source so as to achieve a desirable balance between long term funds and short term funds, and between debt capital and equity capital

- try to ensure that ordinary shareholders obtain the returns they expect, in the form of either dividends or capital gains.

Inter-related decisions in financial management

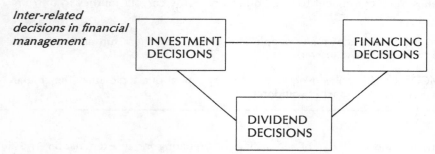

Risk management. Investments are risky, and investors in companies accept some risk to obtain a financial return. The size of the expected return is related to the degree of perceived risk. Financial management deals with

- achieving a suitable balance between risk and return, with both investment decisions and financing decisions (gearing levels)

- where possible, minimising risk for example by means of insurance, and treasury instruments such as forward exchange contracts for foreign exchange.

Cash and working capital. Financial management deals not just with long term investments and long term sources of funds, but also with the management of cash, other short-term assets and short term liabilities. Working capital should be kept to an efficient minimum, but without putting the liquidity (cash flows) of the business at risk.

Some companies are 'cash rich', and might hold cash not just for transactions purposes and precautionary purposes, but also for potential speculation (takeover bids for a cash consideration, etc). Large cash surpluses, even if temporary, should be invested for an optimum return.

The stock market. The study of financial management focuses mainly on public companies whose shares are quoted on a stock market. This is partly because the principles of the subject are most clearly evident through the workings of a free stock market, as well as because of the importance of public companies in business affairs.

Many of the principles of financial management, however, can be adapted and applied to private companies and businesses, and not-for-profit organisations such as government institutions.

The subjects covered in this book. The subjects covered in this book by multiple choice questions do not cover the *full* range of financial management. There are no questions on

● planning objectives and the business environment, or
● the public sector.

Performance measurement is covered in several chapters, with stock market ratios, working capital ratios and gearing analysis etc, but the complete interpretation of published reports and accounts is the subject of a separate book in the Password series.

If you are studying for a particular financial management syllabus or examination, the book will test your knowledge of the core elements that you will need to learn and that provide the essential bedrock for building up a more interpretative understanding of the subject. Check your syllabus, however, and do not attempt any questions dealing with topics that you do not need to know - for example, not all students need to learn Modigliani and Miller's theories of capital gearing, and not all students need to be able to *calculate* beta factors for the Capital Asset Pricing Model.

Aims of the book

This book is designed:

● to develop your knowledge of Financial Management through repeated practice on questions covering all areas of the subject. There are nearly 300 questions in this book.

● to enable you to assess your standard of knowledge or ability in Financial Management by providing an objective test with these questions

● to explain any errors you are making, by means of comments and solutions to the questions

● to help with your revision of the subject by means of short chapter notes and comments to some of the solutions

The multiple choice approach

A multiple choice question is in two parts.

- The *stem* sets out the problem or task to be solved. It may be in the form of a question, or it may be an unfinished statement which has to be completed.

- The *options* are the possible responses from which you must choose the one you believe to be correct. There is only one correct option (called the *key*); the other, incorrect, options are called *distractors*.

There are various ways in which you may be asked to indicate your chosen response. If you meet with MCQs in an examination, you should obviously read the instructions carefully. In this book, you will find that the options are identified by the letters A, B, C, D. To indicate your choice, draw a circle round the letter you have chosen.

The notes

In Section 1 of this book each chapter begins with brief notes which are designed to refresh your memory of the subject area and get you thinking along the right lines before you begin to tackle the questions.

The notes are *not* a substitute for a textbook: Password assumes that you are already broadly familiar with the topics covered in the chapter. Nor do they give you answers to all the questions.

- The notes are a *reminder* of the key points in each topic area. If your studies have left you feeling that you can't see the wood for the trees, the notes may help to bring the important issues into focus.

- They provide brief *guidance* on particularly knotty points or areas which often cause problems for students.

The questions

The questions are arranged roughly in the order of the key areas highlighted by the notes. But it is difficult, and undesirable, to keep topics completely separate: there's a great deal of overlapping.

The general principle has been for questions *on each topic* to get progressively harder. The result of this is that within a single chapter the level of difficulty will rise, and then fall back to begin rising again. So if you have trouble with two or three questions, don't assume that you have to give up on the whole chapter: there may be easier questions ahead!

Try to work through a whole chapter before turning to the solutions. If you refer to the marking schedule after each question you will find it almost impossible to avoid seeing the answer to the next question, and the value of the book will be lessened.

However, the length of each chapter is variable. Some are quite short, but others are very long. We have taken the view that there is no point in dividing up longer chapters into two just for the sake of making chapters shorter, and so some chapters contain about 40 questions (for example on the valuation of quoted securities). In these cases you might decide to tackle the questions in a chapter in several different sessions, over a period of time, and check your answers at the end of each session.

Finally, don't rush your answers. Distractors are exactly what their name suggests: they are meant to look plausible and distract you from the correct option. Unless you are absolutely certain you know the answer, look carefully at each option in turn before making your choice. You will need a calculator and a pen, and paper for rough workings would be helpful, although you could use the blank space on each page for any rough workings that you need to do.

The marking schedules

The marking schedules indicate the correct answer to each question and the number of marks available. You should add up the marks on all the questions you got right and compare your total with the maximum marks available.

At the foot of each marking schedule there is a rating, which is intended to be helpful in indicating the amount of work you still need to do on each topic. You'll need to use your discretion in interpreting your rating, though. The book may be used by a very wide range of readers, from non-accountancy college students and students of professional, business and accountancy courses, to qualified accounts personnel with years of practical experience. A mark of 10 out of 35 might be worryingly low for an experienced accountant or financial manager, while representing a very creditable achievement for someone at an earlier stage of his studies.

The comments

The answers to purely factual questions generally need no explanation, but for most questions there is a commentary or a numerical solution, usually set out in some detail.

These comments will frequently describe why a particular option is correct and (more commonly) set out the calculations leading to the correct answer. Distractors are usually chosen to illustrate common misconceptions, or plausible, but incorrect, lines of calculation. The comments will often highlight what is wrong about particular distractors and this should help in clarifying your ideas about topics that you may have misunderstood.

Conclusion

Password Financial Management is designed as an aid both to learning and to revision. It is not primarily aimed at those who are already expert in the subject. So don't expect to score 100%. And don't despair if your marks seem relatively low. Choosing the wrong answer to a question is not a failure, if by studying the solution and comments you learn something you did not know before. This is particularly relevant if you are using the book at an early stage in your studies, rather than in the final stages of revision.

And if you *do* score 100%? There are 14 other Password titles to get through...

x

SECTION 1
NOTES AND QUESTIONS

CHAPTER 1

THE FIRM'S INVESTMENT DECISIONS

This chapter covers the following topics:

- Discounted cash flow (DCF) and net present value (NPV)
- DCF and inflation
- DCF and taxation
- DCF: risk and uncertainty
- Capital rationing
- DCF and financing decisions
- Adjusted Present Value method of project evaluation (APV)

1. Discounted cash flow (DCF) and net present value (NPV)

1.1 It is assumed that you are already familiar with the basic principles of discounted cash flow (DCF), and that you know how to calculate a net present value (NPV) and an internal rate of return (IRR) or DCF yield.

1.2 The NPV investment criterion is based on the principles that (1) £1 today is worth more than £1 tomorrow, and (2) a safe £1 is more valuable than a risky £1. The extent to which £1 today is worth more than £1 in the future depends on the distance in time to the future cash flow and the appropriate cost of capital for discounting. Future cash flows are discounted to a present value, to give them comparability.

1.3
> The NPV rule for investments by public companies is that any project with a positive NPV should be undertaken (provided that capital is available) because the market value of the company and of its ordinary shares in particular should increase by the amount of the NPV.

1.4 The NPV method of project evaluation and selection is therefore preferable to other investment decision techniques; in particular:

(a) payback - although a maximum acceptable payback period might be applied in practice

(b) accounting rate of return

(c) internal rate of return (IRR) - although IRR is a useful guide to project selection when there is capital rationing in the current time period (year 0).

1.5 Some 'reminders' about DCF techniques are listed here, and you should check that you know them.

(1) Decision problems to which DCF analysis might be applied are

- decisions whether or not to undertake a project
- choices between mutually exclusive projects
- decisions about how frequently to replace regular operational assets that are replaced at the end of their life - eg company cars.

(2) In DCF, only relevant cash flows are discounted. A relevant cash flow is a future cash flow arising as a direct consequence of the investment decision.

- It can be an extra cash cost, an extra cash revenue, or savings in cash costs or reductions in cash revenue.

- Non-cash items, such as absorbed fixed overheads and depreciation, should be ignored.

(3) For convenience, cash flows are assumed to occur at the *end* of a time period, even though they might have occurred throughout the period. Cash flows occurring early in a time period are assumed to occur at the end of the *previous* time period.

(4) The PV of £1 pa in perpetuity is £1/r where r is the cost of capital as a proportion.

2. DCF and inflation

2.1 Future inflation in prices and costs is inevitable.

(1) If all prices and costs are expected to increase at the same percentage rate, inflation in cash flows can be ignored *provided that* the cash flows are discounted at a real cost of capital.

(2) Alternatively, all prices and costs should be increased to allow for expected inflation, and the inflated cash flows discounted at the money cost of capital. Market rates of interest are a money cost of capital. This approach is especially suitable when costs and revenues are expected to rise in price at different rates.

3. DCF and taxation

3.1 The effect of taxation on cash flows should be included in DCF analysis, with after-tax cash flows discounted at an after-tax cost of capital.

- Taxation on profits is often assumed to be at a standard percentage rate, and (typically) payable one year in arrears. As a general convention, taxation is assessed as a percentage of cash profits, but this is not a hard and fast rule.

- There may be capital allowances on capital equipment purchases. These could be a writing down allowance, but you will need to check the capital allowance details in any problem that you attempt.

3.2 Loan interest costs and the tax allowance on loan interest are usually *ignored* in the cash flow analysis, since the method of financing projects is implicit in the cost of capital, which is an after-tax cost of capital when debt capital is involved.

4. DCF: risk and uncertainty

4.1 Future cash flows cannot be predicted with certainty, and capital expenditure decisions might need to consider the risk or uncertainty involved. Risk should be reflected in the cost of capital, but more specific techniques that might be used include:

- *probability analysis,* and the calculation of an expected value of the NPV (and also perhaps a standard deviation of the NPV).

- *sensitivity analysis,* such as estimating the extent to which cash flows can change for the worse before a project's NPV becomes negative.

- *simulation* techniques and modelling, for large and complex projects.

- applying a cut-off time limit - a maximum payback period or a maximum *discounted payback period.*

5. Capital rationing

5.1 When capital for investments is in restricted supply, a choice must be made between projects that all have a positive NPV.

   (1)   If capital rationing is in the current time period only

      - and projects/investments are *divisible,* the projects for selection should be ranked in descending order of NPV per £1 of current outlay (a highest PV of future net cash flows after year 0, per £1 of current outlay) since this will give the highest achievable NPV

      - and projects/investments are *not divisible,* the feasible combination of projects that give the highest total NPV should be selected.

   (2)   If capital rationing is in more than one time period, a linear programming model can be set up to establish which projects to select, but such a model is based on assumptions of linearity and project divisibility, which might not be valid.

6. DCF and financing decisions

6.1 DCF can be used to decide not only whether or not to undertake a project, but also which method of financing the project might be appropriate. Two techniques to mention in particular are the 'lease versus buy' decision and the adjusted present value (APV) method of evaluation.

6.2 The 'lease versus buy' decision considers whether an item of capital equipment should be purchased, or whether it should be obtained under a leasing or hire purchase arrangement.

Step 1. Establish whether it is worth having the equipment by discounting the project's cash flows at a suitable cost of capital (such as the company's weighted average cost of capital).

Step 2. If the equipment is worth having, compare the cash flows of purchasing, leasing and HP, remembering to consider the differences in taxation by each method, as well as finance payments. The cash flows can be discounted at an after-tax cost of borrowing, and the financing method with the lowest PV of cost will be selected.

7. Adjusted Present Value method of project evaluation (APV)

7.1 The adjusted present value (APV) method of project evaluation is a technique that can be used where the method of financing the project means that using the company's weighted average cost of capital to discount the cash flows would be inappropriate. Instead, a "base-case" NPV is calculated and the positive or negative effects of the selected method of financing are then added to or subtracted from the NPV to reach an APV.

7.2 A project's APV can be described as

(1)   a "base-case" NPV, assuming all-equity finance and a cost of capital appropriate to this

(2)   plus or minus the PV of "side-effects" of undertaking the project, such as

- the PV of the costs of raising the finance

- the PV of the benefits of the 'tax shield', if the project is debt-financed, due to tax relief on loan interest payments. Tax savings to be discounted at the *pre-tax* cost of capital.

Owing to its step-by-step approach of calculating an NPV at an all-equity cost of capital, and then making adjustments for side effects, the APV method is also known as 'project valuation by components'.

QUESTIONS

> You might wish to use discount tables to help you to answer questions in this chapter.

1 Which of the following statements about capital project evaluation is/are correct?

Statement

1 The discount rate for evaluating corporate investments should be determined by prevailing rates of return in the capital markets

2 Cash flows are discounted for two basic reasons: (1) because £1 today is worth more than £1 tomorrow and (2) because a risky £1 is worth more than a safe £1

3 Public companies that invest in projects with a positive NPV will serve the best interests of all their shareholders, even if using cash for current investments prevents the payment of dividends

A Statement 1 only is correct
B Statements 1 and 2 only are correct
C Statements 1 and 3 only are correct
D Statements 2 and 3 only are correct

Circle your answer

A   B   C   D

2 Bowler Soups plc is a UK company that is planning a joint venture in Zimbabwe with a French company. Each of the two companies has agreed to inject £2 million of capital, to finance the following assets.

	£
Plant and equipment	3,500,000
Working capital	500,000
	4,000,000

As part of its capital contribution, Bowler Soups plc will provide plant and equipment to the value of £1,800,000. Of this, one half will be second-hand. Some of this would have to be replaced for £500,000, but the remainder would otherwise be scrapped and sold off for £80,000.

What is the relevant Year 0 cash flow to Bowler Soups plc for the project, with respect to the capital injection of £2,000,000, that should be used in a DCF evaluation?

A £1,400,000
B £1,480,000
C £1,600,000
D £1,680,000

Circle your answer

A   B   C   D

3 The NPV of a project has been estimated as follows.

Discount rate	NPV
10%	+ £48,000
15%	+ £18,000
20%	+ £2,000

Using this data, what is the best approximation of the IRR of the project?

A   20.1%
B   20.4%
C   20.6%
D   21.0%

Circle your answer

A   B   C   D

4 Bagger Cement Ltd has prepared a capital budget programme with four possible projects. The company's cost of capital is 18%, and the four projects have been evaluated as follows:

Project	Capital outlay	NPV at 18%	Internal rate of return
1	£200,000	£30,000	24%
2	£500,000	£45,000	20%
3	£100,000	£21,000	30%
4	£300,000	£40,000	28%

Which project should the company undertake if there is no capital rationing and if, of the four projects, projects 1 and 3 are mutually exclusive and projects 2 and 4 are mutually exclusive?

A   Projects 1 and 2
B   Projects 1 and 4
C   Projects 2 and 3
D   Projects 3 and 4

Circle your answer

A   B   C   D

5 Packer Cards Ltd is planning a three year project, involving an immediate capital outlay of £250,000, for which details are as follows.

(1)

	Year 1	Year 2	Year 3
Annual sales	£500,000	£800,000	£400,000
Sales minus cash costs of sales	£200,000	£350,000	£150,000

(2) An advertising campaign, costing £80,000 in each year, will be undertaken early in the first and second years.

(3) Working capital will build up quickly and will consist of (a) creditors £30,000, (b) stocks £80,000 and (c) debtors = 3 months' sales.

(4) Cost of capital = 14%. Ignore taxation.

What is the NPV of the project, to the nearest £000?

A + £62,000
B + £82,000
C + £88,000
D +£101,000

Circle your answer

A   B   C   D

6 A project has a life of three years. In the first year, it is expected to generate sales of £1,000,000, increasing at the rate of 10% per annum (compound) over the next two years. The cash costs of sales will be 60% of sales value. At the start of each year, working capital is required as follows:

(1) Stock equal to 25% of the cash costs of sales for the year
(2) Creditors equal to 20% of the cash costs of sales for the year
(3) Debtors equal to 20% of sales revenue for the year.

What is the net present value (to the nearest thousand pounds) of the adjustments to cash flows for the working capital changes, discounting at a rate of 15% per annum?

A £(75,000)
B £(86,000)
C £(176,000)
D £(269,000)

Circle your answer

A   B   C   D

7 An all-equity company has 10,000,000 shares in issue, with a market value of £40 million. A project to buy up the operations of another company would earn future net cash inflows with a present value of £24 million. The cost of buying the operations would be £20 million and the finance would be obtained by issuing 5 million shares to new shareholders.

If the project goes ahead, the market price per share for existing shareholders should be expected to rise to

A £4.27
B £4.40
C £4.80
D £6.40

Circle your answer

A   B   C   D

8 Penn Fuller Fink Ltd is considering a three-year project costing £1,000,000. At today's prices, annual sales would be £1,000,000 pa and cash costs would be £600,000 pa.

Price inflation is expected to be as follows:

General price levels   6% pa
Sales prices   4% pa
Project cash costs   8% pa

The money cost of capital is 12% pa.

What is the project's NPV, to the nearest £1,000?

A   -£187,000
B   -£83,000
C   -£57,000
D   +£76,000

Circle your answer

A   B   C   D

---

9 Panner Boyle Linnwater Ltd's weighted average cost of capital is 20% before tax (12% after tax) and is expected to remain at this level into the foreseeable future. The company plans to borrow £20,000 at 10% before tax (6% after tax) to buy equipment which will generate the following cash flows:

	Year 1	Year 2	Year 3	Year 4
Net cash savings before tax (£)	15,000	10,000	15,000	-
Tax paid (£)	-	3,600	2,400	4,000

What is the net present value (to the nearest £10) of the project that should be used in the investment decision?

A   £4,920
B   £7,260
C   £8,120
D   £13,170

Circle your answer

A   B   C   D

---

10 Teak Hettle plc is considering a four-year project involving the purchase of equipment costing £600,000. Tax allowable depreciation would be 25% per year on a straight line basis.

Sales would be £1,200,000 per annum and the cost of sales (including depreciation) would be £900,000 per annum for each of the four years.

Variable costs (all cash expenses) will be one-third of sales, and consist of 25% direct labour costs and 75% materials costs. General fixed overheads (not including depreciation) are absorbed into product costs at the rate of 150% of direct labour costs. All other fixed costs will be incremental expenses.

Tax is 35% of profits, payable one year in arrears. The after tax cost of capital is 16%. What, to the nearest £000, is the NPV of the project?

PV of £1 pa at 16%
Years 1 - 4   2.798
Years 1 - 5   3.274

A   £279,000
B   £563,000
C   £699,000
D   £826,000

Circle your answer

A   B   C   D

11 Corfe Eeyore Potts Ltd is considering a project that would involve buying a machine for £120,000, to earn cash profits before tax of £50,000 pa for three years. At the end of year 3, the machine would be sold for £50,000. The machine would qualify for writing down allowances, which are at the rate of 25% on a reducing balance basis.

Taxation, at 30%, is paid in the same year as the cash flows that give rise to it. The company's cost of capital is 20%.

What is the NPV of the project, to the nearest £1,000?

A -£2,000
B -£31,000
C +£5,000
D +£33,000

Circle your answer

A	B	C	D

12 Mill Cartons plc is considering a three-year 50:50 joint venture with a company in an Eastern bloc country. The joint venture would be capitalised at £1 million or 2 million flotties (the currency of the Eastern bloc country), and Mill Cartons plc's contribution would be in cash.

The expected cash flows from the project are as follows:

Year	Cash flows after tax	End-of-year exchange rate
1	1,500,000 flotties	£1 = 3 flotties
2	3,000,000 flotties	£1 = 4 flotties
3	8,000,000 flotties	£1 = 5 flotties

A law of the country prohibits the payment abroad in dividends each year of more than 25% of a joint venture's cash flows after tax. This prohibition is expected to end after three years. To evaluate this project, Mill Cartons plc would use a cost of capital of 25%.

What is the NPV of the project for Mill Cartons plc, to the nearest £000?

A £232,000
B £245,000
C £350,000
D £452,000

Circle your answer

A	B	C	D

13 Chopin Bagge Ltd is considering the optimal replacement policy for its company fleet of standard motor vehicles. Using the company's cost of capital, which is 10%, estimates have been made of the net present value of the cost of buying, using and selling a car.

If the car is replaced every	The PV of cost for a full 'life cycle' of a car would be
1 year	£15,600
2 years	£27,700
3 years	£42,000
4 years	£60,000
5 years	£69,000

What is the optimal replacement cycle for the vehicles?

A   Every 2 years
B   Every 3 years
C   Every 4 years
D   Every 5 years

Circle your answer

A   B   C   D

14 Nuffin Knupp Mice-Leaves Ltd has made the following estimates of sales for a new product with an expected life of two years:

	High sales	*Average sales*	*Low sales*
Probability	0.4	0.3	0.3
	£	£	£
Year 1	15,000	10,000	8,000
Year 2	20,000	10,000	4,000

Variable costs are uncertain and the following estimates are made for the two year period:

Variable costs as a percentage of sales	*Probability*
80%	0.1
70%	0.2
60%	0.4
50%	0.3

Incremental fixed overheads will be £4,000 per annum if the product is manufactured. The company has a cost of capital of 15% per annum.

What is the expected net present value (to the nearest £100) of making and selling the product over the next two years?

A   £1,000
B   £1,100
C   £4,000
D   £5,200

Circle your answer

A   B   C   D

15 The expected cash flows of a one year project are as follows.

Year 0	Equipment cost		£400,000	
Year 1	*Extra running costs*		*Savings*	
	Probability	£000	Probability	£000
	0.2	400	0.2	700
	0.2	300	0.3	600
	0.6	200	0.5	500

End of year 1. Resale value of equipment = 50% of original cost. The cost of capital is 20% and the expected value of the project NPV is +£25,000.

Savings and running costs are not related or dependent on each other. What is the probability that the NPV of the project will be negative?

A   10%
B   16%
C   20%
D   26%

Circle your answer

A   B   C   D

Data for questions 16 and 17

The following cash flow estimates have been made by a company whose project cost of capital is 20%.

Year 0. Capital equipment cost = £600,000
Year 3. Resale value of equipment = 40% of original cost

Year	Sales	Running costs	Net cash flow
	£000	£000	£000
1	800	600	200
2	1,200	800	400
3	600	500	100

Running costs amount to 50% of sales revenue plus fixed annual costs of £200,000.

The NPV of the project is +£35,208.

16 The estimate of the capital equipment cost is a little uncertain, but the resale value of 40% of original cost at the end of year 3 has been guaranteed by the supplier. Given no change in revenues or running costs, what is the maximum cost that the equipment could have (to the nearest £000) without the project ceasing to be viable?

A   £632,000
B   £642,000
C   £655,000
D   £670,000

Circle your answer

A   B   C   D

17 There is some uncertainty about the level of variable costs. The equipment cost is definitely £600,000, and fixed costs will be £200,000 per annum. Given the expected level of sales, what is the maximum percentage of variable costs to sales that is acceptable for the project to be viable?

A 51.1%
B 51.6%
C 52.3%
D 54.2%

Circle your answer

A   B   C   D

Data for questions 18 and 19

Four investment projects are under consideration. Details are as follows.

Project	Year 0 outlay £	PV of future cash flows £	Profitability index
1	-100,000	+150,000	1.50
2	-300,000	+400,000	1.33
3	-500,000	+650,000	1.30
4	-800,000	+900,000	1.125

Projects 1 and 2 are mutually exclusive. Projects 3 and 4 are mutually exclusive.

18 If the projects are *divisible* (so that undertaking 25% of one project say, would incur 25% of the costs and obtain 25% of the benefits) and investment funds are not in restricted supply, which projects should be undertaken?

A   Projects 1 and 3
B   Projects 1 and 4
C   Projects 2 and 3
D   Projects 2 and 4

Circle your answer

A   B   C   D

19 If the projects are *divisible,* but investment funds are restricted to £500,000, which projects should be undertaken?

A   Project 1 and 80% of project 3
B   Project 1 and 50% of project 4
C   Project 2 and 40% of project 3
D   Project 2 and 25% of project 4

Circle your answer

A   B   C   D

20 Four projects, P, Q, R and S, are available to a company which is facing shortages of capital over the current year but expects capital to be freely available from then on.

Project	P £000	Q £000	R £000	S £000
PV of total capital required over the life of the project	40	50	33	20
PV of capital required in the current year	20	50	30	20
Net present value of the project at the company's cost of capital	20	80	54	42

In what order of preference should the projects be selected if the company wishes to maximise net present values and none of the projects can be deferred?

A P, S, Q, R
B Q, S, R, P
C S, R, Q, P
D S, P, R, Q

Circle your answer

A   B   C   D

Data for questions 21 - 23

Fuller Foot Hare Ltd wishes to purchase a new machine, which will cost £100,000. The machine will help the company to make extra profits and will qualify for capital allowances. It will be sold after 3 years for £40,000.

Taxable profits for each year of the machine's expected life (allowing for the eventual sale of the machine), are as follows.

Year	Cash profits £	Capital allowances £	Taxable profits (tax at 35%) £
1	75,000	25,000	50,000
2	70,750	18,750	52,000
3	60,250	16,250	44,000

Tax is paid one year after the profits giving rise to the tax charge. The company's after-tax cost of capital is 15%.

21 What is the NPV of the project, to the nearest £1,000?

A + £4,000
B + £24,000
C + £38,000
D + £51,000

Circle your answer

A   B   C   D

22 Instead of buying the machine, the company could obtain it under an operating lease agreement. A lease agreement for 3 years would involve the payment of £30,000 per annum at the beginning of each year. The after-tax cost of borrowing is 10%. Using this discount rate, by how much (to the nearest £000) would the cost of the option to buy differ from the cost of the option to lease, in terms of PV of cost?

A   Leasing is cheaper, by a PV of £28,000
B   Leasing is cheaper, by a PV of £14,000
C   Leasing is cheaper, by a PV of £3,000
D   Buying is cheaper, by a PV of £2,000

Circle your answer

A   B   C   D

23 A third option is to buy the machine on hire purchase, as follows.

(1)   Down-payment of £30,000
(2)   Three more annual payments of £30,000
(3)   The interest part of the annual payments, for tax purposes, would be

1st annual payment	£10,000
2nd annual payment	£7,000
3rd annual payment	£3,000

Using the after-tax cost of borrowing of 10% as the discount rate, by how much (to the nearest £000) would the cost of the hire purchase option differ from the cost of the leasing option? Tax is at 35%.

A   Leasing is cheaper by a PV of £10,000
B   Leasing is cheaper by a PV of £27,000
C   HP is cheaper by a PV of £3,000
D   HP is cheaper by a PV of £13,000

Circle your answer

A   B   C   D

24 An all-equity company is considering a project that would cost £9,975,000. The finance would be raised by placing a new issue of shares. Placing costs would be 5% of the funds raised. The annual cash flows from the project would be £2,400,000 in perpetuity. The company's cost of capital is 16%.

What is the adjusted present value (APV) of the project, to the nearest £000?

A   £3,786,000
B   £4,500,000
C   £4,526,000
D   £5,025,000

Circle your answer

A   B   C   D

25 A company is considering a new project that would earn cash profits before tax of £5,000,000 per annum for three years. Tax, 30% of cash profits, will be payable one year in arrears of the profits. The cost of the project would be £7,500,000 and the finance would be obtained by obtaining a five year loan at 10% interest, for which annual repayments would be as follows.

End of year	Capital repayment	Interest	Total payment
	£000	£000	£000
1	2,500	750	3,250
2	2,500	500	3,000
3	2,500	250	2,750

Loan issue costs would be £100,000. The loan would significantly alter the company's gearing. Its current weighted average cost of capital is 12%, but if the company were all-equity financed, its cost of capital would be 13%.

What is the adjusted present value of the project, to the nearest £100,000?

	Cost of capital			
	7%	10%	12%	13%
PV of £1 pa, years 1-3	2.624	2.487	2.402	2.361
PV of £1 pa, years 2-4	2.452	2.261	2.144	2.089

A   £1,300,000
B   £1,400,000
C   £1,500,000
D   £1,600,000

Circle your answer

A   B   C   D

CHAPTER 2

THE STOCK MARKET. LONG TERM FUNDS

This chapter covers the following topics:

- Capital markets
- Securities and long term funds
- Return on securities
- Other sources of long term funds

1. Capital markets

1.1 A *capital* market is a financial market in which long-term capital is bought and sold, or lent and borrowed. A stock market is a capital market for stocks and shares.

A financial market where short term capital is borrowed and lent is a *money* market.

1.2 The role of a stock market for companies is to

- bring companies and investors together, whereby

  o investors put new long term funds into a company and
  o a company can raise capital for investing in its business

- provide a 'second hand' market for stocks and shares, whereby

  o investors can sell their stocks or shares if and when they wish to do so
  o other investors can acquire existing stocks or shares in a company.

A readily available 'second hand' market gives existing stocks and shares greater liquidity, which makes them very much more attractive as investments.

1.3 Further roles of a stock market are to

- enable the owners of a company to realise some of their investment by bringing their hitherto private company to the market

- allow companies to take over other companies by issuing new shares as the purchase consideration. Stock market companies can therefore use their market status to finance expansion through acquisitions.

1.4 Not all companies seek a stock market quotation for their shares

> **Reasons for 'remaining private' might be**
>
> - insufficient size
> - insufficient past trading record
> - no requirement for extra capital or rapid growth; adequate private funding
> - to avoid burdens of stock market regulations
> - to avoid pressures of stock market investors' expectations for earnings and dividend growth
> - to avoid widespread share ownership; to retain ownership in the hands of a few individuals; to avoid takeover threats.

1.5 In the UK, the activities of the capital markets are regulated by the Financial Services Act, which gives regulatory powers over the financial services industry, including capital markets, to the Securities and Investment Board (SIB). The SIB has delegated its regulatory powers to a number of Self-Regulatory Organisations (SROs), and the SRO for the International Stock Exchange is the Securities Association. The main rules of The Stock Exchange are set out in the "Yellow Book" - 'Admission of Securities to Listing'. Similar rules for Unlisted Securities Market companies are set out in the "Green Book".

1.6 In the UK, a company can bring its shares to the market for the first time (in a 'flotation') by means of

   (1)   an offer for sale (at either a set price, or (much more rarely) by tender)
   (2)   a placing
   (3)   a prospectus issue
   (4)   a Stock Exchange introduction.

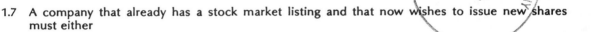

1.7 A company that already has a stock market listing and that now wishes to issue new shares must either

   (1)   make the issue a *rights issue*, whereby existing shareholders are invited to subscribe for all the new shares in proportion to their existing shareholdings; or

   (2)   obtain prior approval from shareholders for any other method of share issue (for example, to finance a takeover with a share-for-share exchange as the method of compensation).

Rights issues will be unpopular with investors when there are poor prospects for high returns.

2. Securities and long term funds

2.1 Companies, whether public or private, obtain long term funds from a variety of sources.

   - New issues of equity shares, preference shares, loan stock or bonds
   - Retained profits
   - Bank borrowing (medium-term)

Retained profits are the main source of new equity funding.

2.2 The government raises long-term capital by issuing bonds (gilt-edged securities or gilts) or by inviting individuals to invest in National Savings. The Stock Exchange is the capital market for gilts in the UK.

2.3 You should also be aware of

- *bonus issues (scrip issues)* of shares, which are a way of increasing the number of shares in issue, but without raising any extra capital, by converting reserves into new share capital

- *stock splits*, which are another way of increasing the number of shares in issue without raising any extra capital, by dividing up existing shares into larger quantities with a smaller nominal value (eg a £1 share can be split into 4 shares of 25p each)

- *scrip dividends (stock dividends)*, which involve the issue of new shares to existing shareholders as a dividend payment, in lieu of a cash dividend.

2.4 *Loan stock and bonds*

(1) *'Bonds'* is a term used to describe various forms of long-term debt.

(2) Loan stock is long term debt capital raised by a company for which interest is paid, usually half-yearly and commonly at a fixed rate of the nominal value of the stock.

(3) *Debentures* are a form of loan stock, legally defined as the written acknowledgement by a company of a debt, usually given under seal and normally containing provisions about the payment of interest and eventual repayment of capital.

(4) Loan stock/debentures might be redeemable or irredeemable. Redemption dates for redeemable stock might cover a period of time; they must be redeemed by the latest specified date, but can be redeemed at the option of the company at any time after the earliest specified date.

2.5 Bonds or loans come in a variety of forms. For example

- *floating rate* debentures are loans on which the coupon rate of interest can be varied at regular intervals, in line with changes in current market rates of interest.

- *zero coupon bonds* are bonds issued at a large discount to their eventual redemption value, but on which no interest is paid. Investors obtain all their return from the capital gain on redemption

- *convertible loan stock* gives their holders the right, if they wish, to convert their stock into shares at a predetermined rate at a future date. There may be a number of 'future dates' for conversion, each with a different conversion rate for stock into shares. Convertible loan stock, because of the attraction of the option to convert into equity, will usually be issued at a lower rate of interest than current interest rates on 'ordinary' loan stock.

2.6 Loans might be *secured* or *unsecured.*

- Mortgage loans are loans secured on property

- Bank loans might have a fixed charge over certain fixed assets (eg property) and a floating charge over changeable assets (eg stocks and debtors) which 'crystallise' if the bank wishes to use its security for repayment of an outstanding loan

- Companies might be able to issue *subordinated debt* or *junior debt* which is debt over which 'senior debt' takes priority. In the event of the company going into liquidation, holders of senior debt would be entitled to repayment out of realised assets of the company before holders of junior debt receive any payment. Junior debt is more risky for investors, and so carries a higher rate of interest. The term *'junk bonds'* has been used, mainly in the USA, to describe unsecured junior debt issued by companies to raise finance.

2.7 *Share warrants.* These are another form of security, often issued by companies as an 'add-on' to a new issue of loan stock to make the issue more attractive to investors. Warrants give their holder the right to apply for new shares in the company at a fixed 'exercise' price at a future date.

2.8 *Share options: traded options*

A *call* option gives its owner the right (but not the obligation) to buy shares at a fixed 'exercise price' or 'striking price'.

A *put* option gives its owner the right (but not the obligation) to sell shares at a fixed price.

- In the case of European options, the options can only be exercised on one particular day in the future

- In the case of American options, the options can be exercised at any time before a particular day in the future.

2.9 Companies can issue call options themselves, perhaps in a share option scheme for employees. In addition, there is a large volume of trading in options that have been created by dealers on specialised options exchanges: these are known as 'traded options'. Investors can buy call or put options and if they wish to do so before the expiration date, sell them. In the UK, options are traded for shares in a number of large companies.

3. Return on securities

3.1 Investors expect to earn a return on their securities.

- Ordinary shareholders will obtain their return from *dividends.* Over a shorter period of time, return can be measured by dividend received in the period plus any increase in the market value of the share (or minus any fall in share value).

- Similarly, preference shareholders will obtain their return from preference dividends, and irredeemable loan stock holders will earn *interest.*

- With redeemable loan stock, return is measured by (1) interest up to the date of redemption and (2) the redemption value of the stock. Return on the stock is the *discounted yield* that equates the cost of investment in the stock with the present value of future interest payments and cash receivable on redemption.

- With convertible loan stock, return is measured by (1) interest up to the date of conversion into equity and (2) the market value of the shares into which the stock can be converted, if conversion is profitable. Return on the stock is the discounted yield that equates the cost of investment in the stock with the PV of interest payments and market value of the shares on conversion.

4.   Other sources of long term funds

4.1   Companies can raise funds from other sources in addition to retained profits and stock market issues. These include:

- bank loans

- private loans (fairly common with small private companies, where the proprietors or their relatives contribute funds in the form of loans)

- loans or equity capital from venture capital organisations, such as the 3i Group and BES fund organisations

- government grants.

Leasing is also a form of finance for fixed assets.

QUESTIONS

1 Which of the following UK capital markets are operated and supervised by The International Stock Exchange?

Market
1. Primary market
2. Unlisted Securities Market
3. Gilts market
4. Over-the-counter markets
5. National Savings

A Markets 1 and 2 only
B Markets 1, 2 and 3 only
C Markets 1, 2, 3 and 4 only
D Markets 1, 2, 3 and 5 only

Circle your answer

A   B   C   D

2 Under the terms of the Financial Services Act 1986, only 'authorised persons' are allowed to carry on investment business. All members of a recognised Self-Regulatory Organisation (SRO) are authorised persons. The SRO which represents The Stock Exchange is

A The International Stock Exchange

B the Securities and Investments Board (SIB)

C the Financial Intermediaries, Managers and Brokers Regulatory Association (FIMBRA)

D the Securities Association

Circle your answer

A   B   C   D

3 An arrangement whereby a company's shares obtain a quotation and listing on The Stock Exchange, and most of the shares that are made available are bought by a small number of institutional investors (such as pension funds and insurance companies), is known as

A a placing
B an offer for sale
C a prospectus issue
D a Stock Exchange introduction

Circle your answer

A   B   C   D

4 Which of the following factors are potential *disadvantages* of flotation?

Factor
1. Having to write off the costs of flotation against the company's profit for the year
2. The pressures of being expected by investors to achieve continual growth in profits, earnings and dividends

Continued....

3. Dilution of control and ownership
4. The need to comply with stringent Stock Exchange regulations

A   Factors 1, 2, 3 and 4
B   Factors 2, 3, and 4 only
C   Factors 3 and 4 only
D   Factor 4 only

Circle your answer

A   B   C   D

---

5 Suppose that Somer Halliday plc, an unquoted company, has obtained a Stock Exchange listing, with its shares offered to the general public by means of an offer for sale. Not all of the shares put on offer were bought by the public, and these unsold shares were bought instead under a previous agreement by a number of financial institutions. This agreement by the institutions to purchase Somer Halliday plc's unsold shares is known as

A   a placing
B   sponsorship
C   underwriting
D   an introduction

Circle your answer

A   B   C   D

---

6 For which of the following reasons might a public company revert to private company status?

Reason
1. To avoid shareholder expectations of annual growth in EPS and dividends
2. To avoid the danger of a takeover
3. Because the plc's share price was over-valued

A   Reason 1 only
B   Reasons 1 and 2 only
C   Reasons 1 and 3 only
D   Reasons 2 and 3 only

Circle your answer

A   B   C   D

---

7 For dealings on the UK International Stock Exchange, the year is divided into 24 time periods called Accounts, of either 2 or 3 weeks' duration. An investor purchases shares through a broker. When, normally, must he pay for them?

A   When the contract note is received

B   Within 7 days of the date of the contract note

C   On the last day of the Account in which they were purchased

D   On Settlement Day during the next Account

Circle your answer

A   B   C   D

8 When a company decides to make a rights issue of shares, the main advantage of issuing the new shares at a *deep discount* is

A to improve the prospects for a successful issue

B to avoid concerns about a fall in the cum rights share price

C to avoid a large increase in the share premium account

D to avoid having to pay underwriting costs

Circle your answer

A   B   C   D

9 Hairport de Lay plc is to make a rights issue of one share at £1.60 for every three existing shares. There is a current dividend payment due of 4p per share, but the new shares will not qualify for this. The current price per share just prior to the rights issue is £2.12 cum dividend.

What is the theoretical ex rights price per share?

A £1.95
B £1.96
C £1.99
D £2.00

Circle your answer

A   B   C   D

10 Sandy Beech plc has announced a 1 for 4 rights issue at a subscription price of £2.50. The current cum rights price per share is £4.10:

What is the theoretical value of the right per existing share?

A 8p
B 32p
C 40p
D £1.28

Circle your answer

A   B   C   D

Data for questions 11 - 12

Date Ripper plc is a new company that is making its first public issue of shares. It plans to do so by means of an offer for sale by tender. The following tenders have been received.

Price tendered per share £	Number of shares applied for at this price
3.00	50,000
2.90	100,000
2.80	250,000
c/fwd	400,000

Continued...

Price tendered per share £	Number of shares applied for at this price
b/fwd	400,000
2.70	500,000
2.60	1,000,000
2.50	1,700,000
2.40	2,400,000
	6,000,000

The company has decided already that partial acceptance would mean allotting to each accepted applicant an equal proportion of the shares applied for.

11 If the company decides to issue exactly 3,000,000 shares, how much money would be raised?

A £7,500,000
B £7,550,000
C £7,800,000
D £7,840,000

Circle your answer

| A | B | C | D |

12 Ira Viller, an investor, tendered for 66,000 shares at a price of £2.50, and submitted a cheque for £165,000. If the company issues 3,000,000 shares, how many shares will he be allocated, and what return payment would he receive?

	Number of shares allocated	Return payment
A	3,960	£154,704
B	3,960	£155,000
C	39,600	£66,000
D	55,000	£27,500

Circle your answer

| A | B | C | D |

13 Which one of the following best describes the term "coupon rate" as applied to debenture stock?

A The annual interest received on the face value of the units of the stock

B The annual interest received divided by the current ex-interest market price of the stock

Continued...

C   The total rate of return on a stock, taking into account capital repayment as well as interest payments

D   The minimum rate of interest required to maintain the market value of the stock at or above par value

Circle your answer

A   B   C   D

14   A participating preference share is a preference share which

A   has the right to be converted into ordinary shares at some future date

B   entitles the shareholder to a share of residual profits

C   carries forward the right to preferential dividends, if unpaid, from one year to the next

D   entitles the shareholder to a fixed rate of dividend

Circle your answer

A   B   C   D

15   Bonds that are issued by a company at a large discount to their eventual redemption value, but on which no interest is paid until redemption, are called

A   deep discount bonds
B   zero coupon bonds
C   equity bonds
D   floating rate bonds

Circle your answer

A   B   C   D

16   Dick Chores plc has in issue some 8% Debenture Stock 1997/1999. Suppose that when 1997 arrives, interest rates are stable and are expected to remain stable for the foreseeable future, with companies able to borrow and investors able to lend at 10% per annum. How would the debentures be redeemed, on the assumption that the company will finance the redemption of the stock by issuing new loan stock?

A   At the earliest specified date in 1997, by choice of the company

B   At the earliest specified date in 1997, by choice of the stock holders

Continued...

C   At the latest specified date in 1999, by choice of the company

D   At the latest specified date in 1999, by choice of the stock holders

Circle your answer

A   B   C   D

17 Deferred equity can be described as

A   shares that are entitled to dividend only after the main class of ordinary shares has been paid a dividend

B   securities that are not yet ordinary shares, but could be converted into ordinary shares at a future date

C   a class of ordinary shares that has less voting rights than another class of ordinary shares in the same company

D   a golden share

Circle your answer

A   B   C   D

Data for questions 18 - 21

Kemp Sights plc's summarised balance sheet is as follows. Revenue reserves include profits for the year just ended.

	£ million
Fixed assets	300
Net current assets	150
	450
Financed by	
Ordinary shares (£1 par value)	100
Share premium account	50
Revenue reserves	300
	450

The current market price per share is £2.

The company's directors are giving some consideration to a scrip issue, a stock split and a scrip dividend.

18 What effect would a 4 for 5 scrip issue have on the balance sheet?

	Ordinary shares	Shares premium	Revenue reserves
A	+ £80m	No effect	- £80m
B	+ £80m	+ £80m	- £160m
C	+ £125m	- £50m	- £75m
D	+ £80m	- £50m	- £30m

Circle your answer

A   B   C   D

19 The directors want to pay a dividend of £40 million. What would be the effect on the balance sheet of a 1 for 5 scrip dividend as a means of paying such a dividend?

	Net assets	Ordinary shares	Share premium	Revenue reserves
A	- £40m	+ £20m	- £20m	- £40m
B	No effect	+ £20m	No effect	- £20m
C	No effect	+ £20m	+ £20m	- £40m
D	No effect	+ £40m	No effect	- £40m

Circle your answer

A   B   C   D

20 Which of the following reasons could explain a decision to pay a scrip dividend rather than a cash dividend?

Reason
1. To avoid the need to pay out cash, especially if the company is 'cash hungry'
2. To keep the company's gearing level down
3. To give shareholders the chance to either increase their shareholding or obtain a cash return

A	Reason 1 only
B	Reasons 1 and 2 only
C	Reasons 1 and 3 only
D	Reasons 1, 2, and 3

Circle your answer

A   B   C   D

21 Ignoring any scrip dividend, what effect would a 1 for 1 stock split have on the company's balance sheet?

	Ordinary shares	Share premium	Revenue reserves
A	No effect	No effect	No effect
B	+ £100m	No effect	- £100m
C	+ £100m	- £50m	- £50m
D	+ £100m	+ £100m	- £200m

Circle your answer

A   B   C   D

22 Which of the following statements about share warrants is *incorrect*?

A Warrants give the holder the right to subscribe for new shares in the company at a future date

B The exercise price (subscription price) will be based on a formula related to the share's market value at the start of the exercise period

C Warrants may be issued as part of a package with unsecured loan stock, but then detached from the stock

D Warrants are bought and sold separately before the exercise period, but if they are not exercised by the end of this period, they will become worthless

Circle your answer

A   B   C   D

23 Which of the following statements is correct?

Traded options

A might be issued by a company in association with the issue of unsecured loan stock, giving option holders the right to subscribe for new shares in the company at a fixed price at a future date

B might be negotiated between investors and dealers, giving the investor the right to either buy or sell a quantity of existing shares in the company at a fixed price at a future date

C are investments written by dealers on an options market, and purchased by investors to hedge or speculate, since they give the right to either buy or sell a quantity of existing shares in the company at a fixed price at a future date

D might be issued by a company giving employees the right to subscribe for new shares in the company at a fixed price at a future date

Circle your answer

A   B   C   D

24 An American call option on a company's share gives the holder the right, at a fixed price, to

A buy the share within a given period of time

B buy the share on a specified date

C sell the share within a given period of time

D sell the share on a specified date

Circle your answer

A   B   C   D

25 In early March, the ordinary shares of Goggleson Flippers plc stood at 469p, their 470p support level having been broken. There is a traded options market in the shares, and the April 500p puts are priced at 47p. Which of the following conclusions can be drawn?

A The options will only become profitable if the share price rises by more than 78p before the exercise date in April

B The options will only become profitable if the share price rises by more than 31p before the exercise date in April

C The options will stay in profit if the share price falls by less than 16p before the exercise date in April

D The options will move into profit if the share price falls by more than 16p before the exercise date in April

Circle your answer

A   B   C   D

26 At 1 January, the equity shares of Rick Pool plc had a market value of 80p each. There are 40 million shares in issue.

The summary P & L account for the year to 31 December is as follows.

		£000	£000
Profit after tax			8,000
Ordinary dividend	- interim paid	800	
	- final proposed	2,400	
			3,200
Retained profits			4,800

During the year, a final dividend of 5.5p per share from the previous year was paid. At 31 December, the equity share price was 85p.

Continued...

What was the return for equity shareholders in the year to 31 December, based on the start-of-year share value?

A 15.6%
B 16.3%
C 23.1%
D 31.3%

Circle your answer

A   B   C   D

27 Beckett and Spade plc is partly financed by two issues of redeemable loan stock, on both of which annual interest has just been paid.

Stock 1 12% Debentures redeemable at par at the end of two more years. Current market value per £100 of stock is £95.

Stock 2 8% Debentures redeemable at 110 at the end of two more years. Current market value per £100 of stock is also £95.

An investor is considering whether to invest £190,000 in each of these stocks. Ignoring personal taxation, will he achieve a target yield of 15% on these stocks?

	Stock 1 Yield above or below 15%	*Stock 2* Yield above or below 15%
A	Below	Below
B	Below	Above
C	Above	Below
D	Above	Above

Circle your answer

A   B   C   D

28 The 12% convertible loan stock of Wind Sofas plc is quoted at £140 per £100 nominal immediately after payment of the annual interest. The earliest date for conversion is in two years time, at a rate of 40 ordinary shares per £100 nominal loan stock. The share price now is £2.50.

What is the average annual rate of growth in the share price that would be necessary for loan stockholders to achieve an overall rate of return of 8% compound over the next two years, including the proceeds of conversion? Ignore taxation.

A 6.0%
B 8.5%
C 8.8%
D 13.0%

Circle your answer

A   B   C   D

29 The 10% of convertible loan stock of Walter Skeese plc has a current market value of £120 per £100 nominal value of stock. Annual interest has just been paid. The earliest date for conversion is in 4 years' time, at a rate of 50 ordinary shares per £100 nominal loan stock. The share price is now £1.90. Ignore taxation.

Continued...

What is the minimum average annual growth in the share price that would be needed to provide loan stock holders with a return of 9% per annum compound over the next four years, including the proceeds of conversion?

A   5%
B   7%
C   8%
D   16%

Circle your answer

A   B   C   D

30 At the present moment, the yield on index-linked gilts is 2%, the yield on long-dated government stocks is about 7% and the rate of inflation for the foreseeable future is about 6% per annum.

Approximately how much per annum would the government have to pay in interest per £100 of index-linked gilts?

A   £2
B   £4
C   £7
D   £8

Circle your answer

A   B   C   D

31 Leasing is a term that describes schemes whereby companies can obtain the use of capital assets without having to finance their purchase. Which of the following schemes might be described as leasing?

Scheme
1.   A printing company obtains delivery of a printing machine from a manufacturer. A finance house purchases the machine from the manufacturer, and the printing company arranges to make quarterly payments for the use of the machine to the finance house, for a five year period. The printer is responsible for maintenance and upkeep of the machine. The finance house retains ownership.

2.   As in scheme 1 above, except that the printer pays 25% of the cost of the machine and at the end of the 5 year period, becomes the legal owner of the machine.

3.   A local government authority wishes to raise capital and does so by selling a freehold property that it owns to an insurance company, and renting the property back for a 50 year period with four-year rent reviews.

4.   A company obtains office equipment under a non-cancellable rental agreement whereby it makes regular rental payments to a finance house that purchases the equipment from the manufacturer. The finance house retains ownership of the equipment, and is responsible for servicing and maintenance.

A   Scheme 1 only
B   Schemes 1 and 3 only
C   Schemes 1, 3 and 4 only
D   Schemes 1, 2, 3 and 4

Circle your answer

A   B   C   D

32 Morter Botes Ltd is a profitable subsidiary of the Rubadingi Group, which the directors of the group holding company have decided to sell off. The subsidiary's senior managers have approached a venture capital organisation for help with financing a management buyout. In addition to (1) the expected return and (2) uncertainty about the future profitability of the company, to which of the following considerations will the venture capital organisation's management have most regard?

A   Security and guarantees for their lending

B   50% financial participation by the managers involved in the buyout

C   That there should be no participation in the scheme by any other venture capital organisation

D   An 'exit route' for their investment

Circle your answer

A   B   C   D

33 Which of the following statements is correct?

Statement
1.   Venture capital organisations might provide loan capital rather than equity funds to a company.
2.   Secured medium-term bank loans are a form of venture capital.

A   Statement 1 only is correct
B   Statement 2 only is correct
C   Statements 1 and 2 are both correct
D   Neither statement is correct

Circle your answer

A   B   C   D

34 Under which of the following circumstances might a venture capital organisation be willing to invest in a company?

Circumstance
1.   Management buyout
2.   Business development scheme
3.   Business start-ups
4.   To help a company where an owner wants to realise all or part of his investment

A   Circumstance 1 only
B   Circumstances 1 and 2 only
C   Circumstances 1, 2 and 3 only
D   Circumstances 1, 2, 3 and 4

Circle your answer

A   B   C   D

35 An entrepreneur has formed a company to develop a new invention, and has taken up 60,000 shares at £1 each. He has persuaded an investor to take up 60,000 shares for £300,000.

The company will make no profits for four years, but in the fifth year it is expected that annual earnings will be £1,000,000, at which stage the entrepreneur hopes to bring the company to the Unlisted Securities Market. A P/E ratio of 12 is anticipated.

At the end of the first year, the company needs an extra £300,000 of capital. A venture capitalist is willing to provide this by purchasing new shares in the company provided that he can expect his investment to increase in value eightfold in four years.

If the venture capitalist agrees with the predictions of earnings of £1,000,000, a USM launch and P/E ratio of 12, what proportion of the total share capital would he require and how many shares would be allotted to him?

	Proportion of share capital	Number of shares
A	20.0%	30,000
B	20.0%	24,000
C	33.3%	60,000
D	33.3%	40,000

Circle your answer

A   B   C   D

CHAPTER 3

STOCK MARKET RATIOS

This chapter covers the following topics:

- EPS
- Fully diluted EPS (FDEPS)
- P/E ratio
- Dividend yield and dividend cover

---

1. EPS

1.1 The existence of current market prices enables investors to

- measure and compare the returns on various stock market investments
- relate the amount of returns that are being earned to the market value of the investments.

In this chapter, we shall concentrate on the stock market ratios that are used to measure and compare *equity* returns.

1.2 *Earnings per share (EPS)* are the after-tax profits available for *ordinary* shareholders, *excluding* any extraordinary items in the P & L account, divided by the number of ordinary shares in issue and ranking for dividend.

1.3 EPS is a measure of profit performance, which can be used to judge progress (growth) from one year to the next. The usefulness of EPS for measuring profit performance over time explains why extraordinary items are excluded, since these would distort comparative figures.

1.4 Comparisons of EPS between one year and the previous year are also affected by changes in the issued share capital during the year. Adjustments are made to the EPS figures to make comparisons more 'fair' and direct. Two examples are given below.

1.5 *EPS and the issue of new shares for cash at full market price*

If a company issues new shares for cash at a current market price after x months of the year, the EPS for the year is calculated by adjusting the number of shares in issue during the current year to a weighted amount. Suppose that the new shares are issued after 3 months of the year.

	Number of shares in issue	Proportion of year	Weighting
Before the new issue	A	3/12	0.25A
After the new issue	B	9/12	0.75B
	Weighted number of shares		0.25A + 0.75B

The EPS is calculated by dividing total earnings by this weighted number of shares. This gives a direct comparison with the previous year's EPS.

1.6 *EPS and rights issues*

Rights issues involve a new issue of shares at a price below their market value. Shares after the rights issue cannot therefore be compared directly with shares before the issue, because they have different values and (implicitly) different 'earning power'.

(1) The EPS for the *previous* year must be multiplied by the fraction

$$\frac{\text{theoretical ex-rights price}}{\text{market price on last day of quotation cum rights}}$$

(2) To obtain an EPS for the *current* year, we must adjust the number of shares in issue to arrive at an appropriate weighted total.

    (a) Multiply the number of shares *before* the rights issue by
        (i)   the fraction of the year before the date of issue, and
        (ii) by the fraction

$$\frac{\text{market price on last day of quotation cum rights}}{\text{theoretical ex-rights price}}$$

    (b) Multiply the number of shares *after* the rights issue by the fraction of the year after the date of issue

    (c) Add the figure in (a) to the figure in (b) to arrive at a total number of shares

    (d) Divide total earnings by this weighted total of shares in (c).

2. Fully diluted EPS (FDEPS)

2.1 A fully diluted EPS can be measured where the company has issued securities that might be converted into ordinary shares at some future date, such as convertible loan stock, share warrants, or share options.

2.2 The FDEPS measures what the EPS would be, based on earnings in the period under review, if the company's ordinary shares were increased to their maximum number by the exercise of all existing share options and warrants, and the conversion of existing convertible loan stock etc. Since the FDEPS will usually be less than the EPS, it is a 'watered down' or 'diluted' earnings figure. It gives investors an appreciation of by how much EPS might be affected if and when the options, warrants or conversion rights are exercised.

2.3 Total earnings are increased by

- the savings in interest (net of tax) from the conversion of loan stock into shares
- the addition to profits (net of tax) from investing the cash obtained from the exercise of share options or warrants. This is estimated on the assumption that the cash is invested in $2\frac{1}{2}$% Consolidated Stock at their market price on the first day of the period to which the FDEPS calculation relates.

$$\text{FDEPS} = \frac{\text{Adjusted earnings}}{\text{Maximum number of ordinary shares}}$$

3. P/E ratio

3.1 The P/E ratio for a share is the ratio of its market price to its EPS. P/E ratios can be used to

- compare the market values of shares in different companies
- assess the stock market's expectations of future earnings growth in a company.

3.2

1. A well-established listed company is likely to have a higher P/E ratio than a company with a recent stock market listing, since it is more 'well known' and perceived as less risky.

2. A bigger company is possibly likely to have a higher P/E ratio than a smaller company in the same industry and with the same growth expectations. A larger size implies a smaller investment risk.

3. Companies in low-risk industries or high-growth industries will have higher P/E ratios than companies in high-risk or low-growth industries.

4. Individual companies which are expected to achieve a high EPS growth into the future will have a higher P/E ratio than comparable companies with low EPS growth expectations.

5. Dividend policy can affect P/E ratios, with investors willing to pay more *perhaps* for shares in a company with a high dividend distribution policy.

4. Dividend yield and dividend cover

4.1 *Dividend yield* relates the dividend per share to the market value per share. In the financial press, dividend yield is grossed up (by adding the appropriate tax credit) to calculate the yield. This makes dividend yield comparable with interest yields on loan stock.

4.2 *Dividend cover* measures the ratio of distributable profits to actual ordinary dividend

$$\frac{\text{Maximum possible dividend that could be paid to ordinary shareholders out of the year's profit}}{\text{Actual dividend out of profits to ordinary shareholders}}$$

If there were no extraordinary items, EPS ÷ net dividend would equal dividend cover.

QUESTIONS

1   Penn plc is to acquire the entire share capital of Dink plc. The consideration is one new share in Penn for every two existing shares in Dink. The combined group expects to save £20,000 per annum (net of tax) on administration costs as a consequence of the takeover.

Extracts from the pre-acquisition budgets of both companies are as follows.

		Penn	Dink
		£000	£000
Profit after tax		300	60
Share capital:	£1 shares		200
	50p shares	400	

What will be the budgeted EPS of the Penn and Dink group after the acquisition?

A	38.0p
B	40.0p
C	42.2p
D	47.5p

Circle your answer

A   B   C   D

2   Heaton plc has made an offer of one of its shares for every two of Darrow plc. Synergistic benefits from the merger would result in increased after tax earnings of £4 million per annum.

Extracts from the latest accounts of both companies are as follows.

	Heaton plc	Darrow plc
Profit after tax	£120m	£20m
Number of shares	400 million	100 million
Market price of shares	170p	75p

Assuming that the price of Heaton plc's shares rises by 10p after the merger, the price earnings ratio of the Heaton and Darrow group after one year will be

A	5.63
B	5.79
C	6.25
D	7.50

Circle your answer

A   B   C   D

Data for questions 3 - 6

The following data are based on an extract from the 'share service' pages of the financial press.

Stock	Price	Dividend net	Cover	Yield gross	P/E
Prefects plc	260	7.2	2.8	W	12.7
Kane plc	140	8.2	3.1	7.8	X
Lessens plc	430	D_1	Y	6.0	15.0
Classes plc	MV	D_2	3.0	Z	7.0

None of these companies had any extraordinary gains or losses in their accounts.

The rate of Advance Corporation Tax is 25/75.

3   What is the missing value W for yield gross?

A   2.8%
B   3.7%
C   9.6%
D   10.4%

Circle your answer

A   B   C   D

4   What is the missing value X for P/E?

A   5.5 times
B   5.8 times
C   17.1 times
D   17.9 times

Circle your answer

A   B   C   D

5   What is the missing value Y for cover?

A   1.1
B   1.3
C   1.5
D   1.7

Circle your answer

A   B   C   D

6

What is the missing value Z for yield gross?

A 3.1%
B 3.6%
C 4.8%
D 6.3%

Circle your answer

A	B	C	D

7

The recently reported profits of Ohm Works plc were as follows.

	£000	£000
Profit on ordinary activities		5,750,000
Tax on profit on ordinary activities		1,200,000
Profit on ordinary activities after tax		4,550,000
Extraordinary loss	(800,000)	
Tax on extraordinary loss	200,000	
		(600,000)
		3,950,000
Ordinary dividend		(1,850,000)
Retained profits		2,100,000

Number of shares: authorised 20,000,000
                             issued 18,000,000

What are the earnings per share (EPS)?

A 19.75p
B 21.94p
C 22.75p
D 25.28p

Circle your answer

A	B	C	D

8

The recently reported profits of Ice Cool plc were as follows.

	£million
Profit on ordinary activities after tax	126
Minority interests	20
	106
Preference dividend	15
	91
Ordinary dividend	(30)
Retained profits	61

Ordinary shares, authorised and issued   250 million

What are the earnings per share (EPS)?

A 36.4p
B 42.4p
C 44.4p
D 50.4p

Circle your answer

A	B	C	D

41

9 In the year to 31 December 19X1, Ed Master plc had earnings per share of 50 pence, with a share capital of 12 million shares. The company made an issue of 6 million new shares on 1 May 19X2 to finance a major acquisition, and a further issue of 2 million new shares on 1 October to finance a second acquisition. The total earnings of the enlarged group in the year to 31 December 19X2 were £9,000,000.

What was the EPS in 19X2?

A   45.0p
B   52.9p
C   54.5p
D   58.1p

Circle your answer

A   B   C   D

Data for questions 10 and 11

Black Borden Chork plc makes a 1 for 4 rights issue on 1 April 19X2, at a subscription price of £2. The market value per share on the last day of quotation cum rights was £3.

There were 8 million shares in issue before the rights issue, and throughout 19X1. Total earnings in the year to 31 December 19X1 were £3,200,000. Total earnings in the year to 31 December 19X2 were £4,000,000.

10 What is the EPS for 19X2, as it would appear in the company's accounts for the year ended 31 December 19X2?

A   40.0p
B   41.5p
C   42.1p
D   42.7p

Circle your answer

A   B   C   D

11 What is the corresponding EPS for 19X1, as it would appear in the company's accounts for the year ended 31 December 19X2?

A   37.3p
B   40.0p
C   42.9p
D   50.0p

Circle your answer

A   B   C   D

12 The results of Price Gibbon Day plc for the year ended 31 March 19X2 were as follows.

	£
Profit on ordinary activities after tax	2,500,000
Extraordinary profit after tax	400,000
Profit after tax for the financial year	2,900,000
Preference dividend	200,000
Ordinary dividend (paid and proposed)	1,200,000
Retained profits for the year	1,500,000

What is the dividend cover?

A 1.92 times
B 2.07 times
C 2.08 times
D 2.25 times

Circle your answer

A   B   C   D

13 Musstrye Ardour plc is a small public company with 10,000,000 5p ordinary shares in issue. Its results for the year just ended are as follows.

	£	£
Profits on ordinary activities after tax		800,000
Extraordinary losses net of tax		(100,000)
		700,000
Dividends: interim (paid)	100,000	
final (proposed)	300,000	
		400,000
Retained profits		300,000

The market price per share is currently 80p cum div. What is the P/E ratio?

A 9.5
B 9.6
C 10.0
D 11.0

Circle your answer

A   B   C   D

14 The following data relates to shares of Gowan Gnome Thyme plc at the end of the day on 27 May 19X2.

Share price

		Closing prices, 27 May		
High for year	Low for year	Buying price	Mid-market price	Selling price
240p	190p	210p	220p	230p

The earnings per share for the year to 31 December 19X1 were 15p.

Continued...

What is the P/E ratio for the company that would be reported in the financial press on 28 May 19X2?

A   14.0
B   14.3
C   14.7
D   15.3

Circle your answer

A   B   C   D

15 Haig Rades and Beague Rades plc are listed companies in the same industry. Their P/E ratios and share prices are shown below.

	P/E ratio	Current share price ex div
Haig Rades plc	10	£6.00
Beague Rades plc	16	£4.80

Which of the following statements will best explain the higher P/E ratio of Beague Rades plc?

A   Beague Rades plc is a much larger company than Haig Rades plc

B   Beague Rades plc has higher EPS growth prospects than Haig Rades plc

C   Beague Rades plc is regarded as a higher risk investment than Haig Rades plc

D   Beague Rades plc retains a higher proportion of its annual post-tax profits than Haig Rades plc

Circle your answer

A   B   C   D

16 On 2 January 19X1, the All-Share Price Index stood at 1,000. On 2 January 19X7, the Index stood at 1,500. This 50% increase in average share prices can be attributed to changes in the average P/E ratio between 19X1 and 19X7, and also to *which* of the following factors?

A   Increase in total corporate earnings
B   Increase in total dividends paid
C   Increase in real asset values of companies
D   Increase in average earnings per share

Circle your answer

A   B   C   D

17 Hale Lovell plc has 20 million ordinary shares in issue. In the year to 31 December 19X3 total earnings were £6 million. The company also has in issue £9,240,000 of 10% convertible loan stock. The conversion rights are:

Date	Price per share £
30.6.X4	2.10
30.6.X5	2.20

The rate of corporation tax is 35%. What was the fully diluted earnings per share (FDEPS) for the year to 31 December 19X3?

A 27.1p
B 27.3p
C 28.4p
D 28.6p

Circle your answer

A	B	C	D

18 Mornan Assemblies plc has 20 million ordinary shares in issue. In the year to 31 December 19X3, total earnings were £8 million. The company also has in issue share options to selected employees. Details of these share options are as follows.

Date issued	Number	Exercise price
3 February 19X1	500,000	£1.50
20 May 19X2	300,000	£1.80

The price of $2\frac{1}{2}$% Consolidated Stock on 31 December 19X3 was £20 per cent. The rate of corporation tax is 30%.

What is the fully diluted earnings per share for the year to 31 December 19X3?

A 38.6p
B 39.0p
C 39.2p
D 39.3p

Circle your answer

A	B	C	D

19 Syon Slessons plc had 3,000,000 £1 ordinary shares in issue at 31 December 19X1. Pre-tax profits for 19X1 were £1,260,000. There are no extraordinary items in the P & L account. The rate of corporation tax on profits is 35%.

On 1 January 19X2, the company issues £1,000,000 of 10% convertible loan stock with the option to convert the stock into equity in 4 years' time at a conversion price of £3.33 per share. The capital raised from the loan issue would add £150,000 to annual profits (ignoring interest charges).

By how much must annual pre-tax profits grow from 19X6 onwards, above the 19X1 level, to avoid a dilution in EPS from 19X6 onwards below the 19X2 level?

Continued...

A   £126,000
B   £135,750
C   £189,150
D   £291,000

Circle your answer

A   B   C   D

20 Marta Borde plc has 9 million ordinary shares issued and fully paid, with a current market value of £3 each. Earnings are 16p per share in the year just ending. The company wishes to redeem £8 million of 12% loan stock at par with funds raised from a rights issue, but also wants the EPS to rise to 20p.

If corporation tax is 35%, which of the following rights issue arrangements would enable the company to achieve its objectives, if the rights issue and redemption of the loan stock occur at the start of the year?

A   A 1 for 3 rights issue at a price of £2.67
B   A 2 for 5 rights issue at a price of £2.22
C   A 4 for 9 rights issue at a price of £2.00
D   A 1 for 2 rights issue at a price of £1.78

Circle your answer

A   B   C   D

CHAPTER 4

THE COST OF FUNDS

This chapter covers the following topics:

- Cost of equity
- Cost of loan stock and other debt capital
- Weighted average cost of capital

1. Cost of equity

1.1 The cost of equity is the return that ordinary shareholders expect to receive from their investment. It is appropriate to measure this in terms of

- either the net dividend that the company pays (dividend valuation model of the cost of equity)

- or the net dividend that the company pays plus any capital gain on the share in a one year time span (capital asset pricing model valuation of the cost of equity)

1.2

Dividend valuation model: no dividend growth

$$r = \frac{d}{MV}$$

r = cost of equity, d = annual (net) dividend
MV = market price of the share, ex div.

1.3

Dividend valuation model: dividend growth of g per annum expected, with g expressed as a proportion

$$r = \frac{d(1 + g)}{MV} + g$$

1.4 With either dividend valuation model, it should be clear that r, d and MV are closely inter-related. If r increases but d is unchanged, MV will fall. If d rises but r is unchanged, MV will rise, and so on.

1.5

> **Capital asset pricing model**
>
> $$R_s = R_f + \beta(R_m - R_f)$$

R_s = expected return on the share (cost of equity)
R_f = risk free rate of return
R_m = market rate of return
β = beta factor of the company's equity shares.

The beta factor will be covered in more detail in a later chapter.

2 Cost of loan stock and other debt capital

2.1 The cost of loan stock, debentures or bank loans is the return which the company must provide its lenders.

2.2 *Cost of debt capital ignoring taxation*

- Irredeemable loan stock $r = \dfrac{i}{MV}$

  r = cost of loan stock, i = interest, MV = market value of loan stock ex-interest.

- Bank overdraft (if permanent) or variable rate loan

  $r = \dfrac{i}{MV}$

  i = interest at current rates (or fixed rate equivalent)
  MV = amount or market value of the loan

- Redeemable loan stock. Cost of loan stock (pre-tax) = the internal rate of return of the following cash flows

Year	Item	Cash flow £
0	Market value of loan	(MV)
1-n	Annual interest till redemption of loan in year n	i per annum
n	Redemption value of loan	RV

2.3 *Cost of debt capital allowing for taxation.* Since interest charges are allowable expenses in calculating corporation tax, loan capital has the advantage of reducing a company's tax bill, and the after-tax cost of capital is the appropriate cost of capital to calculate.

- When the rate of tax is t, the after-tax cost of irredeemable debt capital and variable rate loans is the pre-tax cost multiplied by a factor $(1 - t)$,

  $r = \dfrac{i(1 - t)}{MV}$

- In the case of redeemable loan stock, tax relief is allowable on the interest payments, but not on the payment to redeem the loan capital on maturity, and so the IRR cash flow calculations should be adjusted accordingly (see 2.2 above), with $i(1 - t)$ as the cash flow in either (1) years 1 - n or (2) years 2 to (n + 1), depending on assumptions about the timing of tax savings.

3. Weighted average cost of capital

3.1 The weighted average cost of capital (WACC) of a company's capital structure is the average of the cost of its equity, preference shares and various forms of permanent/long term loans, *weighted* to allow for the market value of each of these capital items.

3.2

Item	Market value £	Cost	Hash total
Equity	a	x	ax
Preference shares	b	y	by
Loan stock	c	z	cz
	a+b+c		(ax+by+cz)

$$\text{WACC} = \frac{(ax+by+cz)}{(a+b+c)}$$

3.3 If a company keeps its capital structure more or less unchanged over time, its WACC can be regarded as its opportunity cost of capital/marginal cost of capital, and this cost of capital can be used to evaluate the company's investment projects with discounted cash flow (DCF) analysis.

QUESTIONS

1 Curran Bunn plc has 14% irredeemable loan stock in issue. Investors require a gross yield of 12% on this stock. The corporation tax rate is 35% and the basic rate of income tax is 25%. What is the cost of the loan stock to the company?

A   7.80%
B   9.00%
C   9.10%
D   10.50%

Circle your answer

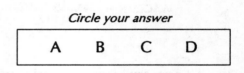

2 Sultan Pepper plc issued its 12% irredeemable debentures at 102. The current market price is 95. The company is paying corporation tax at a rate of 40%.

The current cost of capital to the company of these debentures is

A   7.1%
B   7.2%
C   7.6%
D   12.6%

Circle your answer

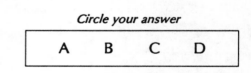

3 Cook Humber plc has £10 million of 12% loan stock in issue which is redeemable in 3 years' time at par. Interest for the year has just been paid and the loan stock has a market value of £97.20 per £100 nominal value of stock. The rate of corporation tax is 35%.

What is the approximate after tax cost of this loan stock to the company?

A   7%
B   8%
C   9%
D   10%

Circle your answer

A   B   C   D

4 Letty Sleef plc's irredeemable loan stock has a coupon rate of 10% and pays interest of £5 per £100 nominal stock on both 1 January and 1 July each year. If the cum interest price on 31 December is £92, what is the annual cost of the loan capital to the company? Ignore taxation.

A   10.9%
B   11.2%
C   11.5%
D   11.8%

Circle your answer

A   B   C   D

5 The balance sheet of Roland Butta plc is as follows.

	£
Fixed assets	21,000,000
Net current assets	3,000,000
	24,000,000
15% Debentures	4,000,000
	20,000,000
Ordinary shares of 25p each	10,000,000
Profit and loss account (retained profits)	10,000,000
	20,000,000

The company has paid a consistent dividend of 10 pence each year, and this rate of payment is expected into the indefinite future. The price per share is currently 50 pence cum div, with the annual dividend for the previous year about to be paid in four days' time.

Using the dividend valuation model, what is the cost of capital of Roland Butta plc's

(1) ordinary shares
(2) retained profits?

	Shares (1)	Retained profits (2)
A	20%	Nil
B	20%	20%
C	25%	Nil
D	25%	25%

Circle your answer

A B C D

6 The ordinary share price of Pam K Kroll plc is currently 200p. Dividend is paid once a year, and has very recently been paid for the previous year. The net dividend for the year was 5p and a 20% annual growth rate in perpetuity is expected for dividend payments in the future.

Using the dividend growth model, what is the cost of capital of Pam K Kroll plc's equity?

A 22.5%
B 23.0%
C 23.1%
D 23.3%

Circle your answer

A B C D

7 The ordinary shares of Barbara Q Dribb plc have a market value of 125 pence each cum div. The annual dividend for the year, which is about to be paid, is 5 pence per share. The expected annual growth rate in dividends is 10% per annum into the foreseeable future, so that the dividend payable at the end of next year is expected to be 5.5 pence, and so on.

The cost of capital for Barbara Q Dribb plc's ordinary shares, using the dividend growth model, is

A   14.2%
B   14.4%
C   14.6%
D   15.0%

Circle your answer

A   B   C   D

8   The dividends and earnings of Bayle Eaves plc over the last 5 years have been as follows.

Year	Dividends £	Earnings £
19X1	300,000	713,000
19X2	316,500	735,000
19X3	334,500	764,000
19X4	361,000	794,000
19X5	379,000	834,000

The company is financed entirely by equity, and there are 2,000,000 shares in issue, each with a market value of £1.18 ex div.

On the assumption that the data for 19X1-19X5 provides a basis for estimating future trends, what is the cost of equity?

A   16%
B   21%
C   22%
D   23%

Circle your answer

A   B   C   D

Data for questions 9 - 11

The following data relates to the ordinary shares of Lye Cheese plc.

Current market price, 31 December 19X1	250p
Market price one year ago, 31 December 19X0	227p
Earnings per share, 19X1	57.73p
Dividend per share, 19X1	35p
Expected growth rate in dividends and earnings	10% per annum
Average market return	20%
Risk-free rate of return	13%
Basic rate of income tax	30%
Beta factor of Lye Cheese plc's equity	1.5

9 The estimated cost of Lye Cheese plc's equity, using the dividend growth model and market price, is

A   24.0%
B   25.4%
C   30.0%
D   32.0%

Circle your answer

A   B   C   D

10 The estimated cost of Lye Cheese plc's equity, using the capital asset pricing model (CAPM), is

A   19.5%
B   23.5%
C   30.0%
D   30.5%

Circle your answer

A   B   C   D

11 The difference between the cost of equity using the dividend growth model and the cost of equity using the CAPM, is attributable to which one of the following causes?

A   The CAPM allows for a premium for financial risk, which the dividend growth model does not

B   The CAPM allows for a premium for business risk, which the dividend growth model does not

C   The CAPM calculates return as future share price changes as well as dividend, whereas the dividend growth model allows for expected future dividends only

D   The CAPM valuation of the cost of equity is based on expected return, excluding alpha values, rather than actual returns in any year

Circle your answer

A   B   C   D

12 Consider the following two statements.

Statement 1. When interest rates are high, the yield on loan stock will exceed the yield on equities.

Statement 2. The cost of equity reflects the opportunity cost of investment for ordinary shareholders. This cost varies from one company to another because of differences in the perceived business risk and financial risk of different companies.

Are these statements correct or incorrect?

	Statement 1	Statement 2
A	Correct	Correct
B	Incorrect	Incorrect
C	Correct	Incorrect
D	Incorrect	Correct

Circle your answer

A   B   C   D

13 Suppose that the yield curve has been steeply inverted, and as a consequence of the persistently high short term interest rates, the bond market eventually comes under pressure and bond prices start to fall. What is the likely consequence for equity share prices and equity yields?

	Equity prices	Equity yields
A	Will fall	Will rise
B	Will fall	Will fall
C	Will be unaffected	Will be unaffected
D	Will rise	Will fall

Circle your answer

A   B   C   D

14 Holly Voyle plc is undertaking a project to build a road/bridge over the Deepwatermouth Estuary. The project will take 4 years to complete, after which revenues will be earned from toll fees. Private capital has been subscribed, in the form of ordinary share capital, to finance the project. Share prices are currently £2.05 each. Shareholders expect dividends from their shares to be nothing for four years, then 100 pence per share at the end of year 5, and then 100 pence per share per annum in perpetuity.

What is the cost of Holly Voyle plc's equity?

A	16%
B	18%
C	20%
D	22%

Circle your answer

A   B   C   D

15 An all-equity company pays out all its earnings as dividends. Its shareholders on average have a tax rate of 35% on each additional £1 of income. *After all personal taxes*, these shareholders require a return of 18%. If an imputation tax system is in operation with a standard tax rate of 25%, what is the appropriate cost of equity capital for the company to use when evaluating post-corporation tax cash flows, to the nearest 1%?

A	18%
B	21%
C	24%
D	28%

Circle your answer

A   B   C   D

16 What is the cost of equity capital for Ray Viola plc from the data given below, using the Capital Asset Pricing Model?

Ray Viola plc

Current price per share on Stock Exchange	264 pence
Current annual net dividend per share	24 pence
Expected average annual growth rate in dividends	10%
Beta coefficient of X plc shares	0.80
Expected rate of return on risk-free securities	9%
Expected return on the market portfolio	14%

A 13.0%
B 14.3%
C 16.0%
D 20.0%

Circle your answer

A   B   C   D

17 Burton Mushrooms plc, an all-equity company, has just paid a dividend of 36p per share for the year in which earnings per share were 48p. The shares in issue are currently quoted at £2.50 each ex div.

Assuming that retained earnings contribute towards earnings and dividend growth, that the dividend/earnings ratio is expected to remain constant into the future and that the share's price reflects these expectations, what is the cost of capital of Burton Mushrooms plc and what is the expected annual growth rate in dividends?

You should use the formula

$$r = \frac{d(1 + br)}{MV} + br$$

where b is the proportion of earnings retained.

	Cost of capital	Growth rate in dividends
A	19.2%	4.8% pa
B	20.2%	5.0% pa
C	23.3%	7.7% pa
D	28.8%	12.0% pa

Circle your answer

A   B   C   D

18 A company has a dividend cover of 1.5 times and a P/E ratio of 4.5 (based on its shares' ex-dividend price). The most recent financial analysis of the company indicates a current and prospective 8% per annum growth in shareholders' funds resulting from retained earnings. What is the best estimate of the company's cost of equity capital?

A 14.8%
B 16.0%
C 22.8%
D 24.0%

Circle your answer

A   B   C   D

19 Consider the following statements.

Statement 1. The cost of capital is an opportunity cost of finance, because it is the minimum return that investors in the capital require.

Statement 2. The cost of funds retained by depreciation is ignored in calculating a weighted average cost of capital (WACC) because these funds can be taken as having a cost equal to the company's WACC.

Are these statements correct or incorrect?

	Statement 1	*Statement 2*
A	Correct	Correct
B	Correct	Incorrect
C	Incorrect	Correct
D	Incorrect	Incorrect

Circle your answer

A	B	C	D

20 A tax-paying company is financed in equal proportions by equity and debt capital. The interest on debt capital is tax deductible, and the corporation tax rate is 35%. What will be the effect of an increase in the rate of corporation tax on the value of the company?

A The value of the company will fall

B The value of the company will be unaffected

C The value of the company will rise

D The value of the company will rise or fall, depending on the extent of the increase in tax rate

Circle your answer

A	B	C	D

21 Mex Turbs plc has the following capital structure.

	£m
40 million ordinary shares of 50p	20
Reserves	120
11% loan stock	30
	170

The loan stock is irredeemable and has a current market value of 98 (ex interest). The company's rate of corporation tax is 40%. Its cost of equity has been estimated at 18% per annum. The current market price per share is 108p ex div.

The company's weighted average cost of capital, for investment appraisal purposes, is

A 11.4%
B 13.4%
C 15.2%
D 16.3%

Circle your answer

A   B   C   D

Data for questions 22 and 23

The balance sheet of Cory and Urr plc is as follows

	£000
Fixed assets plus net current assets	108,000
Long term liabilities	
10% irredeemable loan stock	28,000
	80,000
Ordinary shares of £0.50	20,000
Reserves	60,000
	80,000

Ordinary shares have a current market value of 90p, and annual dividends are expected to remain at 18p in perpetuity. The loan stock has a current market value of £71.43 per £100 nominal value of stock.

The rate of corporation tax is 35%.

The company includes in its current liabilities a bank borrowing facility at variable interest rates which is renewed every 6 months. It can be assumed that £10 million of this borrowing is needed on a permanent basis by the company. The interest rate currently being charged for borrowing under this facility is 16% per annum.

22 What is Corry and Urr plc's current weighted average cost of capital (approximately)?

A 13.5%
B 15.2%
C 16.1%
D 17.6%

Circle your answer

A   B   C   D

23 Suppose that Cory and Urr plc now raises £675,000 net of issue costs from a 1 for 4 rights issue. The share price after the issue falls to £0.85 on expectations of future annual dividends of 17p per share. Given no other changes in capital structure, what would the company's weighted average cost of capital now become?

A	13.8%
B	15.1%
C	15.7%
D	16.5%

Circle your answer

A   B   C   D

---

24 Kahn Flowers plc's equity has a beta factor of 0.9. The company is financed by a mixture of equity, preference shares and irredeemable long term debt capital, as follows.

Ordinary shares:	40 million shares, market value £2 per share
7% Preference shares of £1 each:	20 million shares, market value 50p per share
12% Debt capital	£20,000,000, market value £80 per £100 nominal value

If the market rate of return is 18%, the risk-free rate of return is 12% and the rate of corporation tax 35%, what is the company's weighted average cost of capital?

A	15.6%
B	15.7%
C	15.9%
D	16.7%

Circle your answer

A   B   C   D

---

25 Tony Quarter plc is an all-equity-financed company with 30 million shares, each with a market value of £0.80. The annual dividend on the shares is expected to be 16 pence per share in perpetuity.

The company is considering a new investment that would be financed by a loan of £20 million at an interest rate of 12%. After payment of interest, all the extra profits from the investment would be used to increase annual dividends.

As a consequence of the change in financial structure, the cost of equity would rise to 25%.

If we define the marginal cost of capital as the return that is needed to maintain the company's equity his investment at its existing value, what would be the marginal cost of the project's capital for Tony Quarter plc? Ignore taxation.

A	12%
B	15%
C	17%
D	18%

Circle your answer

A   B   C   D

CHAPTER 5

THE VALUATION OF MARKET SECURITIES

This chapter covers the following topics:

- A theory of share values and bond values
- The efficient markets hypothesis
- Technical analysis and fundamental analysis
- Dividend policy and share values
- The market value of traded share options

1. A theory of share values and bond values

1.1 A well-established theory of share values is that an equilibrium price for any bond or share on a stock market is

- the future expected stream of income from the security
- discounted at a suitable cost of capital.

> Equilibrium market price is thus a present value of a future expected income stream.

1.2 *Share values*

The annual income stream for a *share* is the expected dividend every year in perpetuity. Even if an investor expects to *sell* his shares at some time in the future, the price he will get is the PV of the expected future dividend stream in perpetuity, and so (on the assumption of insignificant transaction costs for selling/buying shares) we can safely ignore expected capital gains on share sales, and use dividend streams to value shares.

1.3
> The PV of £1 per annum in perpetuity from year 1 onwards is 1/r, and so if there is no expected dividend growth, the ex div price per share will be:
>
> $$MV \text{ ex div} = \frac{d}{r}$$
>
> where   d is the annual dividend (in perpetuity)
>   r is the cost of share capital, which is the return expected by the shareholders

The cost of equity capital *might* be estimated using the Capital Asset Pricing Model.

1.4 | If there is an expected *dividend growth* of g per annum, where g is a proportion or percentage

$$\text{MV ex div} = \frac{d_0 (1 + g)}{(r - g)}$$

Where d_0 is the dividend recently paid in the current year, and $d_0 (1 + g)$ is therefore next year's dividend.

1.5 The estimated growth rate might be

- based on historical growth rates in the past, projected into the future
- or based on the formula: $g = bR$

  where b is the proportion of annual earnings that are retained in the business, and
          R is the expected annual return (%) on these re-invested profits.

  Both b and R are assumed to be constant each year.

1.6 *Bond values.* The same theory is applied to derive an equilibrium price for marketable bonds.

The market price should be the present value of

- all future interest receivable up to the date of redemption of the bonds
- and any redemption value when the bonds are eventually redeemed.

This future income stream should be discounted at the appropriate cost of capital, which should be the investor's marginal cost of capital, although the *company's* pre-tax or post-tax cost of capital might be used in examination problems.

(1) *MV of irredeemable debt*

$$\text{MV ex int} = \frac{K}{i}$$

where K is the annual interest and i is the cost of capital

(2) *MV of redeemable debt*

$$\text{MV ex int} = \frac{K_1}{(1+i)^1} + \frac{K_2}{(1+i)^2} + ... + \frac{K_n}{(1+i)^n} + \frac{V_n}{(1+i)^n}$$

Where $K_1, K_2 ...K_n$ is the interest receivable at the end of each time period up to redemption, at the end of period n, and V_n is the redemption value at the end of period n.

1.7 Convertible loan stock valuation

MV ex int will be *at least* the *higher* of

(1) $\quad \dfrac{K_1}{(1+i)} + \dfrac{K_2}{(1+i)^2} + ... + \dfrac{K_n}{(1+i)^n} + \dfrac{V_n}{(1+i)^n}$

and (2) $\quad \dfrac{K_1}{(1+i)} + \dfrac{K_2}{(1+i)^2} + ... + \dfrac{K_{(n-1)}}{(1+i)^{(n-1)}} + \dfrac{S_n}{(1+i)^n}$

where S_n is the current market value of the shares into which the loan stock can be converted. Formula (2) assumes that there would be no interest payable on the stock in the year of conversion, if the investor's decision is to convert the stock into shares, and so the final interest payment would be in year (n-1).

2. The efficient markets hypothesis

2.1 How do investors obtain their estimates of future dividends from shares? Obviously, much depends on the information that is available to them. This consideration leads us into the efficient markets hypothesis.

2.2 We can introduce a second consideration too. Is it possible for investors to 'out-guess' the market, and to make a profit by anticipating share price changes ahead of the rest of the market, and buying or selling shares to make money from their foresight?

2.3

> An efficient market is one in which information is widely available to all investors, at a low cost, and all the available, relevant information is already reflected in share prices and bond prices.

- The *weak-form* efficient markets hypothesis is that share prices reflect all the information about companies that is contained in the record of past share prices.

- The *semi-strong form* efficient markets hypothesis is that share prices reflect not just all the information that is contained in the record of past share prices, but also all publicly available information, such as announcements of earnings and dividends, earnings forecasts, announcements of mergers or takeovers and changes in accounting practice.

- The *strong form* efficient markets hypothesis is that share prices reflect not just all the information in the record of past share prices and all publicly available information, but also *all* the information that can be obtained from very thorough 'fundamental analysis' of companies and the economy etc.

2.4 Whatever form of efficiency the markets show,

- current share prices reflect all the information that the market 'uses'
- share prices change only when new information becomes available.

2.5 Since the future is uncertain, just what new information will emerge must be unpredictable. It follows that share price changes, when they occur in response to new information, could be either up or down. The *random walk* theory of share price changes, that share price movements occur randomly, up or down, supports the efficient markets hypothesis.

2.6 If the market *does* have strong form efficiency, it will be impossible for any investor in the long term, except by luck, to 'out-guess' the market and make profits by buying and selling shares with better 'insider knowledge' than others about how share prices will change.

3. Technical analysis and fundamental analysis

3.1 There are two types of investment analysts.

- *Fundamental analysts* study a company and its business, and attempt to uncover information about its current and future performance, in order to obtain an assessment of the value of the company's shares.

- *Technical analysts or chartists* study the share price movements in the past of a company's shares, and look for patterns or cycles in these price changes, and upper or lower 'resistance levels' for prices - a breach of a resistance level, with the share price rising above or below it, would be interpreted as a significant shift in the pattern of price movements.

3.2 These analysts compete with each other to provide good and accurate information, which means that information is widely available to investors.

- Fundamental research ensures that *all* relevant information is available
- Technical research ensures that information about past price changes is available, so that significant 'upswings' or 'downswings' in a share's price will quickly become known and the current share price will then jump immediately and bring the trend or cyclical price movement to an end.

4. Dividend policy and share values

3.3 A company's directors will have a policy for

- what proportion of profits to pay out as dividends and what proportion of profits to retain for reinvestment
- what rate of dividend growth to aim for, with the help of reinvesting retained profits.

3.4 Their choice of policy might affect their company's share price.

- A high dividend payout ratio gives shareholders more current income (on which individual shareholders pay income tax)

- A high retentions ratio should provide for future earnings and dividend growth, which ought to improve the current share price and so give investors a capital gain (on which capital gains tax would be payable if an individual investor chose to sell the shares).

It could be argued that either (1) a high dividend payout ratio or (2) a low dividend payout ratio, could improve share prices, depending to a large extent on the preferences of shareholders.

3.5 Aspects of dividend policy to consider are:

- taxation for shareholders
- the law on distributable profits
- the strong preference of investors for dividends to remain at least stable, and not to be reduced from one year to the next, even if profits fall
- inflation, and the need to retain some profits just to preserve the real value of the company's equity capital.

3.6 An argument was put forward by Modigliani and Miller that the dividend policy of a company is *irrelevant* to its share price. They argued that in a perfect and efficient capital market with no taxes, if a company pays a high dividend, it can replace the money it has paid out with an issue of new shares. There will be some loss of capital value to existing shareholders, but this will be exactly equal to the amount of dividend they receive.

> By making dividends higher, there will simply be an offsetting capital loss for existing shareholders, and so the new position of shareholders is the same, whatever the dividend payment ratio (0% to 100%).

3.7 MM's arguments can be criticised because markets are not perfect in reality. The arguments have also be criticised because differences in the rate of tax between dividends and capital gains will give shareholders a preference for one or the other. However, when the rates of tax on dividends and capital gains are the same, MM's 'irrelevancy' argument about dividend policy and share prices becomes much more potent.

4. The market value of traded share options

4.1 Estimating a value for traded share options is done in a different way from estimating an equilibrium price for shares. It is fairly straightforward to work out the value of a call option or put option when the expiration date for the options has been reached.

> *Value of options at expiration*
>
> (1) Call option value = Market price of share - Exercise price
> (2) Put option value = Exercise price - Market price of share

4.2 But what about an option's value *before* expiration date?

At any time, a call option might be

- in-the-money: share price higher than the exercise price
- out-of-the-money: share price lower than the exercise price

An option will *not* have a negative value, because the option holder can simply choose not to exercise it, and the options will lapse (unused) after their expiration date.

4.3 An investor can use options to hedge against unfavourable movements in the share price (or to speculate on share price movements). Dealers who 'write' and sell options to investors, and who create a market in traded options, sell options at a price, and so investors who use options incur a cost of hedging or speculating in the price that they pay for them.

4.4 *The Black-Scholes formula (for option valuations)*

> The following notes are only relevant if you are *required* to know about the Black-Scholes option valuation formula.

A theoretical relationship between the *current* market value of a call option and a put option on shares in the same company was developed by Black and Scholes who argued that an investor would get an identical pay-off from either:

(1) buying a call option in the company's shares and also investing cash now in risk-free investments to earn enough by the option's expiration date to buy the shares at their exercise price; or

(2) buying the share now and also buying a put option to sell the shares at the same exercise price as in (1) above.

> The Black-Scholes formula is
>
> Value of call + Present value of exercise price = Value of put + Share price now

The PV of the exercise price found by discounting the exercise price at the expiration date at the *risk-free* rate of interest.

4.5
> The value of an option increases with
>
> - the volatility of the share price and
> - the time to expiration date for the option.

4.6 The Black-Scholes option valuation formula *is* used in practice by traded option dealers, with the benefit of computer programs or specially-programmed calculators.

QUESTIONS

1 Broken Boans plc has issued the following bonds.

£2 million   of zero coupon bonds, redeemable at par after 5 more years
£2 million   of floating rate debentures, issued a year ago at par with interest rates revised every six months.
£2 million   of 9% irredeemable loan stock.

The gross return currently required by all bond investors is 10% per annum. What will be the total market value of these bonds to the nearest £100,000? Ignore taxation.

A   £4.8 million
B   £5.0 million
C   £5.8 million
D   £6.0 million

Circle your answer

| A | B | C | D |

2 The required return on a share is 18% per annum. It is expected that in one year's time a dividend of 8 pence will be paid and the share price will be 80 pence. What will the current share price be, according to the theory of share values?

A   68p ex div
B   75p ex div
C   75p cum div
D   76p cum div

Circle your answer

| A | B | C | D |

3 The shares of Crack Tribb plc have a current market price of 74 pence each, ex div. It is expected that the dividend in one year's time will be 8 pence per share. The required return from net dividends on these shares is 16% per annum.

According to the theory of share values, if the expected growth in future dividends is by a constant annual percentage, what is this expected annual dividend growth?

A   0.4% per annum
B   3.5% per annum
C   3.8% per annum
D   5.2% per annum

Circle your answer

| A | B | C | D |

4 Grays d'Elbo plc has just paid an annual ordinary dividend of 20p per share. The dividend is expected to rise by 10% per annum (compound). The cost of equity is 15%.

According to the dividend valuation model, what should be the market value per share ex div in one year's time?

Continued...

A   440p
B   464p
C   484p
D   506p

Circle your answer

A   B   C   D

5   8% loan stock in Rooney Nose plc is redeemable after 3 more years at 105%. Interest is paid annually, and the next payment is due after one year. The cost of this debt capital to the company is 12% net of tax. Tax payments occur in the same year as the cash flows which give rise to them. Company taxation is at the rate of 35%.

What is the equilibrium price per £100 of the stock?

A   £57.37
B   £61.07
C   £83.53
D   £87.23

Circle your answer

A   B   C   D

6   Bach Cakes plc is considering whether to issue a 15 year 9% redeemable debenture at par in a market where similar securities are yielding 11% per annum. What is the minimum redemption premium (to the nearest pound) on £100 of debt that the company would have to offer? Assume debenture interest would be paid annually. Ignore taxation.

The present value of £1 per annum at a discount rate of 11%:

    Years 0-14   = 7.98
    Years 1-15   = 7.19

Present value of £1 at the end of year 15 at 11% = £0.21.

A   £15
B   £30
C   £34
D   £68

Circle your answer

A   B   C   D

7   The price of Stefan Sore plc's shares is currently £40 per share ex div. The most recent annual dividend was £3.00 per share.

If the company's cost of equity is 10% pa, what is the implicit constant annual dividend growth rate?

A   2.33%
B   2.44%
C   2.50%
D   9.23%

Circle your answer

A   B   C   D

8 Hake and Legge plc has 40 million shares in issue, and its capital structure has been unchanged for many years. Its dividend payments in the years 19X1 to 19X5 were as follows.

End of year	Dividends
	£000
19X1	2,200
19X2	2,578
19X3	3,108
19X4	3,560
19X5	4,236

Dividends are expected to continue to grow at the same average rate into the future. According to the dividend valuation model, what should be the market price per share at the start of 19X6 if the required return on the shares is 25% per annum?

A £0.96
B £1.10
C £1.47
D £1.73

Circle your answer

A   B   C   D

9 The shares in Neil Igament plc earn an annual dividend, and a dividend of 14p per share has just been paid. The expected future growth rate in dividends has been 15% per annum and investors require a return of 22% (based on net dividends).

Information is now obtained indicating that the expected future annual growth rate in dividends will be 13% only, not 15%. By how much should the share price fall, given no change in investors' required return?

A   31 pence
B   44 pence
C   51 pence
D   54 pence

Circle your answer

A   B   C   D

10 Paul Damstring plc has 10 million shares in issue. Dividends for the year just ended were £2 million. Owing to a downturn in the economy, the company has taken certain rationalisation measures, and future dividends are now expected to be as follows.

End of year 1   £1 million
Subsequently rising by 20% per annum (compound) for 2 years (years 2 and 3) and then by 10% per annum (compound) from year 4 onwards.

Investors require a return of 15% on these shares. According to the dividend valuation model, what should the market price per share be, based on these future dividend expectations?

A   £2.17
B   £2.36
C   £2.56
D   £3.85

Circle your answer

A   B   C   D

11 Carter Ledge plc's dividends are generally expected to increase by 15% per year for 3 years, by 8% in the following year and then to remain constant at the year 4 level for every year thereafter. The dividend per share in the year just ended was 11.5 pence.

The cost of equity capital is 18%. What should be the market price per share?

A   84p
B   87p
C   97p
D   108p

Circle your answer

A   B   C   D

12 The cost of capital in ordinary shares of Hanklin Plaster plc is 21% per annum.

Dividend is paid half yearly, as follows:

Interim dividend (end of month 6)	15p
Final dividend (end of month 12)	25p
	40p

There is no annual dividend growth. A final dividend has just been paid. What is the current equilibrium market price per share?

A   178p
B   184p
C   190p
D   400p

Circle your answer

A   B   C   D

13 The following data relate to an all-equity financed company, Bruce Chinn plc.

Dividend just paid	£180,000
Earnings retained and invested	60%
Return on investments	15%
Cost of equity	20%

What, according to the theory of share values, should be the market value of the company (to the nearest £1,000)?

A   £900,000
B   £1,363,000
C   £1,636,000
D   £1,784,000

Circle your answer

A   B   C   D

14 An investor has an effective marginal tax rate on capital gains of 30%. The standard rate of income tax is 25%. Assuming the imputation system applies, which of the following is the highest marginal rate of income tax at which the investor prefers dividends to capital gains, according to the theory of share values?

A 25%
B 30%
C 47%
D 55%

Circle your answer

A   B   C   D

15 Bond prices have fallen in the stock market. What would you expect to happen to share prices and long term borrowing by companies?

	Share prices	New issues of loan stock
A	Would fall	Would decrease
B	Would fall	Would increase
C	Would rise	Would decrease
D	Would rise	Would increase

Circle your answer

A   B   C   D

Data for questions 16 and 17

Burr Steerdrum plc has been achieving the following annual results.

	£
Profit before interest	1,000,000
Interest on £2,500,000 12% loan stock	300,000
	700,000
Tax at 30%	210,000
Earnings and dividends	490,000

The loan stock has a market value at par, and the cost of equity is 19.6%. There are 1,000,000 shares in issue.

The company is now considering a project costing £1,000,000 which would add to profits by £200,000 per annum in perpetuity before interest and tax. All earnings would continue to be paid as dividends.

The share price will respond immediately to any change in expected future dividends. Tax on profits will remain at 30%.

16 By how much will the share price change if the project is undertaken, financed entirely by new debt capital, so that the cost of debt remains unchanged but the cost of equity rises to 22%? The share price will:

Continued...

A   fall by 2p
B   rise by 25p
C   rise by 43p
D   rise by £1.38

Circle your answer

A   B   C   D

17 By how much would the share price change if the project is undertaken, financed entirely by new equity capital by issuing new shares (at the current market price), so that the cost of debt remains unchanged but the cost of equity in the company falls to 17%? The share price will

A   fall by 13p
B   rise by 15p
C   rise by 21p
D   rise by 86p

Circle your answer

A   B   C   D

18 The following are abstracts from a notice published in the financial press:

'Notice is hereby given that Coe Verdin Spots plc will redeem on 15 September 19X5 all of its outstanding 9% Convertible Debenture Stock 19X8 at the redemption price of 100% of the principal amount plus accrued interest from 15 May to 15 September 19X5.

As the alternative to redemption, the debenture holders have the right, on or before the close of business on 15 September 19X5, to convert their debentures into ordinary shares of Coe Verdin Spots plc at the conversion price of £12 per share. Upon conversion of debentures no payment or adjustment will be made for interest accrued thereon'.

What is the minimum market price per share at which debenture holders upon conversion would receive ordinary shares having a higher market value than the cash they would receive on redemption (ignoring any taxation implications)?

A   £12.00
B   £12.36
C   £12.45
D   £12.72

Circle your answer

A   B   C   D

19 Hitchin Parts plc has 2 million ordinary shares in issue, and 25,000 units of convertible debentures each with a nominal value of £100 and a coupon rate of 8%, payable yearly. Each £100 unit may be converted into 25 ordinary shares at any time until the date of expiry 5 years from now. Any remaining unconverted debentures will then be redeemed at 105. The pre-tax rate of interest on a 5-year debt security is 10%.

What will be the *minimum* value for £100 of the debentures if the current share price is (1) £3.70, and (2) £4.40?

Continued...

PV of £1 pa for 5 years at 10% = 3.79
PV of £1 at the end of year 5 at 10% = 0.62

	(1) Current share price £3.70	(2) Current share price £4.40
A	£92.5	£ 95.4
B	£95.4	£110.0
C	£92.5	£110.0
D	£95.4	£ 95.4

Circle your answer

A   B   C   D

20 Ed Lice plc has 8% convertible loan stock in issue which becomes convertible at the end of two more years at the rate of 40 ordinary shares per £100 of stock. The market perceives two possible outcomes for dividend growth in the future.

Outcome		Probability
1	Dividend growth 5% per annum in perpetuity	0.3
2	Dividend growth 10% per annum in perpetuity	0.7

Convertible loan stock holders require a return of 15% and ordinary shareholders want a return of 20%. (Ignore taxation). An annual dividend of 30p per share has just been paid. Annual interest on the stock has just been paid.

What is the expected market value of £100 of the convertible loan stock (to the nearest £1)?

A £102
B £106
C £110
D £118

Circle your answer

A   B   C   D

21 Pinzon Needles plc has just raised £20 million of extra funds by issuing new shares. These are expected to increase earnings by £6 million in the first year. 47.6% of earnings will be retained each year, in order to achieve dividend growth on the additional investment of 10% per annum. Dividends will be paid annually at each year end. The beta factor of the additional investments is 1.10, the market return is 20% and the risk free rate of return is 10%.

By how much should the issue of new funds add to the total equity value of Pinzon Needles plc (to the nearest £100,000)?

A £20.0 million
B £26.0 million
C £28.6 million
D £34.5 million

Circle your answer

A   B   C   D

22 The return on a share is measured by the dividend and share price appreciation during a period, as a percentage of the share price at the start of the period.

During 19X1, the following data related to the return on shares in Armenia Sling plc.

Price per share at the start of the period	250p
Dividend paid during the period	20p
Share's measured beta	1.15
Share's measured alpha	-6%
Market return in the period	20%
Risk-free rate of return in the period	12%

What was the share price at the end of the period?

A   268p
B   272.5p
C   283p
D   288p

Circle your answer

A   B   C   D

23 The data below has been used to estimate a beta factor for shares in Torner Mussles plc.

	Stock market index	Torner Mussels plc Share price £	Dividend £
31.12.X0	1,500	1.40	Nil
31.12.X1	1,810	1.83	Nil
31.12.X2	1,970	2.10	Nil
31.12.X3	1,900	1.94	Nil
31.12.X4	2,280	2.43	Nil

From this data, the variance of market returns is 0.0151 and the covariance of the market rate of return and the return on Torner Mussels plc's shares is 0.0192. The stock market index is expected to rise by 10% in 19X5. The risk free rate of return is 6%.

What is the share price for Torner Mussles plc that should be expected at the end of 19X5, if the company pays no dividend in the year?

A   £2.62
B   £2.65
C   £2.70
D   £2.74

Circle your answer

A   B   C   D

24 An investor who makes all his investment decisions just by analysing historical share price movements as a basis for predicting future price changes is acting as if he believed that the stock market has

A   weak form efficiency
B   semi-strong form efficiency
C   strong form efficiency
D   no efficiency at all

Circle your answer

A   B   C   D

25 Which of the following statements about the strong-form efficient markets hypothesis are correct?

Statement
1. It implies the ability to forecast future share price changes
2. It implies that share prices are valued fairly, and this is evidenced by continual rises and falls in market prices.

A Statements 1 and 2 are both correct
B Statement 1 only is correct
C Statement 2 only is correct
D Neither statement is correct

Circle your answer

A	B	C	D

26 Which are the correct concluding statements to the following propositions of random walk theory?

First proposition
The random behaviour of share price changes occurs because
1. investors are rational and competitive
2. the stock market behaves irrationally

Second proposition
Prices of a company's shares fluctuate randomly from day to day
3. and changes in share price on any day are independent of price changes on the previous days
4. but there is a tendency for share price changes up or down to persist for several successive days.

The correct concluding statements are

A 1 and 3
B 1 and 4
C 2 and 3
D 2 and 4

Circle your answer

A	B	C	D

27 Which of the following statements about the efficient markets hypothesis are correct?

Statement
1. The weak form of the hypothesis implies that it is impossible for an investor to earn superior returns by looking at patterns in share price changes.

2. The semi-strong form of the hypothesis implies that it is impossible for an investor to earn superior returns by studying company reports and accounts, newspapers and investment journals etc.

3. The strong form of the hypothesis implies that since security prices reflect all available information, there is no way that most investors can achieve consistently superior returns.

Continued....

A   Statements 1 and 2 only are correct
B   Statements 1 and 3 only are correct
C   Statements 2 and 3 only are correct
D   Statements 1, 2 and 3 are all correct

Circle your answer

A   B   C   D

28 Wharton Fingers plc has just made a public announcement that it plans to launch a new product on to the market that should reduce the volatility of its reported annual profits. On the same day Saliva plc, a food products manufacturer, has publicly announced that it has withdrawn substantial stocks of its product from its retailer customers because of a reported food poisoning incident.

If neither of these items of information had been made public before, what effect should they now have on the companies' share prices, assuming that the stock market has semi-strong form efficiency?

	Wharton Fingers plc share price	*Saliva plc share price*
A	Decrease	No change
B	No change	Decrease
C	Increase	No change
D	Increase	Decrease

Circle your answer

A   B   C   D

29 Which of the following statements is/are correct?

Statement
1.   If, over time, a company's P/E ratio remains constant, dividends are a constant proportion of earnings, and dividends grow annually, the ratio of market price to dividends will also be constant.

2.   According to the strong form efficient markets hypothesis, changes in the stock price index should be an important leading indicator of economic change.

A   Statements 1 and 2 are both correct
B   Statement 1 only is correct
C   Statement 2 only is correct
D   Neither statement is correct

Circle your answer

A   B   C   D

30 In October 1987 there was a sudden and dramatic fall in share prices on most of the world's stock exchanges, with share prices falling by 25% - 30% or more. What implications for the efficient markets hypothesis can be drawn from this collapse in prices?

A   The hypothesis remains valid. Share prices were responding suddenly to unforeseen new information that became available

Continued...

B The hypothesis is discredited because the principle that there is a single 'true' value for a share's price at any point in time cannot be completely valid

C The share price collapse was a temporary phenomenon, because share prices recovered from their October 1987 low points within about two years

D The hypothesis is discredited because in an efficient market, the fall in share prices would not have been so dramatic or sudden.

Circle your answer

A	B	C	D

31 Bandy Jing plc is financed entirely by issued share capital of 8 million ordinary shares of 50 pence each nominal value. Their market price is currently £1.50, just prior to a 1 for 4 rights issue at £1 per share.

The finance raised will be invested immediately in a project that has an expected net present value of + £3 million.

What are the best estimates of the likely share price after the rights issue if the market shows (1) weak form efficiency and (2) strong form efficiency with the expected NPV of the project known and believed by investors.

	(1) Market has weak form efficiency	*(2) Market has strong form efficiency*
A	£1.40	£1.50
B	£1.40	£1.70
C	£1.50	£1.50
D	£1.50	£1.70

Circle your answer

A	B	C	D

Data for questions 32 and 33

Coot plc has 1 million shares in issue and Grays plc has 4 million.

Day
1. Market value per share is £2 for Coot and £3 for Grays
2. Grays' management decide to make a cash takeover bid for Coot, at a price of £3 per share, with the purchase consideration in cash. The takeover will produce savings with a present value of £4 million. Grays announces its takeover bid but makes no public announcement of the expected savings
10. Grays announces details of the expected savings

32 Assuming that the market is semi-strong form efficient, and only the data above is relevant to share prices, what would be the share price of Coot and Grays on (1) day 2 and (2) day 10?

		Day 2	Day 10
A	Coot price	£2	£3
	Grays price	£3	£3.25
B	Coot price	£3	£3
	Grays price	£2.75	£3.25
C	Coot price	£3	£3
	Grays price	£3	£3.75
D	Coot price	£3	£3
	Grays price	£2.75	£3.75

Circle your answer

A   B   C   D

33 Assuming instead that the market is strong form efficient, and only the data above is relevant to the share prices, what would be the share price of Coot and Grays on (1) day 2 and (2) day 10?

		Day 2	Day 10
A	Coot price	£3	£3
	Grays price	£2.75	£3.25
B	Coot price	£3	£3
	Grays price	£3	£3.25
C	Coot price	£3	£3
	Grays price	£3.25	£3.75
D	Coot price	£3	£3
	Grays price	£3.75	£3.75

Circle your answer

A   B   C   D

34 Lorn Gleggs is an individual investor, resident in the UK, and Shortbody Ltd is a UK company. Each owns shares in Media Mite plc, a UK listed company. Details of their tax positions are given below

	Lorn Gleggs	Shortbody Ltd
Marginal rate of		
Income tax	30%	-
Corporation tax	-	35%
Tax on capital gains	Nil	30%

The rate of advance corporation tax is 3/7.

At present, Media Mite plc adopts a full distribution policy, but is considering a change to a policy of retaining all its earnings.

Continued...

According to the theory of share values, what would be the likely attitude of the shareholders to this proposed change of dividend policy, considering only their tax position?

	Lorn Cleggs	Shortbody Ltd
A	Indifferent	Prefers old policy
B	Indifferent	Prefers new policy
C	Prefers new policy	Prefers old policy
D	Prefers new policy	Prefers new policy

Circle your answer

A   B   C   D

35 The management of Slipper Disc plc is trying to decide on the company's dividend policy. The maximum annual dividend that can be paid this year is 8p per share. Retaining a proportion of profits would allow the company to reinvest earnings in order to achieve dividend growth. Four options are being considered.

	Current dividend	Annual dividend growth
Option A	8p (100% of earnings)	0% per annum
Option B	6p (75% of earnings)	6% per annum
Option C	4p (50% of earnings)	8% per annum
Option D	2p (25% of earnings)	$12\frac{1}{2}$ % per annum

The return required on net dividends is 16% per annum. Which option would maximise the value of the company's shares?

A   Option A
B   Option B
C   Option C
D   Option D

Circle your answer

A   B   C   D

36 Modigliani and Miller derived the following formula in their analysis of the relevance of dividend policy to a company's share price.

$$nP_0 = \frac{1}{1+p}[(n + m)P_1 - I + X]$$

Where
- P_0 = market price at time 0
- P_1 = market price at time 1
- n = number of shares at time 0
- m = number of new shares sold at time 1
- p = capitalisation rate for the company
- I = total new investments during period 1
- X = total profit of the company during period 1

What is implied by this formula?

Continued...

A   Dividend policy is irrelevant to the share price

B   Dividend policy is relevant to the share price, and to maximise this price, there should be 100% retained earnings

C   Dividend policy is relevant to the share price, and to maximise this price, there should be a 100% dividend payout and no retained earnings

D   The formula has no bearing on the relevance or irrelevance of dividend policy to the share price

Circle your answer

A   B   C   D

37 Which of the following statements lends most support to the theory that the pattern of dividend payout is irrelevant to the valuation of ordinary shares?

A   The marginal rate of tax on dividends is generally different from the rate of tax on capital gains

B   Shareholders may sell part of their holding in order to obtain cash for current consumption

C   The discount rate for investors tends to increase with time because of uncertainty

D   Investors tend to prefer steady growth in annual dividends

Circle your answer

A   B   C   D

38 The current price of a share is 160p. An analyst has estimated that the probability distribution of the share's price in three months time will be:

Share price (p)	140	150	160	170	180
Probability of occurrence	0.15	0.20	0.30	0.25	0.10

Call options on the share can be purchased with an expiry date of three months and an exercise price of 150p.

What is the expected value of a combined holding of one call option in three months' time? Ignore the time value of money.

Continued...

A   Nil
B   9.5p
C   10p
D   11p

Circle your answer

A   B   C   D

39 The Put-Call parity is stated as

A   Value of call + Share price =
    Value of put + PV of Exercise Price

B   Value of put + Share price -
    Value of call = PV of Exercise Price

C   Value of put + Value of call =
    Share price - PV of Exercise Price

D   Value of put + Value of call -
    Share price = PV of Exercise Price

Circle your answer

A   B   C   D

40 The value of call option will increase as

A   the underlying share price falls
B   the volatility of the underlying share price
    increases
C   the time to maturity decreases
D   interest rates increase

Circle your answer

A   B   C   D

41 An investor holds put options giving him the right to sell 1,000 shares in Feely Nunn Wells plc for £2,000. Which of the following graphs correctly shows how the value of the put options at expiration date will depend on the share price?

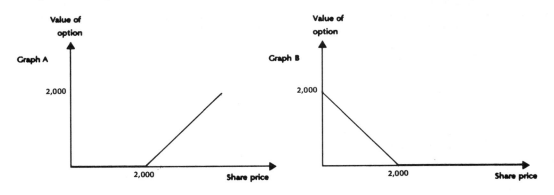

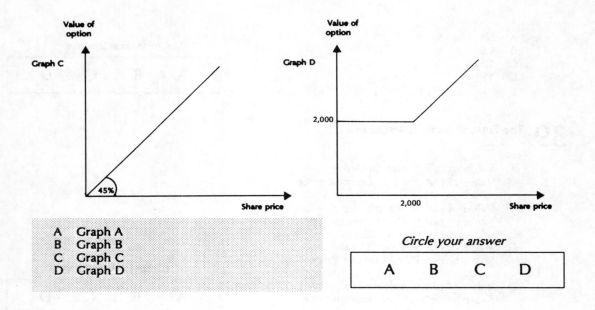

A   Graph A
B   Graph B
C   Graph C
D   Graph D

Circle your answer

A   B   C   D

42 Call options in Fanny Bone plc have an exercise price of 200 pence, which is their current market value. Their expiration date is in one year's time. Investors are assumed to be indifferent to risk and their expected return is 10% per annum.

It is expected that by the expiration date, the share price will *either*

(1)   fall to 160 pence or
(2)   rise to 240 pence

According to the Black-Scholes model for option values, what is the current value of one call option?

A   18 pence
B   20 pence
C   27 pence
D   30 pence

Circle your answer

A   B   C   D

CHAPTER 6

GEARING

1. Financial gearing and operating gearing

1.1 Gearing is used as a measure of risk. Financial gearing is a measure of financial risk and operating gearing is a measure of business risk.

1.2 *Financial gearing* measures the ratio of prior charge capital to either

(a) equity, or
(b) total capital

in a company's capital structure.

- Higher financial gearing means that more profits before interest and tax (PBIT) must be earned in order to pay interest (and preference dividend) to holders of prior charge capital.

- With higher financial gearing, a change in PBIT will have a bigger proportional effect on earnings than with lower financial gearing.

1.3 *Operating gearing* is a measure concerned with the relationship in a company between its variable/fixed cost operating structure and its profitability.

- Operating gearing can be measured as the ratio of contribution (sales minus variable costs of sales) to PBIT.

- The implications of operating gearing are best explained with an example.

	Company X	Company Y
	£000	£000
Sales	1,000	1,000
Variable costs	600	300
Contribution	400	700
Fixed costs	300	600
Profit	100	100

These companies have the same sales and the same profit, but differing cost structures. Company Y has a higher operating gearing, with a higher proportion of fixed costs.

o If sales in both companies fell by 10%, profits would fall by £30,000 more in company Y, because its higher operating gearing would cause a bigger fall in contribution (£70,000 compared with £40,000 in Company X).

o Similarly, if sales in both companies rose by 10%, Company Y's profits would rise by a bigger amount, because of its higher operating gearing.

The possibility of rises or falls in sales revenue and volumes means that operating gearing has implications for a company's business risk.

2. Measuring financial gearing

2.1 Financial gearing can be measured in a variety of ways, although every measure is a ratio of either:

(a) prior charge capital to equity capital (including reserves); or
(b) prior charge capital to total capital.

2.2 Prior charge capital consists of preference shares as well as loan stock/debentures/mortgage loans. Short term loans (less than one year to maturity) would generally be regarded as prior charge capital, although a current liability in the balance sheet, on the assumption that the loans will be replaced by new longer-term loans when they mature. Bank overdraft (especially if there is a solid core overdraft) might be included in prior charge capital too.

2.3 Equity capital or total capital might be valued by taking asset values as:

(a) net book value/balance sheet value;
(b) net replacement cost;
(c) original gross cost;
(d) gross replacement cost;
(e) current cost/value.

2.4 Financial gearing can also be measured for public limited companies by taking prior charge capital and equity capital at *market values*.

2.5
> When prior charge capital exceeds equity capital/reserves, the company is said to be high-geared.

3. Interest cover

3.1 Another way of measuring a company's financial risk is to look at interest cover.

$$\text{Interest cover} = \frac{\text{PBIT}}{\text{Interest charges}}$$

A cover of less than 3 times would indicate a very high level of financial risk.

4. Limits in practice to financial gearing

4.1 Financial gearing can reach very high levels, with companies preferring to raise additional capital for expansion by means of loans rather than issuing new equity, but there are limits in practice to what a company's gearing ought to be.

● Restrictions on further borrowing might be contained in the debenture trust deed for a company's current debenture stock in issue

● Occasionally, there might be borrowing restrictions in the Articles of Association

● Lenders might want *security* for extra loans which the would-be borrower cannot provide

● Lenders might simply be unwilling to lend more to a company with high gearing/low interest cover.

● Extra borrowing beyond a safe level will cost more in interest. Companies might not be *willing* to borrow at these rates. The term 'junk bonds' has been used to describe loan stock issued by companies without a high credit rating, which are generally unsecured, but which offer a high rate of interest to investors.

4.2 Very high levels of gearing have been reached by some companies, particularly those in the USA which have undergone a leveraged buyout (LBO). This is a takeover where the funds to pay for the takeover have been raised by the purchaser by issuing loan stock especially for the purpose. Companies which have undergone an LBO have either been:

(a)   saddled with very high interest costs to finance the high level of debt; or
(b)   forced to sell off parts of their business to repay some of the loans.

5. Theories of financial gearing and cost of capital

There are two main theories about the relationship between a company's level of financial gearing and its cost of capital.

● Both theories are concerned with whether there is an 'ideal' level of financial gearing for a company. Any such level will be one at which the company's weighted average cost of capital (WACC) is minimised.

● Both theories agree that

  o the cost of equity is higher than the cost of debt (because of the higher investment risk)

    ○ the cost of equity will increase as a company's level of financial gearing rises, because of the higher financial risk as gearing increases.

6. Traditional theory of gearing and WACC

The traditional theory is that as a company's gearing increases above zero, WACC will

(1)   fall initially, because of the higher proportion of lower-cost debt capital in the firm's capital structure

(2)   but eventually increase when gearing gets above a certain level, because the rising cost of equity offsets the higher proportion of low cost debt

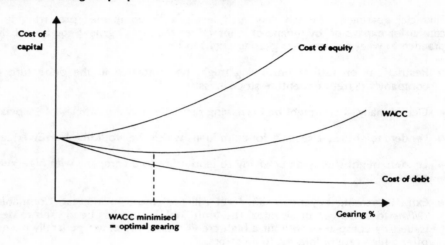

7. Modigliani and Miller's theories about gearing

7.1   An alternative theory of gearing, the net operating income approach, was supported by the US academics Modigliani and Miller.

    ● They argued that if we ignored corporate taxes (and tax relief for companies on interest charges, which reduces the cost of debt capital) the cost of equity would rise as gearing rises so as to *offset exactly* the benefits of the increasing proportion of lower-cost debt capital. The net result is that the WACC is the same at all levels of gearing.

    ● They later modified their theory to allow for corporate taxes (and tax relief on interest charges), and concluded that because of the tax shield for debt interest, a company's WACC will continue to fall as gearing rises, until it is minimised at the level where the company is financed entirely by debt capital.

7.2   *Arbitrage* by investors (buying and selling shares and debt capital to profit from different market prices for the securities of different companies) was a theoretical justification for why their theories are correct. Arbitrage is tested in questions at the end of this chapter.

8. Modigliani-Miller formulae - ignoring taxation

(1) The cost of equity is higher in a geared company than in an equivalent ungeared company, by a measurable amount.

$$K_g = K_u + [(K_u - K_d) \times \frac{D}{V_{eg}}]$$

Where K_g is the cost of equity in a geared company

K_u is the cost of equity in a similar ungeared company

K_d is the cost of debt capital

D is the market value of the debt capital (irredeemable debt) in the geared company

V_{eg} is the market value of the equity in a geared company

(2) Since the WACC is the same in companies regardless of gearing level, the total market value will be the same for companies that are identical in every respect except for their gearing level.

$$V_u = D + V_{eg}$$

V_u is the market value of an all equity company.

$D + V_{eg}$ is the total market value of the identical geared company.

9. Modigliani-Miller formulae - taking corporate taxation into account

(1) The cost of equity is still higher in a geared company than in an ungeared company, but by an amount which must be adjusted (by (1 - t)) to allow for tax relief on debt interest, when the rate of corporation tax is t.

$$K_g = K_u + [K_u - K_d) \times \frac{D}{V_{eg}} (1 - t)]$$

Where t is the rate of corporation tax.

(2) The total value of a geared company (equity plus debt capital) will *exceed* the value of an identical ungeared company, by an amount Dt.

$$V_g = V_u + Dt$$

$$V_g = D + V_{eg}$$

(3)   The WACC in a geared company will be lower than the WACC in an ungeared company by a measureable amount. WACC will fall as gearing increases.

$$\rho_L = \rho_u \left[1 - \frac{tD}{(D + V_{eg})} \right]$$

Where ρ_L is the WACC of the firm if it is levered (geared)

ρ_u is the WACC of the firm if it is unlevered (ungeared).

QUESTIONS

1 Heighway Curd Ltd has a current balance sheet as follows.

	£000
Net fixed assets	800
Net current assets	100
	900
Debt capital	200
	700
Equity and reserves	700

Its budgeted P & L account for next year is as follows.

	£000	£000
Sales		1,600
Variable operating costs	600	
Fixed operating costs	800	
		1,400
Profit before interest		200
Interest		20
Profit before tax		180

If the company now purchased a machine for £200,000, financed by a loan, which would reduce variable costs to 30% of sales, add £70,000 to fixed operating costs, add £30,000 to interest costs, but would *not* add to sales, what would be the change in the company's operating gearing?

A Increase to 36.4%
B Fall to 4.48 times
C Increase to 5.6 times
D Fall to 3.48 times

Circle your answer

A   B   C   D

2 The cost of capital of a company is influenced by the level of business risk in the company's operations. One major factor in business risk is the inherent trading risk in the operations, since some sectors of the economy are more vulnerable than others to downturns in economic activity. Which of the following factors also contribute to business risk?

Factor
1. Stage in the life cycle of the company's product(s)
2. Proportion of fixed costs to total costs
3. Proportion of debt capital to total capital

A Factors 1 and 2 only
B Factors 2 and 3 only
C Factors 1 and 3 only
D Factor 2 only

Circle your answer

A   B   C   D

3 The finance director of Dubble Park plc has estimated that on the basis of last year's results, given the company's current level of gearing, a 10% increase in profit before interest and tax (PBIT) would have increased both profits before tax and earnings by 30%.

By how much would profits before tax and earnings have risen if there had been a 25% increase in PBIT?

A 30.0%
B 45.0%
C 47.7%
D 75.0%

Circle your answer

A	B	C	D

4 The balance sheet of Hoover Taken plc is summarised below.

	£m	£m
Net fixed assets		110
Current assets		90
		200
Bank overdraft	20	
Trade creditors	40	
Other current liabilities	10	
		70
		130
12% debentures		30
		100
£1 ordinary shares		20
8% Preference shares of £1		10
		30
Reserves		70
		100

The company's ordinary shares have a current market price of £1.80 per share, the preference shares have a market value of £0.60 and the debentures are valued at £95 per cent.

Gearing can be measured in a variety of ways. Which of the following gearing ratios might all be used?

A 20.0%, 30.8%, 50.0%, 95.8%
B 30.0%, 50.0%, 67.9%,
C 30.8%, 44.4%, 66.7%, 95.8%
D 44.4%, 104.3%, 111.1%

Circle your answer

A	B	C	D

5 At 1 January 19X1 Terrific Lights plc had long term debt of £5 million and equity and reserves of £10 million (including proposed dividends) giving the company 50% gearing on balance sheet values.

A summarised funds flow statement for the year to 31 December 19X1 is as follows.

	£000	£000
Profit before tax		1,100
Add back depreciation		300
Less loss on sale of asset		(50)
		1,350
Proceeds from sale of asset	150	
New issue of ordinary shares	600	
New issue of loan stock	1,200	
		1,950
		3,300
Purchases of fixed assets	500	
Redemption of loan stock	900	
Tax paid	300	
Dividend paid	400	
		2,100
		1,200

The company's tax liability at 1 January was £250,000, and at 31 December it stands at £350,000.

What is the company's gearing ratio at 31 December?

A   46.9%
B   47.7%
C   48.6%
D   49.1%

Circle your answer

A   B   C   D

6 The interest cover ratio, like the gearing ratio, is often used to assess the financial risk of a company, and an interest cover of less than 3 times would often be regarded as a sign of high risk.

What is the interest cover of the company whose results are shown below?

Multiple Pileup (Carpets) Ltd

	£000
Profit before interest and tax	200
Interest	80
	120
Tax	40
	80
Preference dividend	40
Earnings	40

A 1.0 times	
B 1.5 times	*Circle your answer*
C 2.0 times	
D 2.5 times	A B C D

7 There are limits to the amount of debt capital that a company will be able to raise. Which of the following items will *not* act as such a limit?

A   High interest rates on extra borrowing

B   Limits imposed by covenants made on debentures already in issue

C   Insufficient assets to provide security for an extra loan

D   Borrowing restrictions in the company's Articles of Association

Circle your answer

A   B   C   D

8 Suppose that, for a given level of activity, a firm's ratio of variable costs to fixed costs were lower, and at the same time, its ratio of debt to equity fell. What would be the impact on the firm's financial risk and operating risk?

	Financial risk would	Operating risk would
A	Increase	Increase
B	Decrease	Increase
C	Increase	Decrease
D	Decrease	Decrease

Circle your answer

A   B   C   D

9 Consider the following statements about highly-geared companies.

Statement 1. Until the collapse of the junk bond market in 1989/90, a company could issue high-interest-earning unsecured debt capital and become very highly-geared in order to raise funds to acquire a target group of companies. After the takeover, it would sell off some or all of the purchased group in separate bits at a profit, and use the proceeds to redeem its loans.

Statement 2. If a company is considering a large investment project which it would finance either by retained earnings or by raising new debt capital, it should try to use the marginal cost of investment capital in a DCF evaluation of the project. Since there is no marginal cost to retained earnings, the cost of capital to use should be the after tax cost of debt capital.

Are these statements correct or incorrect?

	Statement 1	Statement 2
A	Correct	Correct
B	Correct	Incorrect
C	Incorrect	Correct
D	Incorrect	Incorrect

Circle your answer

A   B   C   D

10 Rod Humber-Green plc is a company that can earn profits (before interest) of £1,881,000 per year. The company does not retain any earnings. If the company is all-equity financed, the cost of equity will be 18%. For each £1,000,000 of loan stock that is used to finance the company instead of equity, the cost of equity will be as follows.

Amount of loan stock	Cost of equity
£1 million	20%
£2 million	22%
£3 million	24%

The marginal cost of loan stock is 12%. Ignore taxation.

How much loan stock should be in the company's capital structure so as to minimise the company's weighted average cost of capital?

A None
B £1,000,000
C £2,000,000
D £3,000,000

Circle your answer

A   B   C   D

11 Rhodes Works plc is a company that earns profits before interest of £500,000 per year. None of these profits are retained as earnings. If the company is all-equity financed, the cost of equity will be 12%. For each £1,000,000 of loan stock that is used to finance the company instead of equity, the cost of equity and the cost of loan stock will be as follows.

Amount of loan stock	Cost of equity	Cost of all loan stock
£1 million	$12\frac{1}{2}$ %	10%
£2 million	13 %	12%
£3 million	$13\frac{1}{2}$ %	14%

Ignore taxation.

What level of loan stock finance will minimise the company's weighted average cost of capital?

A None
B £1,000,000
C £2,000,000
D £3,000,000

Circle your answer

A   B   C   D

12 According to Modigliani and Miller the cost of equity will *always* rise with increased gearing because

    A   the firm is more likely to go bankrupt

    B   total earnings will fall

    C   the return to shareholders becomes more variable

    D   the tax shield on debt increases the value of the shareholders' equity

Circle your answer

| A | B | C | D |

13 The following details are available about Gavin Waysign plc.

Par value of 12% irredeemable loan stock	£10 million
Tax rate	NIL
Earnings before interest and tax in perpetuity	£6 million per annum

The loan stock's market value is at par, and an otherwise identical all-equity financed company has a cost of equity of 20%.

If Modigliani and Miller's propositions hold, what is the cost of Gavin Waysign plc's equity capital?

A   18.0%
B   20.0%
C   22.7%
D   24.0%

Circle your answer

| A | B | C | D |

14 Occident Report plc has the following capital structure.

	Market value £
Ordinary shares	20,000,000
14% loan stock	10,000,000
	30,000,000

The loan stock is valued at par. The company earns profits after interest of £4 million per year and all such profits are distributed as dividends. It now plans to raise £5 million in new equity, and use this to redeem £5 million of the loan stock. You should ignore issue costs, redemption costs and taxation.

According to Modigliani and Miller's theories, what would be the cost of equity in the company when the capital structure has been changed in this way?

A   16.0%
B   18.0%
C   18.8%
D   19.0%

Circle your answer

| A | B | C | D |

15 Which of the following diagrams is consistent with Modigliani and Miller's propositions on the variation in the weighted average cost of capital (Kw) and the cost of equity (Ke) as gearing increases, in the presence of corporation tax, but in the absence of personal taxes? (Gearing is measured by the value of debt to total value of the firm).

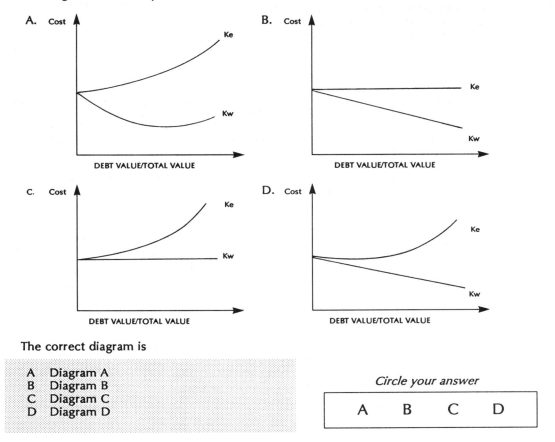

The correct diagram is

16 Which of the following statements is or are correct? They all relate to Modigliani and Miller's theories about capital gearing, allowing for tax relief on loan interest, and to a comparison between a geared company and an ungeared company that is identical with it in every respect except for its capital structure.

Statement

1.   The total value of the geared company will always exceed the total value of the ungeared company.

2.   The total value of equity in the geared company will always exceed the total value of the ungeared company.

Continued...

3.   The market value per share in the geared company will always exceed the market value per share of the ungeared company.

A   Statement 1 only is correct
B   Statements 1 and 2 only are correct
C   Statements 2 and 3 only are correct
D   Statements 1 and 3 only are correct

Circle your answer

A   B   C   D

17 Suppose that Steer plc and Weel plc are *identical* in every respect, with the single exception that Steer plc is all-equity-financed and Weel plc is part-equity-financed and partly financed by £3 million of loan stock (which has a par market value). The market value of Steer plc's shares in total is £6,000,000. The annual profits before interest of both companies is £1,200,000. The rate of corporation tax is 35%.

According to Modigliani and Miller's theory, what will be the market value of the equity shares in Weel plc?

A   £4,050,000
B   £4,950,000
C   £6,360,000
D   £7,050,000

Circle your answer

A   B   C   D

18 An all-equity company has a market value of £120 million. It plans to raise £20 million by issuing debentures, to invest in a project that would have a net present value of £5 million and the same business risk as the company. According to Modigliani and Miller's theory, what will be the value of the company after the project is undertaken, if the corporation tax rate is 35%?

A   £140 million
B   £145 million
C   £147 million
D   £152 million

Circle your answer

A   B   C   D

19 The capital structure of Otto Barnes plc as it appears in its balance sheet is as follows:

	£m
10 million £1 ordinary shares	10
10% irredeemable loan stock	36
	46

The company's earnings before interest and taxes are expected to be £7 million per year in perpetuity. Apart from a corporation tax rate of 25%, there is a perfect capital market. The loan stock is quoted £80 per cent and an otherwise identical all equity company has a cost of capital of 18% per annum.

Continued...

To the nearest £100,000, what should be the market value of the company, according to Modigliani and Miller's theories?

A £10.1 million
B £11.9 million
C £17.3 million
D £38.9 million

Circle your answer

A   B   C   D

Data for questions 20 and 21

One quarter of the total market value of Rhonda Bout plc (equity plus loan stock) consists of loan stock, which has a cost of 12%.

Another company is identical in every respect to Rhonda Bout plc, except that its capital structure is all-equity, and its cost of equity is 18%.

---

20 According to Modigliani and Miller, if we ignored taxation and tax relief on debt capital, what would be the cost of equity in Rhonda Bout plc?

A 18.0%
B 19.2%
C 19.5%
D 20.0%

Circle your answer

A   B   C   D

---

21 According to Modigliani and Miller, if we took taxation into account, and the rate of corporation tax is 40%, what would be the cost of equity in Rhonda Bout plc?

A 18.8%
B 18.9%
C 19.2%
D 19.8%

Circle your answer

A   B   C   D

---

22 A firm has a weighted average cost of capital of 18%, and a ratio of debt value to equity value of 1:2. The rate of corporation tax is 35%; ignore any impact of personal taxes.

If the firm reduces the proportion of debt to equity to one third, what (according to Modigliani and Miller's theory) would be its new weighted average cost of capital?

A 18.6%
B 19.3%
C 20.4%
D 21.8%

Circle your answer

A   B   C   D

95

23 There are three companies in the same industry, DEF plc, GHJ plc and KLM plc. They have exactly the same business and operating characteristics, and even earn the same annual profit before interest and taxation, but their capital structures are different.

The market values of the equity and loan stock in each company are currently as follows.

		DEF plc	GHJ plc	KLM plc
		£m	£m	£m
Equity	(5m shares)	25	(10m shares) 34	(20m shares) 19
Loan stock		15	0	20
		40	34	39

It is thought that the market value of GHJ's shares and the market value of the loan stock in DEF plc and KLM plc are all at their "correct" equilibrium value.

Applying Modigliani and Miller's theory, and assuming corporation tax at 35%, are the shares in DEF plc and KLM plc therefore over-valued or under-valued?

	DEF plc shares	KLM plc shares
A	Over-valued	Over-valued
B	Over-valued	Under-valued
C	Under-valued	Over-valued
D	Under-valued	Under-valued

Circle your answer

A	B	C	D

Data for questions 24 - 27

Leftern Nonely plc is currently financed by 10 million ordinary shares and each share has a market value of £4. The company is all-equity financed, and annual earnings and dividends are currently expected to be £0.80 per share per annum in perpetuity.

The company's management are now considering whether or not to undertake a capital investment project that would cost £10,000,000 and would yield a benefit of £1,950,000 per annum in perpetuity (net of corporate taxes).

The rate of corporate taxation is 35%.

24 If the project is financed by raising new equity capital, what would be its net present value? (Ignore share issue costs).

A	Minus	£3,662,500
B	Minus	£500,000
C	Minus	£250,000
D	Plus	£5,000,000

Circle your answer

A	B	C	D

25 According to Modigliani and Miller's theories, what would be the change in the value of Leftern Nonely plc's equity if the project were financed by raising debt capital of £10,000,000 at an interest rate of 12% per annum? (Ignore charges for raising the new capital).

A	Reduction by	£6,750,000
B	Reduction by	£250,000
C	Increase by	£950,000
D	Increase by	£3,250,000

Circle your answer

A   B   C   D

26 Assuming that the project is undertaken and financed by the 12% loan capital, what (according to Modigliani and Miller's theories) would be the weighted average cost of capital of the company after undertaking the project?

A   17.6% approx
B   18.4% approx
C   18.7% approx
D   20.0% approx

Circle your answer

A   B   C   D

27 Assuming that the project is undertaken and financed by the 12% loan capital, what (according to Modigliani and Miller's theories) would be the incremental cost of capital when compared with the company's previous all-equity state?

A   7.8%
B   12.0%
C   14.7%
D   19.5%

Circle your answer

A   B   C   D

Data for questions 28 - 30

Bonnitt plc and Boot plc are two companies operating in the same industry. Both earn annual profits before interest of £11,700,000. They have the same business risk and are identical in most other respects, and their only differences are in their financial structures and market values.

	Bonnitt plc £000	Boot plc £000
Ordinary shares of £1 (nominal value)	15,000	30,000
Reserves	20,000	40,000
	35,000	70,000
12% loan stock	30,000	0
	65,000	70,000

Bonnitt plc's shares have a market value of £3 each and Boot plc's shares have a market value of £1.95 each. It can be assumed that the share price of Bonnitt plc is correctly valued by the market and that the 12% loan stock has a par market value. All available profits are paid out as dividends.

Suppose that you hold 1% of the equity of Bonnitt plc.

28 Ignoring corporate and personal taxation, how much capital gain could you make by means of arbitrage, following the propositions of Modigliani and Miller, by selling your 1% stake in Bonnitt plc and acquiring a stake in Boot plc, to leave your annual income unchanged?

A	£45,000	
B	£135,000	
C	£157,500	
D	£165,000	

Circle your answer

A   B   C   D

29 Continuing the previous question, what would the share price of Boot plc need to become before arbitrage ceased to be profitable (ignoring transaction costs)?

A	£2.10
B	£2.17
C	£2.47
D	£2.50

Circle your answer

A   B   C   D

30 Now assume corporation tax of 35%, but ignore personal taxation. The profits of £11,700,000 should be assumed to be profits after tax, except that in the case of Grace plc, these profits ignore debt interest and tax relief on the debt interest.

How much capital gain could you now make by selling your 1% stake in Bonnitt plc and acquiring a 1% stake in Boot plc, following the propositions of Modigliani and Miller that take corporation tax into account?

A	£30,000	
B	£60,000	
C	£107,250	
D	£165,000	

Circle your answer

A   B   C   D

CHAPTER 7

PORTFOLIO THEORY.
CAPITAL ASSET PRICING MODEL

This chapter covers the following topics:

- Investment return and risk
- Portfolios and diversification
- Capital Market Line (CML)
- Beta factors
- Capital Asset Pricing Model (CAPM)
- Geared and ungeared betas

1. Investment return and risk

1.1 Investors buy stocks and shares to make a return. Return can be measured by the capital gain on the security, if it goes up in price, plus any dividend or interest received.

$$\text{Return on share in period t} = \frac{\text{Dividend + Capital gain in the period}}{\text{Share price at start of period}}$$

1.2 Companies invest in projects, and make a return from the cash inflows from the project.

1.3 Returns might be higher or lower than expected, and this variability in returns is the cause of investment risk. Some investments are more risky than others, which means that their returns are likely to be more variable and 'erratic'.

1.4 Investments in debt capital are less risky than investments in equity shares, because returns are more certain and stable. However, much debt capital has some risk, since market prices can go up or down and this causes capital gains or losses. Some short-term debt capital is virtually risk-free, such as Treasury bills and eligible bank bills in the UK.

1.5 An investor will be willing to accept more risk for a bigger return. His willingness to trade off risk and return can be described by an indifference curve.

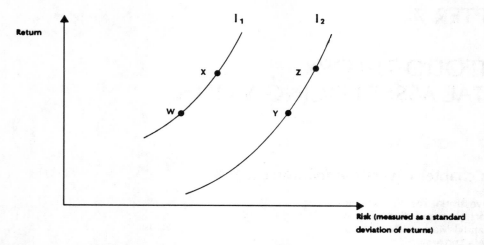

The investor would be indifferent about choosing any investment or portfolio of investments that lie on the same indifference curve.

- W and X have equal merit. The lower return on W is compensated by the lower risk
- Y and Z have equal merit. The lower return on Y is compensated by the lower risk
- W or X will be preferred to Y or Z, because they lie on an indifference curve I_1 that offers a higher return for the same risk or equal return for a lower risk than investments on indifference curve I_2

2. Portfolio and diversification

2.1 Investors can reduce their investment risk by diversifying, and building up a portfolio of investments.

If you are studying financial management for a professional qualification or business studies course, you might have to calculate the return and standard deviation of return (risk) on a small portfolio with just two securities in it. (To minimise risk at any given level of return, portfolios will need to include many more varied investments).

> Questions that follow will test your ability to calculate risk and returns, and will indicate useful formulae where appropriate.

2.2 Some portfolios will offer higher returns or less risk than others. If a graph could plot, for every possible portfolio of securities, the return and associated risk of the portfolio, the dots or crosses representing each portfolio would form an egg-shaped cluster on the graph.

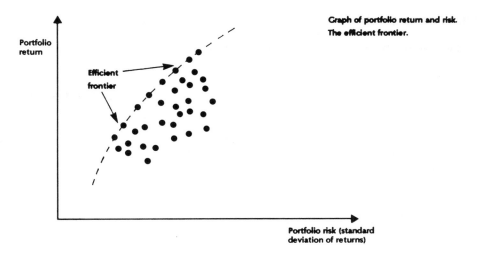

Graph of portfolio return and risk.
The efficient frontier.

Some portfolios would offer either a higher return *or* lower risk in comparison with any other individual portfolios. These 'efficient' portfolios lie along the efficient frontier on the graph.

2.3 An investor should select the portfolio that is on the efficient frontier and touches one of his indifference curves at a tangent, because this will give him an optimal feasible combination of return and risk to suit his preferences. This is portfolio M on the graph below.

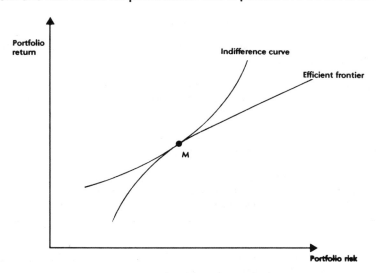

Portfolio M is likely to be the portfolio preferred by all risk-averse investors.

3. Capital Market Line (CML)

3.1 So far, the analysis has ignored risk-free investments.

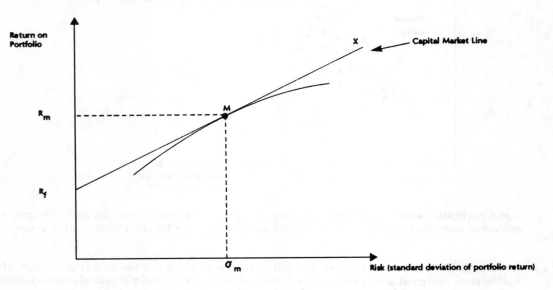

3.2 An investor can choose risky investments in portfolio M or risk-free investments.

- He could combine portfolio M with risk-free investments, to create a portfolio that would be between R_f and M on the line in the graph above

- If he could borrow at a risk-free rate and invest in more of portfolio M with the borrowed funds, he could create a portfolio that would lie between M and X on the line in the graph above.

3.3   If we consider investors as a whole rather than individual investors

         (1)   since all investors would wish ideally to hold portfolio M, and
         (2)   all shares quoted on a stock exchange must be held by investors
         (3)   then all shares quoted on a stock exchange will be in the 'ideal' portfolio M.

3.4 The line R_f - M - X in the graph above is a new 'efficient frontier' of investments for all investors, and this is called the Capital Market Line or CML.

3.5 It is in the nature of the stock market that an investor might succeed in building up a portfolio whose return and risk characteristics would make it lie above the CML. Any such portfolio would be regarded as super-efficient.

Portfolios can also be built up with return and risk characteristics that would put it below the CML. These portfolios are inefficient, and could be improved by altering the composition of the portfolio.

3.6 The slope of the CML can be measured as $\dfrac{R_m - R_f}{\sigma_m}$

The equation for the expected return for any portfolio on the CML is $R_f + \left(\dfrac{R_m - R_f}{\sigma_m} \right) \sigma_p$

where σ_p is the risk (standard deviation of return) of the particular portfolio.

4. Beta factors

4.1 The returns obtained from an individual security are variable, and the reasons for variations could be

(a) factors unique to the company itself or even a single project that the company is undertaking
(b) factors unique to the company's industry
(c) economic factors affecting the country as a whole.

Factors (a) and (b) are risk items that an investor can eliminate by diversifying. Factor (c) is unavoidable, non-diversifiable risk, which is greater for some projects/companies than for others.

4.2 Risk that can be diversified away (and variations in returns which tend to cancel themselves out over time) is called *unsystematic risk*. Non-diversifiable risk is called *systematic risk*.

4.3 The systematic risk of an individual company's shares might be higher or lower than the average risk for the market as a whole. (Similarly, the systematic risk for some projects is greater or less than for others). The relationship between an individual security's risk and the average market risk can be measured as a beta factor or β.

- The market as a whole has a $\beta = 1$
- A risk-free security has a $\beta = 0$
- A security with a $\beta < 1$ has non-diversifiable risk below the market average
- A security with a $\beta > 1$ has a non-diversifiable risk above the market average.

4.4 A security's beta factor can be estimated by comparing returns on the security and average market returns for each time period (each month, say) over a longer period of time. Linear regression techniques can be used.

> Mathematical techniques for calculating security beta factors are dealt with in questions that follow. Suitable formulae will be given in each question, although you might be expected to know these.

4.5 By combining securities into a portfolio, risk is reduced but there will be some non-diversifiable risk.

> The beta factor for a portfolio can be measured as the weighted average of the beta factors of individual securities in the portfolio, with weightings based on the *market values* of the securities in the portfolio.

5. Capital Asset Pricing Model (CAPM)

5.1 The higher the β for a security (or a portfolio, or a project) the greater the return an investor will want from it.

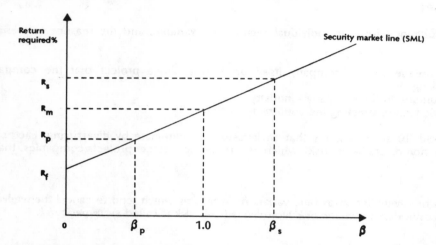

- If the investment is risk-free and $\beta = 0$, the required return will be the risk-free rate R_f
- If the investment has the same risk as the market as a whole, and $\beta = 1$, the required return will be the market return R_m.

5.2
> For an investment with $\beta = \beta_s$, the required return R_s can be stated as
> $R_f + \beta_s(R_m - R_f)$.
>
> Similarly, for a portfolio with $\beta = \beta_p$, the required portfolio return R_p can be stated as $R_f + \beta_p(R_m - R_f)$.

This is the Capital Asset Pricing Model formula.

5.3 The CAPM can be used to estimate the required return on a security, from a portfolio or from a project, for an investor who expects to be able to get rid of unsystematic risk through diversification, and who therefore wishes to assess his required return for a given amount of non-diversifiable, systematic risk.

6. Geared and ungeared betas

6.1 There is a connection between Modigliani-Miller's theories of gearing and CAPM theory, and it is possible to establish a mathematical relationship between the β value of an ungeared company and the β value of a *similar*, but geared, company. (Similar means a company in the same industry with the same operating and business risk characteristics, differing only in their financial gearing).

6.2 The β value of a geared company will be higher than the β value of a company identical in every respect except that it is all-equity financed. This is because of the extra financial risk.

The mathematical relationship between the 'ungeared' and 'geared' betas is:

$$\beta_g = \beta_u \left[1 + \frac{D(1-t)}{V_{eg}} \right] \qquad \dots (1)$$

which is also

$$\beta_g = \beta_u + \beta_u \left[\frac{D(1-t)}{V_{eg}} \right] \qquad \dots (2)$$

where β_g is the beta factor of a geared company - ie the 'geared beta'
β_u is the beta factor of a similar, but ungeared company - ie the 'ungeared beta'
D is the market value of the debt capital in the geared company
V_{eg} is the market value of the equity capital in the geared company
t is the rate of corporation tax

Notice especially in formula (2) that the geared beta is equal to the ungeared beta plus a premium for financial risk which equals

$$\beta_u \left[\frac{D(1-t)}{V_{eg}} \right]$$

QUESTIONS

1 On a graph of the efficient frontier, what do the X and Y axes represent?

	X axis	Y axis
A	Expected return of a security	Beta of a security
B	Expected return of a security	Expected return of the market
C	Expected return of a portfolio	Expected return of the market
D	Expected return of a portfolio	Standard deviation of a portfolio's return

Circle your answer

A   B   C   D

Data for questions 2 and 3

It is proposed to add a new investment to an existing portfolio of investments.

	Existing portfolio	New investment
Market value	£800,000	£200,000
Expected annual return	0.16	0.20
Standard deviation of the expected annual return	0.10	0.12

The correlation coefficient between the expected return on the new investment and the expected return on the existing portfolio is 0.6.

The following formulae are relevant.

(1)   Covariance $XY = r_{xy}\, \sigma_x\, \sigma_y$

(2) $\sigma_p = \sqrt{p^2\, \sigma_x^2 + q^2\, \sigma_y^2 + 2pq\, \text{covXY}}$

2 What is the covariance between the expected return on the existing portfolio and the expected return on the new investment?

A   0.0072
B   0.0192
C   0.0620
D   0.1033

Circle your answer

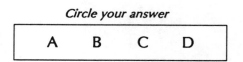

A   B   C   D

3 What would be (1) the expected return and (2) the standard deviation of the expected annual return on the enlarged portfolio?

	Return	Standard deviation
A	0.168	0.096
B	0.168	0.098
C	0.168	0.115
D	0.180	0.142

Circle your answer

A   B   C   D

4 Two securities, P and Q, have the following characteristics.

	P	Q
Mean return	15%	15%
Standard deviation of returns	19%	21%

The correlation coefficient between returns from P and Q is less than 1 and the two securities can be combined to form a portfolio, PQ Portfolio, consisting of equal proportions of P and Q. Which investment should be chosen by investors who are (1) risk averse, and (2) risk seeking?

	Risk averse	Risk seeking
A	P	Q
B	P	PQ Portfolio
C	PQ Portfolio	Q
D	PQ Portfolio	PQ Portfolio

Circle your answer

A   B   C   D

Data for questions 5 and 6

A portfolio consists of 40% security X and 60% security Y. The predicted returns from each security are as follows.

Probability	Predicted return from X	Predicted return from Y
0.3	25%	18%
0.4	20%	15%
0.3	15%	12%

The mean expected return from the portfolio is 17%.

5 What is the portfolio risk, measured as the standard deviation of return, if returns from X and Y have perfect positive correlation?

A 2.94%
B 3.10%
C 3.80%
D 5.37%

Circle your answer

A   B   C   D

6 What is the portfolio risk, measured as the standard deviation of return, if returns from X and Y are perfectly negatively correlated?

A Nil
B 0.15%
C 0.20%
D 0.28%

Circle your answer

A   B   C   D

7 You are considering investing in a portfolio comprising 60% Security X and 40% Security Y. Possible rates of return on these securities have been estimated as follows.

Security	Probability	Return %
X	0.5	30
	0.5	20
Y	0.5	45
	0.5	5

Assuming neutral correlation between possible rates of return on these securities, and an expected return on the portfolio of 25%, what is the risk of the portfolio, measured as the standard deviation of variations from the expected rate of return?

A 8.54%
B 10.31%
C 12.50%
D 17.09%

Circle your answer

A   B   C   D

8 A division of Lornscape Gardiner plc has been allocated a fixed capital sum for capital investment next year. Management has identified four possible projects, W, X, Y and Z, each of equal size and cost, but there are only enough funds to undertake two. Project W and X are mutually exclusive and projects Y and Z are also mutually exclusive.

Portfolio theory will be used to select the two projects for investment, based on an analysis of return and risk. You are given the following data.

Continued...

Probability	Estimated return %			
	Project W	Project X	Project Y	Project Z
0.6	12	8	15	20
0.4	17	23	$12\frac{1}{2}$	5
Expected return (EV)	14	14	14	14

The variance of project returns and covariances of returns from each possible pair of investments are as follows.

Covariance		Variance of returns		
W,Y	- 3.0	W	=	6.0
W,Z	- 18.0	X	=	54.0
X,Y	- 9.0	Y	=	1.5
X,Z	- 46.8	Z	=	54.0

The variance of returns from two projects R and S is given by $Var(pR + qS) = p^2 varR + q^2 varS + 2pq(covRS)$ where p and q are the proportions of each project in the portfolio and $p + q = 1$.

Which combination of projects would the division select?

A   Projects W and Y
B   Projects W and Z
C   Projects X and Y
D   Projects X and Z

Circle your answer

A   B   C   D

9

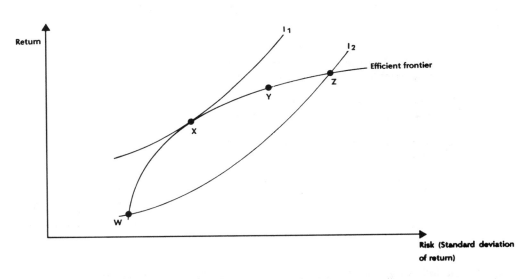

The diagram shows the efficient frontier of portfolios, and two indifference curves I_1 and I_2 for an investor. Which portfolio or portfolios would the investor most prefer out of W, X, Y and Z?

A	Portfolio W or Z only	
B	Portfolio X only	
C	Portfolio X or Y only	
D	Any of portfolios W, X, Y or Z	

Circle your answer

A   B   C   D

10 Characteristics of four portfolios are shown below:

Portfolio	Standard deviation %	Expected return %
A	16	14
B	26	19
C	10	7
D	18	12

Which portfolio *cannot* lie on the efficient frontier?

A	Portfolio A
B	Portfolio B
C	Portfolio C
D	Portfolio D

Circle your answer

A   B   C   D

11 On a graph of the Capital Market Line, what are the Y and X axes?

	Y axis	X axis
A	Standard deviation of a portfolio	Expected return of the market
B	Expected return of a portfolio	Expected return of the market
C	Standard deviation of a portfolio	Expected return of a portfolio
D	Expected return of a portfolio	Standard deviation of a portfolio's return

Circle your answer

A   B   C   D

12 The following data relate to three different portfolios of securities.

Portfolio	Expected rate of return	Standard deviation of return on the portfolio
X	16.5%	5.4%
Y	11.5%	1.2%
Z	16.0%	10.0%

Continued...

The expected rate of return on the market portfolio is 15%, with a standard deviation of 4%. The risk-free rate of return is 9%.

The portfolios which could be regarded as risky or inefficient are:

A   X and Y only
B   X and Z only
C   Y and Z only
D   Z only

Circle your answer

A   B   C   D

13

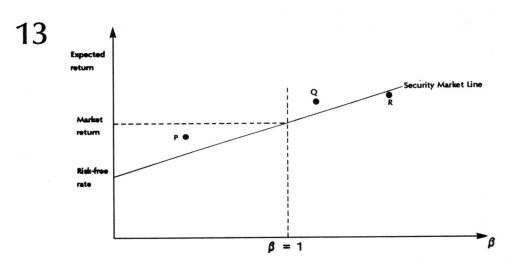

What does the diagram indicate about the pricing of securities P, Q and R?

	Security P	*Security Q*	*Security R*
A	Underpriced	Overpriced	Underpriced
B	Underpriced	Underpriced	Overpriced
C	Overpriced	Underpriced	Overpriced
D	Overpriced	Overpriced	Underpriced

Circle your answer

A   B   C   D

14

An investor intends to borrow funds, at the risk-free rate of 8% per annum, an amount equal to one half of the size of his original funds, and to invest both this and his original funds in the market portfolio. The expected return on the market portfolio is 14% per annum and the standard deviation of return on the market portfolio is 16%.

What is the expected return on his portfolio and his portfolio risk?

	Expected return on portfolio	Portfolio risk (standard deviation)
A	14%	16%
B	17%	16%
C	17%	24%
D	21%	24%

Circle your answer

A   B   C   D

15 Gordon Bench has £1,000,000 to invest in securities and requires an expected return of 24%. The market premium for risk is 8%. If Gordon can achieve this required return by borrowing £250,000 at a risk-free rate and investing the total in the market portfolio, what is the expected return on the market portfolio?

A   17.6%
B   20.8%
C   22.0%
D   26.0%

Circle your answer

A   B   C   D

16 The systematic risk of a project's return is the result of uncertainties in the return caused by

A   factors unique to the project

B   factors unique to the firm undertaking the project

C   factors unique to the industry to which the project belongs

D   nationwide economic factors

Circle your answer

A   B   C   D

17 Which of the following statements is/are correct?

Statement
1. A share's measured beta remains very stable over a period of up to five years or so
2. A share's measured alpha (assuming no dividend payments) represents its rate of price appreciation, and the return (gain or loss) obtained when the market as a whole earned nothing.

A   Statements 1 and 2 are both correct
B   Statement 1 only is correct
C   Statement 2 only is correct
D   Neither statement is correct

Circle your answer

A   B   C   D

18 The beta coefficient of a security measures

   A the correlation between the return on the market index and the return on the security

   B the covariance between the return on the market index and the return on the security divided by the variance of the return on the market index

   C the variance of the return on the security divided by the variance of the return on the market index

   D the standard deviation of the return on the security divided by the standard deviation of the return on the market index

Circle your answer

   A   B   C   D

19 For which of the following reasons might a company that is perceived as 'risky' have a lower beta factor than an equivalent company that is perceived as less risky?

   A The risky company has a lower financial gearing level

   B Inaccuracies in the estimation of beta factors from linear regression analysis or company's returns over time

   C The risky company has lower systematic risk but higher unsystematic risk

   D The risky company is larger in size

Circle your answer

   A   B   C   D

20 Lorn Mower plc is an all-equity company whose shares have a beta value of 1.4. In a month when a dividend of 6p per share was paid, the share price and stock market all-share index values were:

	Share price	All-share index
At the start of the month	100p	400
At the end of the month	95p	408

The return on a risk-free investment in the month would have been $\frac{1}{2}$ %.

Return due to unsystematic risk can be estimated as the difference between actual return and the return predicted by the CAPM. What was the size of return on Lorn Mower plc's shares due to *unsystematic risk* in the month, based on the start-of-month share price and share index value? Ignore taxation.

A	Negative return of 1.6%
B	Negative return of 2.3%
C	Negative return of 7.6%
D	Positive return of 3.4%

Circle your answer

A   B   C   D

21 The financial manager of José Pipe plc has made an analysis over a one year period of the monthly returns on his company's equity shares, and the corresponding returns on the stock market all share index, as follows.

Month	Monthly return on the all share index	Monthly return on José Pipe plc's shares	M²	S²	MS
	M %	S %			
1	+3	+2	9	4	+ 6
2	- 6	- 8	36	64	+ 48
3	- 3	- 6	9	36	+ 18
⋮	⋮	⋮	⋮	⋮	⋮
12	+ 4	+ 5	16	25	+ 20
	+ 15	+ 18	145	278	+ 184

To obtain a regression coefficient for the model y = a + bx, you can use the formula

$$b = \frac{n\Sigma xy - \Sigma x \Sigma y}{n\Sigma x^2 - (\Sigma x)^2}$$

where n = the number of pairs of data used.

Using the data above, what would be the estimated beta coefficient for José Pipe plc's shares for the year?

A	0.54
B	1.20
C	1.28
D	1.31

Circle your answer

A   B   C   D

22 Patty O'Dors has invested its surplus cash in a small portfolio of equity shares, details of which are given below.

Company	Number of shares	Beta value of equity	Nominal value per share	Market value per share	Latest dividend yield	Expected return on equity in the next year
W plc	50,000	1.20	£1	£4.00	5%	18%
X plc	100,000	1.40	50p	£1.40	10%	22%
Y plc	200,000	0.90	25p	£0.80	5%	14%
Z plc	100,000	1.10	£1	£3.00	4%	14%

What is the beta value of the portfolio as a whole?

A   1.09
B   1.16
C   1.21
D   1.30

Circle your answer

A   B   C   D

Data for questions 23 and 24

Paddy Linpool plc has three projects, each lasting one year and in different industries. The net cash flows and beta factors associated with each project are as follows.

	Net cash flow	Beta factor
	£000	
Project 1	+ 100	1.5
Project 2	+ 100	1.4
Project 3	+ 200	0.8

The market return is 13% and the risk-free rate of interest is 8%.

23 What is the total present value of the three projects for the company, to the nearest £000?

A   £352,000
B   £356,000
C   £388,000
D   £400,000

Circle your answer

A   B   C   D

24 What is the overall beta factor for the three projects taken as a portfolio?

A   1.00
B   1.12
C   1.125
D   1.23

Circle your answer

A   B   C   D

Data for questions 25 - 27

Compass Teape plc is considering a new project lasting one year and requiring initial investment of £200,000 which would be raised as equity finance.

The returns from the new project are uncertain and depend on which state of the economy prevails in the coming year. Market values in one year's time are expected to be:

State of economy	Probability	Project's market value	Project internal rate of return	Market returns - stock market as a whole
		£		
I	.3	238,000	19%	30%
II	.5	242,000	21%	20%
III	.2	208,000	4%	5%

Compass Teape plc has a weighted average cost of capital (WACC) of 18%. The beta factor of the company's existing activities is 0.8. The risk-free rate of return is 10%.

---

25 What is the net present value of the project, at the company's current WACC?

A   - £5,650
B   - £1,694
C   Nil
D   + £5,085

Circle your answer

A   B   C   D

---

26 Using the Capital Asset Pricing Model, and measuring the project's beta factor as the covariance of the project's returns with market returns divided by the variance of market returns, what is the project's beta factor?

A   0.60
B   0.66
C   1.05
D   1.99

Circle your answer

A   B   C   D

---

27 Using the Capital Asset Pricing Model to establish a cost of capital for the project, what would be the expected NPV of the project?

A   - £5,809
B   + £686
C   + £1,724
D   + £8,621

Circle your answer

A   B   C   D

28 Will Barrow plc's capital structure comprises share capital with a nominal value of £20 million and a market value of £50 million, plus £10 million of 10% loan stock valued at par. The earnings yield on the equity is 18%, the company's equity beta is 1.20 and the debt beta coefficient is 0.30. The market rate of return on equity is 20% and the risk-free rate of return is 8%.

Using the capital asset pricing model, what should be the rate of return yielded by Will Barrow plc's investments?

A   20.3%
B   20.6%
C   20.8%
D   22.4%

Circle your answer

A   B   C   D

29 Arrow Zabusch, an all-equity company, plans to raise new equity finance which would comprise 10% of the total value of the company's new market capitalisation. The company currently has a beta factor of 1.10 and the new project would cause the beta factor to rise to 1.15.

The return on the market portfolio is expected to be 17% per annum and the risk-free rate of return 7% per annum.

Using the capital asset pricing model, what is the required return per annum on those investments that would be financed with the new equity capital?

A   16%
B   18.5%
C   22%
D   23%

Circle your answer

A   B   C   D

Data for questions 30 and 31

Wood and Fence plc is an all-equity financed company with a beta factor of 0.9. Its management are considering an investment that would increase the company's overall beta factor to 1.0 if it were accepted.

The project would be equity financed, and would comprise 20% of the total market value of the company if it were to be accepted. The project will last for 1 year only, and has an expected return of 25%.

The risk-free rate of return is 6% per annum and the current return on the market portfolio is 16%. Ignore taxation.

30 What is the current weighted average cost of capital (WACC) of Wood and Fence plc and what would be the revised WACC if the project were accepted?

	Current WACC	Revised WACC
A	9%	10.0%
B	15%	15.2%
C	15%	16.0%
D	15%	17.0%

Circle your answer

A   B   C   D

31 What would be the required rate of return from the proposed investment based upon its own risk characteristics?

A   1.0
B   1.4
C   1.5
D   1.9

Circle your answer

A   B   C   D

32 Pru Nunn-Hedges plc has an observed equity beta of 1.26. It is financed entirely by equity. It is estimated that 40% of the current market value of the company is caused by risky growth opportunities which have an estimated beta of 1.80. These risky opportunities are reflected in the overall beta for the company.

What is the estimated beta for the portion of the company's activities which is outside the 60% relating to risky growth opportunities?

A   0.756
B   0.90
C   1.26
D   1.476

Circle your answer

A   B   C   D

33 Triste Hump plc, an all-equity financed company with a market value of £4,000,000 is to consider investing £1,000,000 in a project which will provide a return of £300,000 in perpetuity. The company currently has a beta of 0.9. The project has a beta of 1.5, giving the project a required rate of return of 20.5%.

If the project is accepted, what will be the new beta of the company as a whole?

A   0.94
B   1.02
C   1.04
D   1.06

Circle your answer

A   B   C   D

34 Ferdy Liza Ltd is considering investing in a risky new project which would have a one-year life. The estimated returns on the new project, Ferdy Liza Ltd's existing projects and the market portfolio have been estimated as follows.

Economic conditions	Probability of occurrence	Return from existing projects %	Returns from new project %	Market portfolio returns %	Risk-free returns %
I	0.2	40	60	40	10
II	0.4	20	40	20	10
III	0.4	10	10	10	10

The new project, which has a beta factor of 1.67, will comprise 25% of Ferdy Liza Ltd's total operations, if accepted.

Using the Capital Asset Pricing Model, is the new project worthwhile, and what is the minimum required return for Ferdy Liza Ltd's future projects, assuming that all of these will have the same risk on average as the combination of the existing projects plus the new project?

	Project worthwhile?	Minimum return on future projects
A	Worthwhile	21.675%
B	Worthwhile	23%
C	Worthwhile	26.7%
D	Not worthwhile	26.7%

Circle your answer

A	B	C	D

Data for questions 35 and 36

P plc and Q plc are two companies which are considering merging into one, PQ plc although the merger would not create any extra profits.

P plc is all-equity financed, and has a market value of £70 million. Q plc is financed by a mixture of debt and equity which have a market value of £30 million and £60 million respectively.

The equity beta of P is 1.1. and the equity beta of Q is 1.4. The rate of corporation tax is 30%.

35 Applying Modigliani and Miller's propositions and assuming a corporate tax rate of 40%, what would be the market value of the merged company if PQ plc is to be be all-equity financed?

A £118 million
B £148 million
C £150 million
D £160 million

Circle your answer

A	B	C	D

36 What would be the equity beta of PQ plc if it is an all-equity financed company?

A 1.07
B 1.24
C 1.25
D 1.27

Circle your answer

A   B   C   D

Data for questions 37 and 38

Gould Fisher Pond plc has a beta factor of 1.20 and a debt:equity ratio of 1:4. The rate of corporate tax is 35%, and the impact of personal taxes can be ignored.

37 What would be the beta factor of the company if it changed to being an all-equity company?

A 1.03
B 1.06
C 1.10
D 1.48

Circle your answer

A   B   C   D

38 What would be the beta factor of the company if its debt:equity ratio were changed to 1:2?

A 1.29
B 1.30
C 1.37
D 1.44

Circle your answer

A   B   C   D

Data for questions 39 and 40

Bulb plc is identical in all operating and risk characteristics to Seed plc, except that Seed plc is all-equity financed and Bulb plc is financed by both equity and debt, in the proportion 75%:25% respectively (at market values).

The beta factor of Seed plc is 0.90. Bulb's debt capital is virtually risk-free, the risk-free rate of return is 7% per annum, and the expected market return is 12%.

39 If corporate taxation is assessed at a rate of zero, what is the equity beta of Bulb plc?

A 1.12
B 1.20
C 1.50
D 2.60

Circle your answer

A   B   C   D

40 If corporate taxation is assessed at a rate of 30%, what is the equity beta of Bulb plc?

A 0.83
B 1.06
C 1.08
D 1.11

Circle your answer

A   B   C   D

CHAPTER 8

WORKING CAPITAL MANAGEMENT

This chapter covers the following topics:

- Funds flow management and the operating cycle
- Stock management
- Management of debtors

1. Funds flow management and the operating cycle

1.1 The management of working capital is linked closely with the management of cash. Here, it helps to think of working capital as, principally, stocks, debtors and short term creditors, with cash balances and bank overdrafts as a separate item.

- An increase in working capital ties up funds, and this has consequences for cash flows
- Similarly, a reduction in working capital should speed up the inflow of cash by releasing funds.

1.2 The link between working capital (stocks, debtors and creditors) and cash can be seen in

- a funds flow statement, and
- the operating cycle.

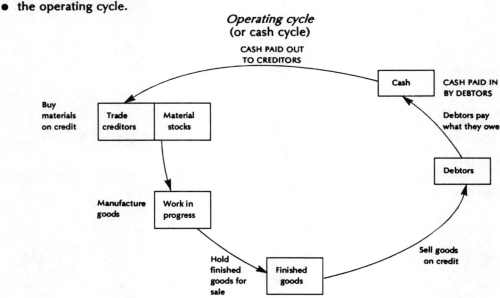

Operating cycle
(or cash cycle)

1.3

> *Cash flows can be improved by*
>
> (1) shorter stock turnover periods
> (2) shorter production cycle
> (3) shorter period of credit for debtors
> (4) longer credit taken from creditors

2. Stock management

2.1 A 'traditional' text book method of controlling the volume of stocks and the stock turnover period is to purchase or produce items for stock in an 'economic' quantity or batch size.

The economic batch quantity is $\sqrt{\dfrac{2cd}{h}}$

where   c is the incremental cost of placing an order (or incremental set-up costs)
             d is the quantity demanded per period
             h is the holding cost per unit of stock per period.

A buffer stock would be held to provide for (1) fluctuations in demand and (2) variable supply lead times/production order cycles.

2.2 More recently, management in some manufacturing companies have been aiming for 'stockless production' and Just In Time (JIT) deliveries, whereby

● materials and parts are delivered from suppliers only just when they are needed
● products are manufactured only just when they are needed for sale to customers

JIT therefore aims towards an 'ideal' level of zero stocks, but with no hold-ups due to stock shortages.

3. Management of debtors

3.1 Companies need to allow credit to boost sales. For example, credit cards help retailers to achieve higher sales. Allowing credit, however, results in

● an interest cost of funds tied up in debtors (rather than immediate cash receipts)
● possibly a bad debt risk.

A suitable balance might have to be found between sales volume, credit allowed, interest costs and bad debts.

3.2 *Discounts for early payment* might be used to shorten average credit periods, reduce the investment in debtors and so reduce interest costs. The benefit in interest costs saved should exceed the cost of discounts allowed.

3.3 Some companies use *factoring organisations* to deal with the management of debtors. Factors provide one or more of the following services:

- administration of debtors - sending out invoices, sales ledger work, collecting payments
- insurance against bad debts
- advances against debtors: typically, clients are advanced up to 80% of the value of invoiced debtors, with repayment to the factors coming when the debtors pay. (Advances incur an interest cost).

3.4 *Credit insurance* - insurance against bad debts - can be an important feature of debtors management, especially for exporting companies. Export credit insurance is available in the UK from ECGD (Export Credits Guarantee Department) or through banks.

QUESTIONS

1 Mew Sickles Ltd uses a computer model for financial planning, which produces a profit and loss account and balance sheet. Within the model, the following relationships hold:

Ratio of fixed assets to working capital	2.0
Current ratio	3.0

The first run of the model uses a sales forecast of £240,000 and a sales:capital employed ratio of 0.5.
What value will the first run produce for current assets?

A £160,000
B £240,000
C £320,000
D £360,000

Circle your answer

A   B   C   D

2 Bagge Pipes Ltd uses a computerised financial model of its operations. By entering the sales forecast and values for parameters, the model will produce a profit and loss account and a balance sheet.

Parameter values:
Net profit margin	25%
Return on capital employed	10%
Ratio of fixed assets to working capital	1:1
Current ratio	1.5:1

The first trial run of the model will use a sales forecast of £960,000.

What value will the first trial run produce for current liabilities?

A £480,000
B £1,200,000
C £1,800,000
D £2,400,000

Circle your answer

A   B   C   D

3 The working capital of Trump Pets Ltd consists of stocks, debtors, cash or bank overdraft and creditors. The following turnover ratios apply.

Debtors	90 days
Stocks	72 days

Assume a 360 day year. Stocks are valued at 50% of sales value.

Continued...

The ratio of creditors to debtors is 0.8, and during a year when sales turnover was £2,000,000 (achieved at an even monthly rate) the current ratio declined to 1.4 at 31 December. The liquid ratio (or acid test ratio) at 31 December was

A   1.00
B   1.05
C   1.25
D   1.50

Circle your answer

A   B   C   D

4 When a company expands too rapidly, it might start overtrading. A symptom of overtrading is

A   a high ratio of current assets: current liabilities

B   high ratio of current assets: proprietors' capital

C   low ratio of current assets: annual sales

D   shorter credit given by trade creditors

Circle your answer

A   B   C   D

5 Pickle Low Ltd needs to hold stocks of material XYZ for resale to customers. Basic data about material XYZ are as follows.

Annual sales demand (50 week year)	3,000 units
Cost of placing and processing a purchase order	£259
Cost of holding one unit of XYZ for a year	£27
Normal delay between placing an order and receiving goods	3 weeks

What is the economic order quantity (EOQ) for material XYZ, and what is the average frequency at which purchase orders should be placed?

	EOQ	Frequency of orders
A	170 units	3 weeks
B	170 units	6 weeks
C	240 units	4 weeks
D	240 units	7 weeks

Circle your answer

A   B   C   D

6 Fife Fern Drumm Ltd has operated a manual system for invoicing customers. On average, the delay between the date of sale and the despatch of the invoice has been as follows.

Working days of delay	% of sales
3	15%
4	35%
5	30%
6	20%

Continued...

If the company computerises its invoicing operation, the delay in sending out invoices will be reduced, as follows.

Working days of delay	% of sales
0	20%
1	70%
2	10%

Annual sales are £15,000,000, spread evenly throughout the year, and the company's cost of capital is 20% per annum. The annual net costs of operating the computer system would be £25,000. There are 250 working days each year.

The net savings from introducing the computer system would be

A £18,800
B £43,800
C £94,000
D £194,000

Circle your answer

A B C D

Data for questions 7 and 8

Cy Low Phones Ltd
Extracts from annual accounts

	£
Stocks: raw materials	250,000
work in progress	115,000
finished goods	186,000
Purchases	1,070,000
Cost of goods sold	1,458,000
Sales	1,636,000
Debtors	345,000
Trade creditors	162,000

7 On the basis of these figures, the length of the working capital cycle (operating cycle) is

A 182 days
B 193 days
C 210 days
D 293 days

Circle your answer

A B C D

8 The company's management believe that if the average debtors collection period were reduced to 45 days, sales would fall by 25%. The company relies heavily on overdraft financing at a cost of 14% per annum. By how much, to the nearest £000, would a reduction in the collection period affect annual profit, assuming that average stocks and creditors vary with sales volume and that the cost of goods sold is variable with sales?

A   Profit would increase by £8,000
B   Profit would fall by £4,000
C   Profit would fall by £10,000
D   Profit would fall by £19,000

Circle your answer

A   B   C   D

9 Wynne Donsomble Ltd sells its services on credit with normal terms of payment being 30 days net. What would be the cost to the company of offering a 2% discount for payment within 10 days of invoice date? Assume a 365 day year.

A   24.3%
B   36.5%
C   37.2%
D   74.5%

Circle your answer

A   B   C   D

Data for questions 10 and 11

String Gunns Humble Ltd is launching a marketing campaign to boost sales, currently £10,000,000 per annum, by 20%. As part of the campaign, credit terms will be eased, and the payment pattern will be expected to change as follows.

	Before the campaign % of gross sales	After the campaign % of gross sales
Cash sales	10%	5%
10 days credit	20%	5%
30 days credit	40%	20%
60 days credit	25%	50%
90 days credit	5%	20%

There will be no bad debts. The company would maintain its policy of allowing a 2% discount for payment in ten days or less. Assume a 360 day year.

10 With the introduction of the campaign the annual costs of discounts allowed should be expected to fall by

A   £28,000
B   £30,000
C   £36,000
D   £40,000

Circle your answer

A   B   C   D

11 The investment in average debtors would increase by (to the nearest £000)

A £725,000
B £738,000
C £885,000
D £886,000

Circle your answer

| A | B | C | D |

12 The monthly sales of Stringer Tar Ltd are £1,000,000, all on credit. If the company switches to a new policy of giving $2\frac{1}{2}$% discount to customers who pay within one month, it believes that the average pattern of payment by customers will change as follows.

Date of payment	No discount	With $2\frac{1}{2}$% discount
After 1 month	10%	70%
After 2 months	10%	10%
After 3 months	80%	20%

The company's cost of capital is 2% per month. What would be the expected present value of a decision to introduce the $2\frac{1}{2}$% discount policy, to the nearest £000?

A £207,000
B £225,000
C £290,000
D £325,000

Circle your answer

| A | B | C | D |

13 Mast Quires Ltd currently achieves credit sales of £140,000 per month. Profits are as follows.

	£
Sales	140,000
Cost of sales (75% variable, 25% fixed)	100,000
Gross profit	40,000
Bad debts (1% of sales)	(1,400)
Other costs	(18,600)
Net profit	20,000

The management think that by increasing the period of credit allowed to customers from 1 month to 2 months, sales will rise by 25%, but bad debts would increase to 5% of sales.

The increase would leave fixed costs, average stocks and average creditors unaffected. The company's cost of capital is 15% per annum.

The new credit policy would increase annual profits, after additional financing costs, by

A £300
B £58,500
C £75,300
D £106,800

Circle your answer

| A | B | C | D |

129

14 The draft budget of Hopp Piraticals Ltd includes the following data.

Profit and loss account (extract)

	£
Sales (all on credit)	5,000,000
Cost of sales	3,400,000
Gross profit	1,600,000
Bad debts	£210,000

End-of-year balance sheet (extracts)

	£
Debtors	900,000
Stocks (vary directly with sales)	300,000
Creditors (vary directly with sales)	250,000

If the company switches to a credit policy of insisting on full payment from customers within one month, bad debts should fall to 2% of sales, but sales would fall by 10% below budget. The extra administrative costs of the new credit policy would be £45,000 per annum. The company's opportunity cost of capital is 20% per annum. All costs of sales vary directly with sales.

By how much would the company gain next year (before tax) by introducing the new credit policy?

A £10,000
B £11,000
C £20,000
D £21,000

Circle your answer

A   B   C   D

Data for questions 15 and 16

Tenner Sachs plc has annual sales of £14,400,000, spread evenly throughout the year. The company's average collection period from debtors is 90 days, and its management hopes to improve efficiency by hiring the services of a factoring company. (Assume a 360 day year).

The factor offers two services.

Service
(1)   *Debts administration and debt collection.* The charge would be $1\frac{1}{2}$ % of the value of invoices sent out, payable annually in arrears. This service would save Tenner Sachs plc in-house administration costs of £64,000 pa.

(2)   *Payments in advance.* The factor would advance Tenner Sachs plc 80% of the value of invoices sent out, but deduct commission of $2\frac{1}{2}$ % of the gross advance. The interest rate on the advances would be 15% per annum, calculated on the net advances.

15 What will be the effective annual factoring cost, as a percentage of the funds improvement caused by factoring, if the factor provides Service 1 only, and the average debt collection period falls to 60 days?

A   6.3%
B   8.3%
C   12.7%
D   18.0%

Circle your answer

A   B   C   D

16 On the assumption that the average debt collection period falls to 60 days, what would be the effective annual cost of the advances against debts service (Service 2) as a percentage of the funds advanced?

A   17.5%
B   17.9%
C   29.6%
D   30.4%

Circle your answer

A   B   C   D

17 Most large retail organisations accept credit cards such as Visa and Access. Compared with payment by cheque, which of the following benefits are obtained by retailers from the use of major credit cards?

Benefit
1.   More sales volume
2.   Fewer bad debts
3.   Quicker cleared funds
4.   Lower bank/credit card company charges

A   Benefits 1 and 2 only
B   Benefits 1, 2 and 3 only
C   Benefits 3 and 4 only
D   Benefits 2 and 4 only

Circle your answer

A   B   C   D

18 Morgan Recital Ltd uses a bank overdraft to finance its export trade. Annual exports of £800,000 are all on open account. Creditors take on average 80 days to pay. The company takes out an export credit insurance policy from ECGD for all its exports, and this costs 55 pence per £100 insured and covers 90% of the risk of non-payment. Bad debts are expected to be 1% of sales. Overdraft interest is at 15% per annum.

What is the total annual cost for exports of ECGD insurance cover, bad debts and interest charges, to the nearest £100? Assume a 365 day year.

Continued...

131

A   £28,100
B   £30,700
C   £31,500
D   £39,100

Circle your answer

A   B   C   D

19 Eyebrow Tastes Ltd has received an export order with a sales value of £30,000. The incremental costs of meeting the order would be £20,000. The overseas customer would want one year's credit, and neither export credit insurance nor a letter of credit is available. There is a 0.35 probability of non-payment.

Eyebrow Tastes Ltd would receive a 10% deposit with the order, but there is only a 50% probability that the customer would pay in one year's time. After one year, if the customer has not paid, an attempt would be made to collect the debt at a cost of £4,000. There is a 0.3 chance that the attempt would be successful and payment would be received quickly. If not, the debt will be written off.

Eyebrow Tastes Ltd's cost of capital is 15% pa.

What is the expected net present value of the order, to the nearest hundred pounds?

A   - £3,500
B   - £2,300
C   - £2,200
D   + £3,000

Circle your answer

A   B   C   D

CHAPTER 9

TREASURY MANAGEMENT AND RISK MANAGEMENT

This chapter covers the following topics:

- Role of the corporate treasurer
- Funding: cash management
- Interest rate exposures: hedging interest rate exposures
- Foreign exchange receipts and payments
- Exchange rate exposures
- Hedging exchange rate exposures

1. Role of the corporate treasurer

1.1 The two principal responsibilities of the corporate treasurer of a large company are

- funding the company's operations
- management of the interest rate and foreign currency exposures of the business.

2. Funding: cash management

2.1 *Yield curve.* Market interest rates differ according to the term of borrowing, from a one day (overnight) borrowing to loan periods of 30 years or more. The yield curve describes how interest rates vary according to the period to maturity of a loan.

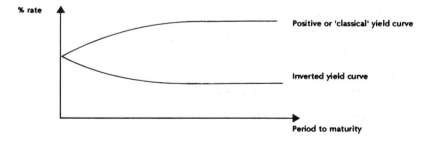

- When short term borrowing rates are higher than longer term borrowing rates, there is an inverted yield curve. An inverted yield curve is likely to be found in countries with current economic problems, such as a high rate of inflation, perhaps facing the threat of recession. Interest rates are expected to fall after the 'temporary' economic problems are resolved.

- When interest rates rise as the period to maturity is longer, we have the classical yield curve. This will be found in countries where the medium/long term economic outlook is much the same as the short term outlook - eg stable, sustained growth with low inflation.

2.2 *Cash management: cash budgets*

- When a company has surplus cash, this can be invested, even in the short term, to earn interest. The treasurer should seek to employ any cash surplus efficiently.

- When a company has a cash deficit (overdraft), the treasurer should try to fund the deficit at the lowest possible cost.

In large multinational companies, the planning, monitoring and control of cash will involve a number of banks and bank accounts, multi-currency facilities and computerised monitoring of cash balances.

2.3 | Cash planning and forecasting involve the need for

- accurate estimates of the *quantity of cash flows*
- accurate estimates of the *timing* of cash flows

2.4 *Cash budgets* or forecasts are prepared for shorter term and longer term periods. Accurate forecasting can enable a corporate treasurer to exploit the yield curve to fund the company's cash requirements as cheaply/profitably as possible.

2.5 *Overcoming problems of forecast cash shortages*

When a company is faced with a cash deficit in excess of its existing borrowing facilities, the treasurer or finance director can try to overcome the problem in a number of different ways:

- increase the size of borrowing facilities
- cancel fixed asset expenditures
- postpone fixed asset expenditures
- suggest a reduction in any dividend that might be due to be announced
- urge efforts to stimulate sales
- urge efforts to reduce running costs
- delay payments to creditors
- make efforts to speed up payments from debtors
- sell investments
- sell any other non-essential fixed assets

2.6 *Obtaining funds*

- *Long term funds* can be raised by issuing new equity, debt or convertible bonds etc.

  o Debt capital might be issued in the domestic currency and on the domestic stock market, or as eurobonds. Eurobonds are bonds denominated in a major currency, with a maturity period of up to 40 years, and issued internationally

- *Bank borrowing* might be

  - bi-lateral - a facility/term loan provided by an individual bank
  - syndicated - a group of banks provide a combined facility/term loan, with each bank taking part of the facility on identical terms

- Borrowing from sources other than banks can be arranged by large companies in the form of bond issues (such as eurobonds, loan stock issues) for long term debt and *commercial paper* for shorter term debt. Commercial paper (CP) is unsecured short term debt, issued in various CP markets around the world, with maturities of mostly in the region of 30 to 90 days although some maturities are up to 270 days.

3. Interest rate exposures: hedging interest rate exposures

3.1 Interest rate exposures for a company fall into four broad categories.

Nature of the exposure

1. Fixed rate versus floating rate debt	Company can get caught paying higher interest rates by having fixed rather than floating rate debt, or floating rather than fixed rate debt, as market interest rates change.
2. Currency of debt	Also a foreign currency exposure. A company can pay higher interest rates by borrowing in a currency for which exchange rates move adversely against the company's domestic currency. Treasurer should seek to match the currency of the loan with the currency of the underlying operations/assets that generate revenue to pay interest/repay the loans.
3. Term of loan	A company can be exposed by having to repay a loan earlier than it can afford to, resulting in a need to re-borrow, perhaps at a higher rate of interest.
4. Term loan or overdraft facility?	A company might prefer to pay for borrowings only when it needs the money (overdraft facility): the bank will charge a commitment fee for a facility. Alternatively, a term loan might be preferred.

3.2 A number of treasury instruments have been devised to help a corporate treasurer to hedge interest rate exposures.

3.3 *Interest rate swaps.* An arrangement whereby two unrelated parties (eg a company and a bank) borrow identical amounts for an identical term, independently of each other, one at a fixed rate and the other at a floating rate of interest. They then swap their interest payments. Swaps can be used by a company to switch from floating rate to fixed rate borrowing, or vice versa.

Example

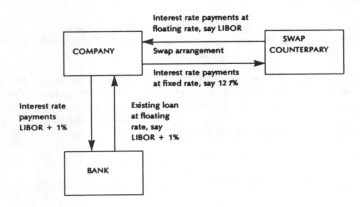

In this example, a company can use a swap to change from paying interest at a floating rate of LIBOR + 1% to one of paying fixed interest of $(12\frac{1}{2}\% + 1\%$ over LIBOR$) = 13\frac{1}{2}\%$.

3.4 Interest rate swaps might be arranged in different currencies, for example between a fixed rate in US dollars and a floating rate in sterling. Where this happens, these currency coupon swaps are normally reversed with the principal eventually swapped back at the original exchange rate. For example, a UK company and a US company can arrange a back-to-back loan and currency swap as follows.

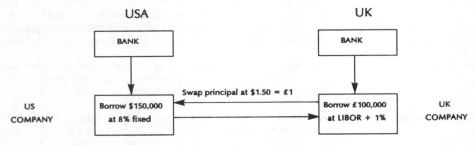

The companies can service each other's debt (interest rate swap) and also exchange the principal, with the UK company taking $150,000 and the US company taking £100,000 (currency swap). Each company will eventually repay the principal on each other's loans at a rate of $1.50 = £1.

3.5 *Financial futures.* A futures contract is an agreement to buy or sell a standard quantity of a particular financial instrument at a specified future date at an agreed price - the price being determined by trading on the floor of a futures exchange.

3.6 For example, a company can contract to buy (or sell) £100,000 of a notional 30 year Treasury bond bearing an 8% coupon in, say, 6 months time, at an agreed price.

3.6 For example, a company can contract to buy (or sell) £100,000 of a notional 30 year Treasury bond bearing an 8% coupon in, say, 6 months time, at an agreed price.

- The futures price is likely to vary with changes in interest rates, and this acts as a hedge against adverse price movements.

- The outlay to buy futures is much less than for buying the financial instrument itself, and so a company can hedge large exposures with a relatively small initial employment of cash.

3.7 *Forward rate agreement (FRA)*. An agreement between a company and a bank which fixes the interest rate in advance for a specific sum of money, which the company will invest or borrow at a specified future date.

3.8 *Interest rate options*. These grant the buyer the right *but not the obligation* to deal at an agreed interest rate (strike rate) at a future maturity date. Options are comparatively expensive to buy.

3.9 *Offset hedging*. A company can offset floating rate borrowings by investing surplus cash in floating rate investments. Increases/decreases in interest rates will affect both liabilities and assets, leaving the company's net income position unchanged.

4. Foreign exchange receipts and payments

4.1 Treasurers of international companies will often wish to exchange one currency for another; for example, to exchange US dollar income for sterling, or to buy Deutschemarks in order to pay a German supplier.

4.2 Foreign currency is bought and sold through banks. Banks will quote spot rates for buying and selling currency.

For example, the US$ - £ rate might be quoted as 1.6100 - 1.6120

The bank will sell US$ at $1.6100 to £1 and will buy US$ at $1.6120 to £1.

4.3 | Of the spot rates quoted, the lower rate is always the bank's selling rate and the higher rates is always the bank's buying rate.

5. Exchange rate exposures

5.1 Exchange rate exposure for companies with assets and/or liabilities denominated in foreign currencies or income/expenditures in foreign currencies can be divided into three categories.

(1) *Translation exposure*. These are potential losses that might occur when foreign currency assets or liabilities are translated into domestic currency for the preparation of the company's consolidated accounts.

(2)   *Transaction exposure.* Where a company has contracted to receive or pay an amount of money in a foreign currency at some time in the future, transaction exposure arises from the risk of adverse exchange rate movements between now and the time of the eventual cash receipt/payment.

(3)   *Economic exposure.* This arises from the effect of adverse exchange rate movements on future cash flows, where no contractual arrangement to receive or pay money has yet been made. This kind of exposure is longer term in nature and difficult to quantify exactly.

6.   Hedging exchange rate exposures

6.1   *Matching the currency of fixed assets and long term liabilities*, to reduce or eliminate translation exposure.

6.2   *Structural hedging.* This involves netting and matching foreign currency inflows and outflows. A company can try to

● buy supplies in the same currencies in which it earns revenue
● use the foreign currency income to pay the supplier.

Matching eliminates transaction exposure, to the extent that matching can be achieved.

6.3   A variety of treasury instruments are available to minimise transaction exposure, such as forward exchange contracts and foreign currency options.

6.4   *Forward exchange contracts*

A forward exchange contract is:

● an immediately firm and binding contract between a bank and its customer
● for the purchase or sale of a specified quantity of a stated foreign currency
● at a rate of exchange fixed at the time the contract is made
● for performance (ie delivery of the currency and payment for it) at a future time which is agreed upon when making the contract. This future time will be either a specific date, or at any time between two specified dates.

6.5   Forward rates are quoted by banks at a premium or discount to the spot rate. The 'ADDIS' rule applies - add a *dis*count to the spot rate, or subtract a premium, to obtain the forward rate.

6.6   Forward rates *do not* represent the FX markets' expectations about what exchange rates will be in the future. The difference between spot rates and forward rates represents interest rate differentials between the two currencies.

Approximately: Spot rate x $\dfrac{1 + \text{interest rate in country A}}{1 + \text{interest rate in country B}}$ = Forward rate

where the interest rate is for the appropriate time period of forward cover.

6.7   *The cost of forward exchange cover*

> The approximate cost (as an *interest percentage*) of forward exchange cover may be calculated by means of the following formula:
>
> $$\frac{\text{Premium or discount x 12 months x 100}}{\text{Number of months forward cover is taken x the forward rate}}$$

Thus, if a company can borrow for one year in sterling at 14% and in US dollars at 11%, and the implied interest rate differential in a one year forward exchange rate contract for £ and $ is $2\frac{3}{4}$%, it would be cheaper to borrow in US dollars and enter a one year forward exchange contract to buy dollars in order to repay the loan after one year, without any risk from foreign currency exposure.

6.8   *Foreign currency options*

> A currency option can be described as a method by which the buyer of the option has the right, *but is not obliged*, to buy or sell a certain quantity of a currency at a specified rate of exchange (the exercise price) within a certain limited time or at the end of that time. The absence of an obligation to buy or sell the currency is what makes it different from (and more expensive to obtain than) a forward exchange contract.

6.9   *Futures*

Some financial futures markets, such as LIFFE, offer foreign currency futures - agreements for the sale or purchase of a standard quantity of a foreign currency at a specified future time and exchange rate. Futures are available in only a limited number of currencies. They are an alternative to forward exchange contracts, but are less flexible, and an initial sum must be paid for the futures. They are not widely used.

QUESTIONS

1 Pointer Law Ltd is a manufacturing company. It purchases materials each month, and holds them in store for two months before they enter production. The production cycle is one month. Finished goods are held for about three months before sale. Three months credit is taken from suppliers.

Sales are expected to be £100,000 in January, rising by £10,000 per month through the year. Material costs amount to 50% of sales.

The budgeted cash payments for materials in June is

A £60,000
B £65,000
C £90,000
D £95,000

Circle your answer

A   B   C   D

Data for questions 2 and 3

George Ment Ltd expects to make sales of £200,000 in January, with sales rising by 2% per month (compound) thereafter.

(1) Materials in the cost of sales amount to 30% of sales value. Materials are purchased one month ahead of requirement and are paid for on 60 days' credit. The production cycle is very short and no stocks of finished goods are held.

(2) Debtors pay as follows

   20% cash with purchase: no discount
   40% on 1 month's credit, with a 3% early settlement discount
   Rest after 2 months
   5% bad debts

---

2 What are the budgeted cash payments in June (to the nearest £000) for materials?

A £62,000
B £64,000
C £65,000
D £66,000

Circle your answer

A   B   C   D

3 What are the budgeted cash receipts (to the nearest £100) in June?

A   £198,500
B   £202,000
C   £202,400
D   £207,100

Circle your answer

A	B	C	D

4 A company has the following long term investments

Holding	Number held	Market price	P/E ratio	Expected annual payout ratio
Eggs Hibbit plc	750,000	£2.40	16	30%
Watt Ness plc	500,000	£1.90	10	60%
2½% Consols (£100 nominal value)	10,000	£30.00	-	-

Dividends and interest are payable twice a year in equal amounts on all three investments, in May and November in each case.

What is the expected total cash income in November from the three investments? (Assume there are no tax adjustments or dividends or interest).

A   £49,125
B   £57,875
C   £70,875
D   £115,750

Circle your answer

A	B	C	D

5 Which of the following statements is correct?

Statement
1. Knowing the size of their usable cash balances can help companies to increase their profits.
2. Companies should be able to ascertain the size of their usable cash balances from their cash book.

A   Both statements are correct
B   Statement 1 is correct
C   Statement 2 is correct
D   Neither statement is correct

Circle your answer

A	B	C	D

6 A company's treasury department wishes to speed up the availability of funds received from customers. The company's bank has offered special clearance of remittances, that would speed up the availability of funds by 2 days, from the current 3 days. The charge for this service would be £3 per clearance. The company's opportunity cost of capital is 15%.

What is the minimum remittance value that would make use of the special clearance facility beneficial?

A £548
B £1,095
C £3,650
D £7,300

Circle your answer

A   B   C   D

7 The following factors will be considered by managers responsible for the cash management of a large company.

Factor
1. Exposure to interest rate movements
2. Inaccurate cash flow forecasts
3. Risk of deteriorating credit rating

Which of these factors will make managers prefer long term to short term debt?

A Factors 1, 2 and 3
B Factor 1 only
C Factor 2 only
D Factor 3 only

Circle your answer

A   B   C   D

8 A company with large amounts of surplus cash may decide to invest it in short-term money market instruments. Which of the following money market investments would carry the *lowest* interest rate?

A Sterling certificates of deposit (CDs)
B Treasury bills
C Finance house deposits
D Local authority deposits

Circle your answer

A   B   C   D

Data for questions 9 and 10

Barry Stirr Ltd has investments in the money markets. It has estimated its operational net cash flows next week to be

Net cash flow	Probability
+ £30,000	0.3
+ £10,000	0.5
0	0.2

Transaction costs for money market deposits or withdrawals are £8 plus 0.05% of the transaction value. Deposits and withdrawals must be £10,000 or in multiples of £10,000. Interest, which is not paid on money withdrawn during the week, is at the rate of 0.25% per week. The company has no other cash balances on which to draw. A decision about investing extra cash in the money markets will be made at the start of the week.

9 If the company deposits a further £10,000 in the money markets at the beginning of the week, the expected value of the net profit or loss to the company in the week from this money market investment decision is

A £4.40
B £7.00
C £9.40
D £19.40

Circle your answer

A   B   C   D

10 The optimum policy for investing in the money markets at the start of the week is

A to invest nothing
B to invest a further £10,000
C to invest a further £20,000
D to invest a further £30,000

Circle your answer

A   B   C   D

11 An agreement between two parties to make interest payments to each other based on each other's underlying debt obligation is

A an interest rate swap
B an interest rate option
C an interest rate future
D a swaption

Circle your answer

A   B   C   D

12 A securities market in which dealers trade in standardised contracts covering the sale or purchase at a future date of a set quantity of financial investments is called

A   an options market
B   an over the counter market
C   a swaps market
D   a futures market

Circle your answer

A   B   C   D

13 Goodmen and Trew plc has an outstanding loan of £20 million from its bank, on which it pays fixed interest of 14% per annum. Its corporate treasurer suspects that interest rates might fall, and arranges a swap with another bank whereby

(1)   the counterparty bank pays the company interest on £20 million at a rate of 13%

(2)   the company pays the counterparty bank interest on £20 million at a rate of LIBOR plus 50 basis points

What is the net rate of interest per annum on £20 million that the company will now be paying?

A $13\frac{1}{2}$%
B   LIBOR + $\frac{1}{2}$%
C   LIBOR + 1%
D   LIBOR + $1\frac{1}{2}$%

Circle your answer

A   B   C   D

14 Wigg plc is a very large international company with a high credit rating that can currently borrow from its bank at a fixed rate of 10% pa or a variable rate at LIBOR. LIBOR is currently 11% pa, but its future movements are uncertain.

Penn plc is less highly-rated and can borrow from its bank at a fixed rate of 12% pa or a variable rate of LIBOR plus 1% pa.

Wigg plc wants to increase its variable interest rate borrowing. Penn plc wants to increase its fixed rate borrowing. Which of the following swap arrangements would enable both to benefit?

		Borrow from bank	Lend to other company
A	Wigg	At fixed rate of 10%	At LIBOR plus $1\frac{1}{4}$%
	Penn	At LIBOR plus 1%	At fixed rate of $11\frac{1}{2}$%
B	Wigg	At fixed rate of 10%	At fixed rate of 11%
	Penn	At LIBOR plus 1%	At LIBOR minus $\frac{1}{2}$%

Continued...

C	Wigg	At LIBOR	At fixed rate of 11%
	Penn	At fixed rate of 12%	At LIBOR minus $\frac{1}{2}$%
D	Wigg	At fixed rate of 10%	At fixed rate of $10\frac{1}{2}$%
	Penn	At LIBOR plus 1%	At LIBOR minus $\frac{1}{4}$%

Circle your answer

A	B	C	D

15 An investor holds a portfolio of shares with a value of £12 million at the end of March. He is worried that by the end of June, when he plans to sell his shares to raise cash, share prices will have fallen. How could he buy or sell FT-SE 100 Index futures on the LIFFE to hedge against this risk of capital loss?

The index value for contracts to be completed at the end of September is 2,400 and the price of futures is £25 per full index point.

	At end of March	*At end of June*
A	Sell 200 futures	Buy 200 futures whatever the share price index
B	Sell 200 futures	Buy 200 futures but only if share price index has fallen
C	Buy 200 futures	Sell 200 futures, whatever the share price index
D	Buy 200 futures	Sell 200 futures but only if share price index has fallen

Circle your answer

A	B	C	D

16 A UK based manufacturing company with spare capacity imports a considerable proportion of its materials and components from abroad, and exports about 20% of its output. The foreign exchange value of sterling declines by 10%.

What will be the consequences for the company's revenues and unit variable costs?

	Revenues	*Unit variable costs*
A	Will rise	Will rise
B	Will rise	Will fall
C	Will fall	Will rise
D	Will fall	Will fall

Circle your answer

A	B	C	D

17 Heavy Dense plc borrowed $120,000 in dollars and one year later repaid $132,000 in dollars. When the loan was acquired, the rate of exchange was $1.50 to the pound and when the loan was repaid the rate was $1.25 to the pound. What was the effective annual cost of the loan in terms of the pounds received and paid by Heavy Dense plc if the company did not hedge against its foreign exchange exposure?

A   8.3% income
B   10.0% expense
C   24.2% expense
D   32.0% expense

Circle your answer

| A | B | C | D |

18 Sally Sitter Ltd has to pay a French supplier 100,000 francs in 3 months time. The company's financial director wishes to avoid exchange rate exposure, and is looking at four options.

Option
1.   Do nothing for three months, then buy the francs at the spot rate.

2.   'Lead' with the payment, and pay in full now, buying the francs at today's spot rate.

3.   Buy francs now, put them on deposit for three months, and pay the debt with these francs plus accumulated interest.

4.   Arrange a forward exchange contract to buy the francs in three months time.

Which of these options would provide cover against exchange rate exposure?

A   Options 1, 2, 3 and 4
B   Options 2, 3 and 4 only
C   Options 3 and 4 only
D   Option 4 only

Circle your answer

| A | B | C | D |

19 Suppose that annual inflation levels are currently at 4% in Japan and 6% in the United Kingdom. If the levels of inflation move during the next year to 3% in Japan and 8% in the United Kingdom, what effect are these changes in inflation likely to have on the relative value of the yen and the pound by the end of next year, according to the purchasing power parity theory of long term exchange rates?

Sterling will decline in value against the yen by

A   2.8%
B   3.0%
C   4.6%
D   5.0%

Circle your answer

| A | B | C | D |

20 The US dollar/sterling spot rate is $1.52 = £1.

One year US interest rates = 8%
One year UK interest rates = 14%

The one year forward exchange rate between the dollar and sterling should be

A	$1.4288 to £1
B	$1.4400 to £1
C	$1.6044 to £1
D	$1.6112 to £1

Circle your answer

A	B	C	D

21 The current US dollar/sterling spot rate is $1.50 to £1, and the dollar is at a premium against sterling for forward exchange contracts?

What would happen to the spot rate and forward rates if interest rates went up in the UK on sterling but not in the USA on the dollar

	Spot rate	*Forward premium*
A	Dollar would weaken	Would increase
B	Dollar would weaken	Would get smaller
C	Dollar would strengthen	Would increase
D	Dollar would strengthen	Would get smaller

Circle your answer

A	B	C	D

22 Plane Tiff Ltd has just purchased goods from Sweden costing 200,000 Swedish krona. It is now 1 April and the supplier must be paid on 15 June. Plane Tiff Ltd's finance director wishes to hedge against foreign currency transaction exposure. Exchange rate details are:

On 1 April	9.90
2 months forward	$1\frac{1}{4}$ ore pm
3 months forward	$1\frac{3}{4}$ ore pm
On 15 June	9.92

How much would Plane Tiff Ltd pay on 15 June to obtain the Swedish currency that it requires, on the assumption that measures were taken on 1 April to hedge against the currency exposure?

A	£20,161
B	£20,228
C	£20,233
D	£20,238

Circle your answer

A	B	C	D

23 George and Dury Ltd must pay a French supplier 35,000 French francs in one month's time. Given the following exchange rates being quoted by the company's bank, what would be the cost of the payment in sterling if the company were to arrange a one month forward exchange contract?

French francs - £ rates: Spot $9.22\frac{1}{4}$ - $9.23\frac{1}{4}$
                                1 month forward $4\frac{1}{2}$ c dis - $4\frac{3}{4}$ c dis

- A £3,771.55
- B £3,776.64
- C £3,810.56
- D £3,813.67

Circle your answer

A   B   C   D

24 The treasurer of Hugh Runderer-Rest Ltd wishes to sell DM120,000 that the company will receive in two months' time from a customer in Frankfurt. The bank's exchange rates are

Spot   1.73 - 2.74
2 months forward $3\frac{1}{4}$ pf - 3pf pm

If the company took out a forward exchange contract, what would it receive in 2 months' time from the exchange of its DM income?

- A £43,321.30
- B £43,360.43
- C £44,280.44
- D £44,568.25

Circle your answer

A   B   C   D

25 Noake Caister Rancer Ltd has just agreed to pay a US supplier $80,000 in 3 months' time. The company has also just sold goods to a customer in the Middle East, and the $50,000 owed will also be received in 3 months' time.

The US$/sterling exchange rates are

Spot $1.5640 - $1.5660
3 months forward   2.62c pm - 2.59c pm

What is the minimum net cost of these transactions, if the company's corporate treasurer is to avoid any foreign exchange transaction exposure?

- A £18,685.48
- B £19,479.25
- C £19,508.39
- D £19,556.95

Circle your answer

A   B   C   D

Data for questions 26 and 27

Seville Lactions plc in the UK has invoiced a US customer the sum of $500,000 receivable in one year's time.

The company's finance director is considering two methods of hedging the exchange risk:

Method

1. Borrowing $500,000 now for one year, converting the amount into sterling, and repaying the loan out of the eventual receipts

2. Entering into a 12 month forward exchange contract to sell the $500,000 and meanwhile borrowing an equivalent amount in sterling

The US dollar-sterling spot rate is 1.6180 - 1.6400

The 12 months forward rate of dollars against sterling is 1.5790

Interest rates for 12 months are: USA 7.5%, UK 11%.

26 What would be the net proceeds in sterling under method 1 (to the nearest £1)?

A £271,341
B £281,129
C £285,274
D £304,878

Circle your answer

| A | B | C | D |

27 What would be the net proceeds in sterling under method 2 (to the nearest £1)?

A £281,824
B £292,907
C £316,656
D £351,488

Circle your answer

| A | B | C | D |

28 Kays Forder Fence Ltd arranges on 1 February to deliver goods to a US customer. The selling price is $40,000, to be paid in 6 months' time on 1 August. The company covers all its foreign exchange transaction exposures by means of forward exchange contracts.

Due to a dispute about the quality of some goods, the payment that is actually received on 1 August is only $30,000, and no further payments are to be made.

Continued...

Exchange rates are as follows

1 February	Spot	$1.6260
6 months forward	1.55c dis	
1 August	Spot	$1.6630

What will be the net receipts from the transaction for the company (to the nearest £1)?

A   £18,234
B   £18,276
C   £18,355
D   £18,628

Circle your answer

A   B   C   D

29   Myler Nodd Friends Ltd wants to borrow £500,000. The company's finance director is considering whether to borrow the equivalent amount in US dollars, because the interest rate on a dollar loan would be just 8% pa, although it would need to convert the dollars into sterling. If the company took out a forward exchange contract to avoid exposure for the loan plus interest, how much would it cost in one year's time to repay the loan with interest, given the following exchange rates?

Spot	$1.5235 - 1.5255
1 year forward	9.50c - 9.40c pm

A   £574,705
B   £575,459
C   £575,912
D   £576,668

Circle your answer

A   B   C   D

30   A large multinational manufacturing company has very large and regular receivables in US dollars and Italian lira.

Which of the following treasury policies would be valid methods of reducing the foreign exchange exposure of the company?

Policy
1.   The company could hedge against its US dollar receivables by establishing a manufacturing facility in Paraguay

2.   The company could hedge against its Italian lira receivables by means of a currency loan in Deutschemarks at 9% pa, rather than a loan in lira at 14% pa (which are the current interest rates on loans in those currencies).

A   Both policies would reduce foreign exchange exposure

B   Policy 1 only would reduce foreign exchange exposure

Continued...

C   Policy 2 only would reduce foreign
    exchange exposure

D   Neither policy would reduce foreign
    exchange exposure

Circle your answer

A	B	C	D

31 The interest rate on a three months' loan in sterling is currently 15% per annum, and interest on an equivalent loan in US dollars is just $8\frac{1}{2}$% per annum.

Rich D'Aver Duct Ltd's finance director thinks it might be cheaper, instead of borrowing £2,000,000 for three months in sterling, to borrow instead in US dollars, and to arrange a forward exchange contract to buy US dollars in 3 months' time for repaying the loan, in order to avoid exchange rate exposure.

Spot rate	$1.5425
3 months' forward rate	2.25c premium

The option to borrow in US dollars and to take out a forward exchange contract

	would be	*because the approx cost of forward exchange cover is*
A	more expensive	5.8% pa
B	more expensive	5.9% pa
C	cheaper	5.8% pa
D	cheaper	5.9% pa

Circle your answer

A	B	C	D

32 The following conditions are present

German interest rate = 1.25% per 3 months
US interest rate = 1.75% per 3 months
Spot rate $1 - 2DM
3 months forward rate premium = 0.5pf (There are 100 pfennigs to 1 DM)

What will be the effect of large-scale covered interest arbitrage activities by international investors?

	Interest rate differential between $ and DM will	*Forward exchange premium for DM will*
A	Increase	Decrease
B	Increase	Increase
C	Decrease	Increase
D	Decrease	Decrease

Circle your answer

A	B	C	D

33 Pohl Leese Witneys plc has entered a transaction that will involve a yen payment exposure arising in six months time. The company's treasurer decides to cover the exposure by means of foreign currency options, and buys a 6 month yen call/sterling put option.

Forward exchange rate	240 yen = £1
Option strike price	240 yen = £1
Option premium	1.2%

What is the worst case exchange rate that the company will have to pay, and what would it do in 6 months' time if the spot rate is 245 yen = £1?

	Worst case rate	Decision in 6 months time
A	237.1	Let option lapse
B	237.1	Exercise the option
C	242.9	Let option lapse
D	242.9	Exercise the option

Circle your answer

A   B   C   D

Data for questions 34 and 35

Prosser Kew Shone plc must make a payment of US$450,000 in six months time. Now is December.

Exchange rates

Spot	$1.7000 - $1.7040
6 months forward	$1.6764 - $1.6809

Money markets
Interest rates for six months

	Borrowing	Lending
US dollars	$6\frac{1}{2}$%	5%
Sterling	$7\frac{1}{2}$%	6%

Foreign currency option prices
Prices are in cents per £1, for a contract size of £12,500

Exercise price $	Call options June	Put options June
1.80	3.6	9.3

Any money market borrowing in December would be invested at the money market rate for six months.

34 Hedging the foreign exchange exposure on the forward exchange market in December would be

    A   cheaper than hedging on the money markets by £8,576

    B   cheaper than hedging on the money markets by £3,294

    C   more expensive than hedging on the money markets by £6,933

    D   more expensive than hedging on the money markets by £13,551

Circle your answer

A	B	C	D

35 Suppose that instead of using the forward exchange market or the money market, the company used currency options. The spot rate in June when the options are exercised is $1.67. What would be the total cost to the company in June, assuming that the options are not paid for until June?

    A   £255,389
    B   £263,922
    C   £283,383
    D   £295,247

Circle your answer

A	B	C	D

CHAPTER 10

GROWTH. MERGERS AND TAKEOVERS. RECONSTRUCTIONS

> ## This chapter covers the following topics:
>
> - Company growth
> - Mergers and takeovers
> - Splitting the business. Share repurchase schemes
> - Liquidations
> - Reconstructions

1. Company growth

1.1 Companies might seek to grow in size and profitability. They are likely to do this by means of a combination of

- internal growth
- external growth (mergers or takeovers).

1.2 Growth must be financed. Companies might use

(1) retained profits (reducing current dividends below what they otherwise would be)
(2) borrowing (issuing loan stock, borrowing from a bank etc)
(3) issues of new shares for cash (perhaps as a rights issue)
(4) issues of new shares or loan stock in exchange for shares in another 'target' company.

The aim of growth by companies ought to be to add to the wealth of existing shareholders.

2. Mergers and takeovers

2.1 Mergers and takeovers are essentially the same thing, except that mergers refer to the joining together of two companies of comparable size, and takeovers refer to the acquisition of a larger company by a smaller one.

2.2 The purchase price must be decided and agreed between the directors/shareholders of the companies involved.

- If the target company's shares have a market price, a successful takeover bid will need to offer a higher price, to win acceptances of the offer.

- If the target company is a private company, estimates of its value will be made. Techniques to help with this assessment include:

  - P/E multiple
  - dividend valuation model
  - CAPM and expected future profits
  - DCF basis of evaluation
  - superprofits assessment
  - asset valuation basis.

  Valuation cannot be exact, and is an 'art' rather than a 'science'.

2.3 The predator company will also wish to consider the purchase consideration, which could be

- cash
- shares in the predator company in exchange for shares in the target company (a share exchange perhaps with a cash alternative)
- new loan stock in the predator company, perhaps convertible into equity at a future date.

2.4 The nature of the purchase consideration (cash or 'paper offer') will affect EPS and share values after the takeover. If the takeover bid involves an all-share offer, and the profits of the enlarged company after the merger are no larger than the profits of the separate companies before the merger

- there will be 'earnings concentration' for the shares that were valued on a higher P/E ratio for the purpose of the takeover

- there will be 'earnings dilution' for the shares valued on a lower P/E ratio.

2.5 If the purchase consideration involves a share exchange, the target company's shareholders will also want to consider how

- dividends and
- asset backing per share

might be affected if they accept shares in the predator company.

2.6 Takeover bids might be welcomed by the directors of the target company, or hostile. In the event of a hostile bid, the target company's directors will take defensive measures to persuade their shareholders to turn down the bid.

2.7 In the UK, the takeover of public companies is subject to the City Code on Takeovers and Mergers. In addition, takeovers that may be against the public interest can be referred to the Monopolies and Mergers Commission (MMC) by the Office of Fair Trading/Department of Trade and Industry. The MMC has the power to stop a takeover.

3. Splitting the business. Share repurchase schemes

3.1 Companies do not always seek growth. Some might seek to

- separate the different parts of their business into independent companies, and give shareholders new shares in each newly established company (eg the fairly recent 'unbundling' of Courtaulds and BAT)

    - repurchase some of its own shares - usually if the company has a large amount of cash for which it cannot find a worthwhile investment use.

4. Liquidations

4.1 Some companies face liquidation rather than the prospect of growth, because of an inability to meet their liabilities when they fall due. In the event of a liquidation, the assets of the business are sold off and distributed, in the following order or 'priority list'

(1) Secured creditors with a fixed charge on certain assets, insofar as the secured assets realise enough money to cover the debt
(2) Liquidation expenses
(3) Preferential creditors (eg up to a given time limit, unpaid income tax, VAT and national insurance; some arrears of unpaid wages and salaries)
(4) Secured creditors with a floating charge on certain assets
(5) Unsecured creditors
(6) Preference shareholders
(7) Ordinary shareholders.

5. Reconstructions

5.1 As an alternative to liquidation, companies might be able to arrange a scheme of reconstruction.

- All creditors threatened with non-payment or only partial payment, as well as shareholders, need to agree to the scheme

- New capital will have to be injected into the company, perhaps by a 'white knight' or by existing shareholders

- The capital structure of the company will be re-built (reconstructed).

5.2 | For a reconstruction to be agreed, the individual parties involved must be confident that they will benefit from the reconstruction more than from a liquidation of the company.

QUESTIONS

1

X plc and Y plc are planning a merger. Shareholders in Y would accept 2 shares in X for every share in Y they hold.

Details are as follows.

	X plc	Y plc
Number of shares	20 million	6 million
Annual earnings	£5 million	£2.2 million
P/E ratio	10	12

As a result of the merger, annual earnings of the enlarged company would be 10% higher than the sum of the earnings of each company before the merger. The expected post-merger P/E ratio is 11.

By how much would the former shareholders in Y gain from the merger?

A £2.97 million
B £3.30 million
C £4.02 million
D £6.27 million

Circle your answer

| A | B | C | D |

2

PQ plc is considering a possible bid for the share capital of RS Ltd, which consists entirely of ordinary shares.

RS Ltd achieves annual profits after tax of £200,000. Additional savings of £80,000 pa before tax would result from a successful takeover. Tax is 50% of profits and is paid in the same year as the profits are earned.

Other data

(1) Annual depreciation charges in RS Ltd's P & L account are £50,000 and are expected to remain at this annual level. Assume that depreciation is an allowable cost for tax purposes.

(2) RS Ltd has a long term loan of £200,000.

(3) PQ plc would put a value to the shares of RS Ltd using DCF. The takeover would be evaluated over 10 years at a 20% cost of capital. The PV of £1 pa for 10 years at 20% is £4.19.

(4) If PQ purchased RS, capital expenditures in RS over the next 10 years, to maintain operations at their current level, would have a PV of £150,000.

What valuation would PQ plc put on the shares of RS Ltd (to the nearest £000)?

A £856,000
B £865,000
C £960,000
D £1,065,000

Circle your answer

| A | B | C | D |

3

Tooth plc's shares are quoted at a market price of £4.20 giving a P/E ratio of 10. The company has just made a takeover bid for Gumm plc, at a price of £3.15 per share, with the suggested purchase consideration being the exchange of 3 new shares in Tooth for every 4 shares held in Gumm. The most recently quoted EPS of Gumm plc is 20p and its share's market price is currently £2.60.

Tooth plc could reduce the dilution in EPS after the takeover in all *but one* of the following ways. Which is the exception?

A   Achieve additional earnings growth as a consequence of the takeover

B   Revalue the assets of Gumm to a realistic current value

C   Sell off parts of Gumm's business after the takeover

D   Buy the shares in Gumm for cash, rather than by exchanging shares

Circle your answer

A	B	C	D

4

An independent accountant has used four different bases to value a company. Where appropriate they reflect the expectations and attitudes to risk of the owners.

Economic value of the business	£4.3 million
Net realisable value of individual assets	£4.5 million
Balance sheet value of assets	£4.7 million
Cost of setting up the business from scratch	£5.0 million

In negotiations with a potential buyer for the company, what is the minimum value the owners should be advised to accept for all of their share capital?

A   £4.3 million
B   £4.5 million
C   £4.7 million
D   £5.0 million

Circle your answer

A	B	C	D

5

The following information relates to two companies, Marco plc and Polo plc.

	Marco plc	*Polo plc*
Earnings after tax	£200,000	£800,000
P/E ratio	16	21

Polo plc's management estimate that were they to acquire Marco plc they could save after tax £100,000 annually on administrative costs in running the new joint company. Additionally they estimate that the P/E ratio of the new company would be 20.

On the basis of these estimates, what is the maximum that Polo plc's shareholders should wish to pay for the entire share capital of Marco plc?

A   £2.4m
B   £3.2m
C   £5.2m
D   £6.0m

Circle your answer

A   B   C   D

6   Going Places plc is a small public company which achieves the following results.

Annual earnings	£2,000,000
Number of shares	10,000,000
P/E ratio	16

The company wishes to raise £6,000,000 to finance an internal growth project which will incur annual fixed costs of £400,000 but earn a contribution of 40% on sales from the project.

The project can be financed either (1) by a rights issue at a 25% discount to the current market price, or (2) by issuing £6,000,000 of new 10% loan capital.

At what level of extra annual sales should the company's shareholders be indifferent between either method of financing, given no change in the P/E ratio whatever financing method is used? Ignore taxation.

A   £2,000,000
B   £2,500,000
C   £3,000,000
D   £3,500,000

Circle your answer

A   B   C   D

Data for questions 7 and 8

Nara plc made profits after tax of £750,000 in the year just ended, and annual profits growth is expected to be 10% pa (compound).

A larger company, Sigh plc, is planning a takeover offer for all the shares of Nara plc. After the further addition to profits in the first year from replacing the current managing director of Nara plc (a substantial shareholder in the company) whose salary is £120,000 pa, with another MD whose salary would be £70,000 pa initially, earnings growth would be expected to remain at 10% pa thereafter (compound). Tax is at 35%.

The cost of capital of Sigh plc for such acquisitions is 20% pa. Its P/E ratio is 12.

7   What is the maximum price that Sigh plc should pay on a DCF valuation basis, for all the shares of Nara plc?

A   £7,825,000
B   £8,250,000
C   £8,575,000
D   £8,750,000

Circle your answer

A   B   C   D

8   If the purchase consideration is in shares of Sigh plc, what is the maximum price that Sigh plc should pay, on a P/E ratio valuation of 12, for all the shares of Nara plc, in order to avoid dilution of EPS?

A   £9,000,000
B   £9,390,000
C   £9,900,000
D   £10,290,000

Circle your answer

A   B   C   D

Data for questions 9 and 10

The directors of Mace plc are considering the acquisition of Dickson Ltd, a much smaller company that is capable of making annual profits after tax of £200,000. The current balance sheet of Dickson Ltd is as follows.

	£	£
Fixed assets (net book value)		800,000
Stocks and work in progress	504,000	
Debtors (less provision of 1% for doubtful debts)	396,000	
Bank balances	20,000	
		920,000
Bank overdraft	50,000	
Trade creditors	490,000	
		(540,000)
		1,180,000
Share capital and reserves		1,180,000

The estimated values of Dickson Ltd's assets are as follows.

	Replacement cost £	Net realisable value £
Fixed assets	850,000	600,000
Stocks and WIP	540,000	580,000

It is generally agreed that 2% of total debtors will be uncollectable.

The cost of capital of Mace plc is 15%.

9 What is the net realisable value of Dickson Ltd?

A £1,048,080
B £1,032,000
C £1,052,000
D £1,582,000

Circle your answer

A   B   C   D

10 On the basis of this data, what is the minimum price that the owners of Dickson Ltd should accept for their shares?

A Net realisable value
B £1,176,000
C £1,262,000
D £1,333,000

Circle your answer

A   B   C   D

11 The directors of a UK company can resist a hostile takeover bid from another company in the same industry by any of the following methods *except* by

A issuing an attractive profits forecast for shareholders, to persuade them that the offer price is too low

B finding a 'white knight' to make a welcome alternative takeover bid

C using an advertising and publicity campaign against the bid, to influence shareholders

D referring the bid to the Monopolies and Mergers Commission

Circle your answer

A   B   C   D

Data for questions 12 and 13

Two companies Scratch plc and Tickel plc, are in the same industry. Current statistics are as follows.

	Scratch plc	Tickel plc
Number of shares in issue	6,000,000	8,000,000
Annual earnings	£3,000,000	£1,000,000
P/E ratio	10	8.3

The companies are exploring the possibility of a merger, which would add £400,000 pa to earnings through cost saving measures.

12 One suggestion is that 100% of the shares of Tickel plc would be exchanged for shares in Scratch plc on the basis of 1 share in Scratch for every 2 shares in Tickel.

What would be the expected dilution in EPS from the merger for existing shareholders in Scratch?

A   6p
B   8.3p
C   10p
D   18.6p

Circle your answer

A   B   C   D

13 A second suggestion is that Scratch's shares should be valued at £5 for the merger and that Tickel's share capital is worth £18,500,000 in total for the purpose of the merger. A certain percentage of the shares of Tickel plc would be exchanged for shares in Scratch plc, but the remaining shares of Tickel should be exchanged for 10% loan stock (valued at par) in the newly-merged company.

Tax on profits is 30%.

How much 10% loan stock would be issued as part of the purchase consideration for Tickel's shares in order to avoid a dilution in EPS from the merger for Scratch's existing shareholders?

A   £4,500,000
B   £10,000,000
C   £15,000,000
D   £18,500,000

Circle your answer

A   B   C   D

14 According to the City Code on Takeovers and Mergers, where control of a public company is acquired by another company, a general offer to all shareholders is normally required. In this context, 'control' means aggregate holdings in the ordinary shares of the target company of

A   25% or more
B   30% or more
C   50%
D   more than 50%

Circle your answer

A   B   C   D

15 WX plc plans to acquire 100% of the share capital of YZ plc.

	WX plc £m	YZ plc £m
Value of assets	120	15
Net profits before tax and extraordinary items	10	3
Equity capital (£1 shares)	50	10

Continued...

The market value of WX plc's equity is £100 million and YZ plc will be purchased for £25 million, to be satisfied by the issue of 5 million shares in WX plc plus £15 million in new loan stock.

According to Stock Exchange regulations for listed companies, what class of transaction would this acquisition be?

A   Class 1
B   Class 2
C   Class 3
D   Class 4

Circle your answer

A   B   C   D

16 The directors of Target plc face a hostile takeover bid, and in planning their defence, they have looked at their share register. An analysis reveals the following.

Category of shareholders	% of total shares
Pension funds	17.6
Insurance companies	30.5
Unit trusts	4.8
Commercial companies	10.0
Nominees	21.3
Individuals	15.8
	100.0

The directors can conclude that the total percentage of shares held by institutional investors is

A   48.1%
B   52.9%
C   74.2%
D   unknown, but between 52% and 74%

Circle your answer

A   B   C   D

17 Buyback plc has very large liquid resources which are invested at an interest rate of 11%. Including investment income, the company makes earnings of £25 million on its 80 million shares. The share price is 300 pence, and the directors propose to repurchase 10 million of its own shares for cash at that price.

The P/E ratio is expected to fall to 9.4 because of the higher financial gearing.

Tax on profits is 35%

The expected equilibrium share price after the share repurchases is

A   269p
B   291p
C   300p
D   307p

Circle your answer

A   B   C   D

18 Water Ltd is a loss-making company. A summarised current balance sheet of the company is as follows, with all assets shown at *net realisable value*.

	£000		£000
Freehold property	120	Creditors	120
Plant and machinery	15	Bank overdraft	100
Stocks	60	Taxation	10
Debtors	50	12% debentures	100
	245	Ordinary shares and reserves	(85)
			245

The 12% debenture holders have a first charge over the freehold property and the bank has a second charge over the freehold property. Liquidation costs would be £15,000. The amount due for taxation would be a preferential creditor in a liquidation.

A reconstruction is being considered, but the bank might opt to put the company into liquidation. How much would (1) the bank and (2) trade creditors receive in a liquidation of the company?

	(1) Bank	*(2) Trade creditors*
A	£60,000	50p in £1
B	£80,000	50p in £1
C	£54,500	54.5p in £1
D	£55,500	55.5p in £1

Circle your answer

A   B   C   D

19 Sinking plc is a loss-making company with 10 million ordinary shares in issue. It is faced with liquidation, because it cannot pay interest on its £4 million of 12% debentures (the company's only debt). The assets of the company would currently realise very little, and the debenture holders have been offered a 'rescue package'. This would involve exchanging their debentures for £3 million of non-interest-bearing convertible loan stock, convertible into 5 million ordinary shares after 3 years. At the end of year 3, the loan stock holders would also have the option of putting the company into liquidation.

Estimates of the company's asset values at the end of year 3 are as follows.

Probability	Going concern value of assets £m	Net realisable value of assets £m
0.2	3	2
0.4	6	4
0.4	15	10

On the basis of this information, what would be the expected value of the convertible loan stock? (Ignore the time value of money).

A	£2.8 million
B	£3.0 million
C	£3.2 million
D	£3.6 million

Circle your answer

A   B   C   D

SECTION 2

MARKING SCHEDULES
AND COMMENTS

1: MARKING SCHEDULE

Question	Correct answer	Marks for the correct answer	Question	Correct answer	Marks for the correct answer
1	C	1	14	A	1
2	D	1	15	D	1
3	C	1	16	C	2
4	A	1	17	C	1
5	B	1	18	C	1
6	B	1	19	A	1
7	A	1	20	D	1
8	B	1	21	D	1
9	A	1	22	D	2
10	C	1	23	C	2
11	A	2	24	B	1
12	B	1	25	B	1
13	A	2			

YOUR MARKS

Total marks available **30**   Your total mark

GUIDELINES - If your mark was:

0 - 11 You do not yet have a sufficient understanding of this important topic area. You need to learn more.

18 - 24 Good. You are still making a few mistakes, but you achieved a fairly solid foundation of knowledge. If you do not need to learn about APV, a mark of 23 or 24 would be very good.

12 - 17 Fair, but there will be several important concepts you are still getting wrong. Check your mistakes carefully.

25 - 30 Excellent mark on this wide-ranging subject area.

COMMENTS

Question

1

Statement 2 is incorrect because a risky £1 is worth *less* than a safe one, and the discount rate used for project evaluation should reflect the amount of business risk or financial risk for the investor.

Statement 3 is correct. The existence of capital markets, which allow shareholders to buy and sell stocks and shares in order to plan their personal cashflows, means that if managers invest in projects with a positive NPV, in order to increase the market value of their company and its shares, *all* shareholders will benefit, regardless of their personal wealth and preferences for dividends or capital gains (retained profits).

2

	£
	£
Cost of new plant and equipment	900,000
Replacement cost of second-hand plant that will be replaced	500,000
Scrap value of unwanted plant	80,000
Working capital injection (2,000,000 - 1,800,000)	200,000
	1,680,000

3

Take the two NPVs closest to zero

$$\text{IRR (approx)} = 20\% + [\frac{2,000}{18,000 - 2,000} \times (20 - 15)] = 20.6\%$$

4

The projects giving the maximum NPV should be selected, since there is no capital rationing.

	NPV
	£
These are	
Between Projects 1 and 3: choose project 1	30,000
Between Projects 2 and 4: choose project 2	45,000
	75,000

Question

5

A cash flow *early* in one year is treated as a cash flow at the end of the previous year, for discounting purposes, to provide greater accuracy in PV calculations.

Item	Year	Cash flow £000	Discount factor at 14%	PV £000
Fixed capital cost	0	(250)	1.00	(250.0)
Working capital	0	(175)	1.00	(175.0)
Advertising	0 and 1	(80) pa	1.88	(150.4)
Cash profit	1	200	0.88	176.0
Change in w/capital	1	(75)	0.88	(66.0)
Cash profit	2	350	0.77	269.5
Change in w/capital	2	100	0.77	77.0
Cash profit	3	150	0.67	100.5
W/capital released	3	150	0.67	100.5
			NPV =	82.1

The working capital changes in years 1 and 2 relate to changes in cash flows caused by changes in debtors.

6

Working capital adjustments are required when project cash flows are estimated for each year as (Sales) minus (Cash costs of sales). The actual cash flows each year will be higher or lower than this, depending on changes in working capital between the start and the end of the year.

Let sales be S

Stocks	= 25% of 60% of S	= 0.15S
Creditors	= 20% of 60% of S	= (0.12S)
Debtors		= 0.20S
Working capital		0.23S

Year		Working capital change £	Discount factor at 15%	PV £
0	(0.23 of £1,000,000)	(230,000)	1.000	(230,000)
1	(+ 10%)	(23,000)	0.870	(20,010)
3	(+ 10%)	(25,300)	0.756	(19,127)
4	(End of project)	278,300	0.658	183,121
				(86,016)

7

Total value of company £40 million + £24 million = £64 million
Number of shares = 15 million
Price per share £4.27

Question

8

Year	Sales £	Cash costs £	Net cash flow £	Discount factor at 12%	PV £000
0			(1,000,000)	1.000	(1,000.00)
1	1,040,000	648,000	392,000	0.893	350.06
2	1,081,600	699,840	381,760	0.797	304.26
3	1,124,864	755,827	369,037	0.712	262.75
				NPV	-82.93

9

The company should generally use its weighted average cost of capital (WACC) to evaluate all its projects (provided they are of equal risk) even though this particular project is to be financed by a bank loan. Since tax cash flows are included, the after tax WACC should be used.

Year	Cash flow £	Discount factor at 12%	PV £
0	(20,000)	1.000	(20,000)
1	15,000	0.893	13,395
2	6,400	0.797	5,101
3	12,600	0.712	8,971
4	(4,000)	0.636	(2,544)
		NPV	4,923

10

Direct labour costs pa = 25% of 1/3 of £1,200,000 =	£100,000
General absorbed fixed overheads = (150%)	£150,000
Annual depreciation	£150,000
Total fixed overheads	£500,000
Cash items in fixed overheads	£200,000
Cash flow before tax each year (in £000) 1,200 - 400 - 200 =	£600,000

Tax each year (in £000) = 35% of (1,200 - 900 + allowance 150) = £157,500

Year	Cash flow £000	Discount factor at 16%	PV £000
0	(600.0)	1.000	(600.0)
1 - 4	600.0 pa	2.798	1,678.8
2 - 5	(157.5) pa	2.412	(379.9)
			698.9

Question

11

Capital allowances

Year	Reducing balance		Writing down allowance	Tax saved (30%)
	£		£	£
1	120,000	(25%)	30,000	9,000
2	90,000	(25%)	22,500	6,750
3	67,500	(25%)	16,875	
End of 3	50,625		625	5,250
Sale price	50,000			
	625			

Project evaluation

Year		Cash flow £	Discount factor at 20%	PV £
0	Machine cost	(120,000)	1.000	(120,000)
1-3	Cash profits	50,000	2.106	105,300
1-3	Tax on profits	(15,000)	2.106	(31,590)
1	Tax saving (capital allowance)	9,000	0.833	7,500
2	Tax saving (capital allowance)	6,750	0.694	4,685
3	Tax saving (capital allowance)	5,250	0.579	3,040
3	Sale of machine	50,000	0.579	28,950
			NPV	-2,115

12

Year	Cash profits after tax	Mill Cartons plc's share (50%)	Dividend for Mill Cartons plc	Mill Cartons plc's share of accumulated retained profits
	flotties	flotties	flotties	flotties
1	1,500,000	750,000	375,000	375,000
2	3,000,000	1,500,000	750,000	1,125,000
3	8,000,000	4,000,000	5,125,000	

Year	Cash flow Flotties	£	Discount factor at 25%	PV £
0		(500,000)	1.000	(500,000)
1	375,000	125,000	0.800	100,000
2	750,000	187,500	0.640	120,000
3	5,125,000	1,025,000	0.512	524,800
			NPV	244,800

Question

13 The information in the question can be used to calculate an equivalent annual cost per annum for each year of the vehicle's life.

Replacement cycle	Total PV of cost		Discount factor at 10%	Equivalent annual cost
	£			£
1 year	15,600	(year 1)	0.909	(17,162)
2 yrs	27,700	(years 1-2)	1.736	(15,956)
3 yrs	42,000	(years 1-3)	2.487	(16,888)
4 yrs	60,000	(years 1-4)	3.170	(18,927)
5 yrs	69,000	(years 1-5)	3.791	(18,201)

A 2 year replacement cycle is the cheapest.

14 EV of sales
Year 1   (In £000 (0.4 x 15) + (0.3 x 10) + (0.3 x 8))   £11,400
Year 2   (In £000 (0.4 x 20) + (0.3 x 10) + (0.3 x 4))   £12,200

EV of variable costs   (0.1 x 80%) + (0.2 x 70%) + (0.4 x 60%) + (0.3 x 50%) = 61% of sales.

Year	Sales	Variable costs	Fixed costs	Net cash flow	Discount factor at 15%	PV
	£	£	£	£		£
1	11,400	6,954	4,000	446	0.87	388
2	12,200	7,442	4,000	758	0.76	576
						964

15

	£000
Equipment cost	(400.00)
PV of resale value (200 ÷1 .2)	166.67
Net PV of equipment cost	(233.33)

Running costs	Savings	Net cash flow	PV (÷ 1.2)		Probability
£000	£000	£000	£000		
400	700	300	250	(0.2 x 0.2)	0.04
400	600	200	*166.67		0.06
400	500	100	*83.33		0.10
300	700	400	333.33		0.04
300	600	300	250		0.06
300	500	200	*166.67		0.10
200	700	500	416.67		0.12
200	600	400	333.33		0.18
200	500	300	250		0.30
					1.00

*NPV is negative, because the present value of the net cash flow is less than the present value of the equipment cost.

Question

The probability of the PV of the net cash flow of savings and running costs being less than 233.33 (ie the project having a negative NPV) is 0.06 + 0.10 + 0.10 = 0.26.

16

		Present values at 20%		
Year	Sales	Variable costs	Fixed costs	Net cash flow
	£000	£000	£000	£000
1	666.67	333.33	166.67	166.67
2	833.33	416.67	138.89	277.77
3	347.22	173.61	115.74	57.87
	1,847.22	923.61	421.30	502.31

Net PV of cost of equipment £

Year 0 cost	(600,000)	=	C
Resale value (£240,000 in year 3)	139,960	=	0.233 C
Net PV of cost	(460,040)	=	0.767 C

NPV of project (in £000) + 502.31 - 460.04 = + 42.27

Solution

The net PV of cost the the equipment is 0.767 of its original cost. The project will only just be viable if this equals £502,310.

Maximum cost permissible = $\frac{£502,310}{0.767}$ = £654,902, say £655,000

17

The project will cease to be viable if the PV of variable costs is £42,270 higher, at (923.61 + 42.27) £965,888.

This maximum permissible variable cost is $\frac{965,888}{1,847,220}$ = 52.29% of sales value

18

The aim should be to maximise NPV. Since projects 1 and 2 are mutually exclusive, and projects 3 and 4 are mutually exclusive, the selection should be

	NPV £
Project 2	100,000
Project 3	150,000
	250,000

Question

19

Since capital is rationed to £500,000, the aim should be to maximise the PV of future cash flows per £1 invested.

Choice	Higher profitability index	Outlay required
		£
Projects 1 or 2	Project 1 (1.50)	100,000
Projects 3 or 4	Project 3 (1.30)	500,000
		600,000

Only £500,000 is available, and project 1 has a higher profitability index than project 3, so the choice ought to be 100% of project 1 and 80% of project 3 to give a total PV of future cash flows of (£150,000 + 80% of £650,000) £670,000, and a total NPV of £170,000.

20

The company should aim to maximise the PV of net future cash flows per £1 of outlay in year 0 (the year of capital shortage).

Project	PV of future cash flows after year 0		Year 0 outlay	Ratio	
		£000	£000		
P	(40 + 20)	60	20	3.0 : 1	2nd
Q	(50 + 80)	130	50	2.6 : 1	4th
R	(33 + 54)	87	30	2.9 : 1	3rd
S	(20 + 42)	62	20	3.1 : 1	1st

Priority sequence S P R Q

(Taking the ratios of NPV to year 0 outlay would give you the same priority sequence)

21

Year	Equipment	Cash profits	Tax	Net cash flow	Discount factor, 15%	PV
	£	£	£	£		£
0	(100,000)			(100,000)	1.000	(100,000)
1		75,000		75,000	0.870	65,250
2		70,750	(17,500)	53,250	0.756	40,257
3	40,000	60,250	(18,200)	82,050	0.658	53,989
4			(15,400)	(15,400)	0.572	(8,809)
					NPV	+ 50,687
					say	+ £51,000

Question

22

Differential cash flows

(1) Buy

Year	Item	Cash flow £	Discount factor at 10%	PV £
0	Machine cost	(100,000)	1.000	(100,000)
3	Trade-in price	40,000	0.751	30,040
(note 1) 2	Tax saved, due to allowance	8,750	0.826	7,228
3	Tax saved, due to allowance	6,563	0.751	4,929
4	Tax saved, due to allowance	5,688	0.683	3,885
			Net PV of cost	(53,918)

Note 1   35% x £25,000, 35% x £18,750 and 35% x £16,250 for years 1, 2 and 3, with the cash effect of the tax saving in years 2, 3 and 4 respectively.

(2) Lease

Year	Item	Cash flow £	Discount factor at 10%	PV £
0 - 2	Lease costs	(30,000) pa	2.736	(82,080)
1 - 3	Tax saved	10,500 pa	2.487	26,114
			Net PV of cost	(55,966)

Buying has a cheaper PV of cost by about £2,000.

WITHDRAWN

23

The company would obtain the same capital allowances as if the machine had been purchased outright.

PV of hire purchase costs

Year	HP payments	Tax reductions due to interest charges in HP	Tax saved due to capital allowances	Net cash flow	Discount factor	PV
	£	£	£	£	10%	£
0	(30,000)			(30,000)	1.000	(30,000)
1	(30,000)			(30,000)	0.909	(27,270)
2	(30,000)	3,500	8,750	(17,750)	0.826	(14,662)
3	(30,000)	2,450	6,563	(20,987)	0.751	(15,761)
4		1,050	5,688	6,738	0.683	4,602
3	40,000 (Sale of machine)			40,000	0.751	30,040
				PV of cost		(53,051)

Since the PV of the cost of the leasing option is £55,966, the HP option is about £3,000 cheaper.

Question

24

Because the company will continue to be all-equity financed, the APV and the NPV are the same.

Capital raised before placing costs £9,975,000 x $\frac{100}{95}$ = £10,500,000

	£
PV of £2,400,000 pa in perpetuity (÷0.16)	15,000,000
PV of outlays in year 0	(10,500,000)
APV and NPV	4,500,000

25

Step 1   Calculate NPV as if the company were all-equity financed. Here the cost of capital will be 13%. Loan issue costs will be considered later.

Year		Cash flow £000	Discount factor at 13%	PV £000
0		(7,500)	1.000	(7,500.0)
1 - 3		5,000	2.361	11,805.0
2 - 4	(tax)	(1,500)	2.089	(3,133.5)
				1,171.5

Step 2   Calculate the PV of the tax shield provided by the loan interest, discounting the tax reliefs at the pre-tax cost of interest (*Assumption:* tax shields are just as risky as the interest payments that generate them.)

Interest	Tax shield 30%	Discount factor at 10%	PV £000
£000			
750	225 (year 2)	0.826	185.9
500	150 (year 3)	0.751	112.7
250	75 (year 4)	0.683	51.2
			349.8

Step 3

	£000
NPV of project if all equity financed	1,171.5
PV of tax shield due to loan interest	349.8
Loan issue costs	(100.0)
APV	1,421.3

2: MARKING SCHEDULE

Question	Correct answer	Marks for correct answer	Question	Correct answer	Marks for correct answer	Question	Correct answer	Marks for correct answer
1	B	1	13	A	1	25	D	1
2	D	1	14	B	1	26	A	1
3	A	1	15	B	1	27	D	2
4	B	1	16	C	1	28	B	2
5	C	1	17	B	1	29	B	2
6	B	1	18	D	1	30	D	1
7	D	1	19	C	1	31	C	1
8	D	1	20	D	1	32	D	1
9	B	1	21	A	1	33	A	1
10	B	1	22	B	1	34	D	1
11	A	1	23	C	1	35	A	2
12	D	2	24	A	1			

YOUR MARKS

Total marks available **40** Your total mark

GUIDELINES - If your mark was:

0 - 14 Quite a lot of basic knowledge was tested in these questions. Your mark suggests that you haven't really begun to learn this subject yet.

24 - 33 Good. Your knowledge has reached the standard you should be aiming for. There are still one or two things you could probably still learn, but you can feel pleased with your mark.

15 - 23 Fair. You know a reasonable amount about this subject, but there are still quite a few gaps in your knowledge that you should try to fill in.

34 - 40 Very good indeed. You have achieved a high standard of knowledge about the stock market and sources of long term funds.

COMMENTS

Question

1   Over-the-counter markets are free from Stock Exchange regulations, but OTC dealers will be members of a Self Regulatory Organisation and are subject to the Financial Services Act.

2   Regulatory powers under the Act are delegated to the SIB. The SIB in turn has granted authorisation to a number of SROs, and the SRO representing The International Stock Exchange is the Securities Association. The International Stock Exchange is also a Recognised Investment Exchange (RIE) under the Act.

3   The most common methods of flotation are placings and offers for sale. Offers for sale are 'bigger' and all the shares are offered to the general investing public. Placings are 'smaller' and although some shares must be made available for the general investing public, most are 'placed' with a small number of institutional investors.

4   The costs of flotation (costs of the accountancy firm, solicitors, market maker/sponsor, printing, advertising, Stock Exchange fees, etc) are written off against reserves and not through the profit and loss account.

6   Some companies have decided to revert from being a plc to being a limited company (eg Virgin, Really Useful Group). They have usually cited among their reasons (a) their disillusionment with pressures from investors for 'short term' results (Reason 1) (b) the serious *under*valuing of the company's shares by investors (so Reason 3 is incorrect) and (c) hence a serious danger of an unwelcome takeover bid (Reason 2).

7   Settlement Day is the Tuesday 11 days after the end of the previous Account (which ends on a Friday). This is when shares purchased during the previous Account must normally be paid for. This means that investors have about 2-4 weeks after buying shares before they must pay for them, which is a peculiarity of the UK stock market.

8   When shares are issued at a deep discount to their current market price, it becomes much more likely that existing shareholders will exercise their rights to realise the value of their rights. This avoids the need to have the issue underwritten. This was the reason, for example, why Barclays Bank made a rights issue at a deep discount in 1988. Share issues at a deep discount are fairly rare.

178

Question

9

	£
Three current shares have an ex div value of (x 2.08)	6.24
One new share - subscription price	1.60
Theoretical ex rights value of four shares	7.84
Theoretical ex rights price per share (÷ 4)	£1.96

10

	£
Current value of 4 shares (x £4.10)	16.40
Subscription price for 1 share	2.50
Theoretical value of 5 shares ex rights	18.90

	£
Theoretical ex rights price (£18.90 ÷ 5) =	3.78
Subscription price	2.50
Theoretical gain on 4 current shares	1.28
Theoretical value of right per existing share (÷ 4)	32p

11

Price	Number of shares applied for at this price	Cumulative applications
£		
3.00	50,000	50,000
2.90	100,000	150,000
2.80	250,000	400,000
2.70	500,000	900,000
2.60	1,000,000	1,900,000
2.50	1,700,000	3,600,000

Cumulative applications, working downwards in prices tendered, reach 3,000,000 at a price of £2.50. The issue price will therefore be £2.50 and £7,500,000 will be raised.

12

There are 3,600,000 applications at or above the price the company must choose in order to issue 3,000,000 shares. The issue price will be £2.50 and all investors who have tendered £2.50 or more will receive (3,000,000 ÷ 3,600,000) = 5/6 of the number of shares they have applied for.

Ira Viller will therefore receive 55,000 shares, costing (x £2.50) £137,500, and so will receive a return payment of £27,500 since his cheque in payment for the shares had been £165,000.

Question

15 Zero coupon bonds are rare. Floating rate bonds, which are bonds on which the interest rate is altered periodically to bring it into line with current market rates of interest, become more attractive to both borrowers and lenders when market interest rates are volatile.

16 The company will be paying 8% on the existing stock whereas replacement borrowing would cost 10%. The redemption date for loan stock is at the option of the company, not the stockholders, and the company should choose to delay the redemption until as late as possible, to minimise interest costs.

17 An example of deferred equity, defined in answer B, is convertible loan stock. The term deferred equity is not used to describe different classes of shares (answers A and C).

Confusingly, however, 'deferred ordinary shares' are a class of ordinary shares which are not entitled to dividend unless profits rise above a certain level, or until after a certain period of time has elapsed. Deferred ordinary shares may be held by founders of the company. However, this class of shares is *not* what is meant by the term 'deferred equity'.

A golden share is a share with special voting rights or powers attached, and a golden share in a company that has been privatised might be held by the government, with the right perhaps to prevent an unwelcome takeover of the company by a foreign multinational.

18 The bonus issue (scrip issue) is four new £1 shares for every 5 shares currently held. New shares with a nominal value of £80 million will be created. The full £80 million could be taken out of revenue reserves (answer A) but it is much more likely that the share premium account of £50 million will be eliminated first, leaving just £30 million to take out of the distributable profits in revenue reserves.

19 The payment of a £40 million dividend means that revenue reserves must be reduced by £40 million. The new shares created have a nominal value of £20 million (1 for 5 issue) but a market value of £40 million. The difference between the market value of the scrip dividend and the nominal value of the newly-created shares is credited to the share premium account.

No cash is paid out with a scrip dividend, and so net assets are unaffected.

Question

20 Reason 1 is perhaps the most obvious one. The company is paying out a dividend to reward shareholders, but not in cash. However, the shares that are created and issued can be sold, and so shareholders can obtain a cash return by selling their share allocation (reason 3). By paying a scrip dividend rather than a cash dividend, equity plus reserves are not reduced, and so an increase in gearing is avoided (reason 2).

21 A 1 for 1 stock split would replace the 100 million shares of £1 with 200 million shares of 50p each. The total nominal value of the shares would be unaffected. Similarly, the share premium account and revenue reserves would be unaffected. A stock split, like a scrip issue, might be used by a company whose market share price is high, so that issuing more shares will bring the share price down to a more 'convenient' level, and perhaps improve their marketability. A scrip issue would probably be preferred when the company has a sizeable share premium account that it can 'write off', whereas a stock split would probably be preferred when a bonus issue would result in a large reduction in distributable reserves.

22 Answer B is incorrect. The exercise price for share warrants is a fixed price.

The market value of share warrants will be related to the difference between (a) the exercise price and (b) the expected future market price of the company's shares when the exercise period begins.

23 Traded options are available for a fairly restricted number of 'blue chip' company shares, and are bought and sold on the traded options market. Statement B, which is similar, describes negotiated options. Companies might have share option schemes for employees (statement D) but these are a different type of share option. Companies do *not* issue traded or negotiated options, and so statement A is incorrect too.

24 A *European* option can be exercised on only one date, as distinct from an American option, which can be exercised at any time before that date.

25 Traded options give the holder the right, but not the obligation, to (a) buy (call option) or (b) sell (put option) a quantity of shares at a fixed price at an exercise date in the future. They are for three, six or nine months and are almost always for 1,000 shares.

The put options give their holders the right to sell shares in Goggleson Flippers plc at a price of 500p in April. An investor would have to pay 47p now to buy these options, and so put options for 1,000 shares would cost £470. The investor might believe that share prices will fall before the exercise date is reached, and if the share price falls below 453p, they become profitable. For example, if the share price falls to 450p, the investor can buy shares at this price, and exercise his put options and sell them for 500p. After deducting the cost of the options, he would make a profit of 3p per share.

Question

If the share price remains above 453p, but below 500p the put options would still be exercised, but the investor would make a net loss after deducting the cost of the options.

If the share price rises above 500p, the options will be worthless, and the investor would lose in full his 47p per option.

Options give an investor a chance to hedge - or speculate - on share price changes for a relatively small outlay, the cost of the options.

26   Return = dividend received + capital gain (or minus capital loss)

	pence
Final dividend from previous year received	5.5
Interim dividend	2.0
Capital gain (85 - 80)	5.0
Return	12.5

Return based on start-of-year values = $\dfrac{12.5}{80}$ = 15.6%.

27   Discounted cash flow techniques are needed here. In each case, since the market price is £95 per £100 nominal value of stock the investor could buy stock with a nominal value of £190,000 ÷ 0.95 = £200,000.

Stock 1

Year	Item	Cash flow	Discount rate at target 15%	Present value
		£		£
0	Cost of investment	(190,000)	1.00	(190,000)
1	Interest (at 12%)	24,000	1 ÷ 1.15	20,870
2	Interest	24,000	$(1 \div 1.15)^2$	18,147
2	Redemption of stock	200,000	$(1 \div 1.15)^2$	151,229
				+ 246

Stock 2

Year	Item	Cash flow	Discount rate at target 15%	Present value
		£		£
0	Cost of investment	(190,000)	1.00	(190,000)
1	Interest (at 8%)	16,000	1 ÷ 1.15	13,913
2	Interest	16,000	$(1 \div 1.15)^2$	12,098
2	Redemption of stock (at 110)	220,000	$(1 \div 1.15)^2$	166,352
				+ 2,363

The net present value is positive in both cases, and so the investor will earn a yield in excess of 15% on both stocks.

Question

28

	£
Current cost of £100 of stock	140.00
Yield required, year 1 (8%)	11.20
	151.20
Yield received	(12.00)
	139.20
Yield required, year 2 (8%)	11.14
	150.34
Yield received	(12.00)
Proceeds required from conversion into shares	138.34

Minimum share price required (÷ 40 shares) £3.46

Annual minimum growth rate in share price required $\sqrt{\dfrac{3.46}{2.50}} - 1 = 8.5\%$

29

The return on investing £120 in £100 of stock over 4 years must be at least £120 x (2.09)^4 = £169.39 by the end of year 4.

The value of interest receivable, compounded at 9% per annum to the end of year 4, will be

		£
Received at end of year 1	£10 x (1.09)^3	12.95
year 2	£10 x (1.09)^2	11.88
year 3	£10 x 1.09	10.90
year 4		10.00
Value of returns from interest payments		45.73
Minimum total return required		169.39
Minimum required value of shares on conversion		123.66
Minimum required value per share, end of year 4 (÷ 50)		£2.4730
Current share price		£1.9000
Growth factor required over 4 years		1.3016
Average annual growth factor		1.0680

This means average growth of 6.8% per annum, or approximately 7%.

30

Index-linked gilts are government stocks in which the annual return for investors is set at a 'real' level in excess of the rate of inflation, which is here 6% per annum, giving a yield of (approximately) 8% per annum or £8 per £100 of stock.

31

Scheme 2 describes hire purchase, which is not leasing. Eventual ownership by the user of the equipment is a key difference between hire purchase and leasing.

Scheme 1 describes a *finance lease* arrangement. Scheme 3 describes a *sale and leaseback* arrangement. Scheme 4, which many businessmen think of as 'renting', is an *operating lease* arrangement.

Question

32 Venture capital organisations will accept more investment risk than banks, and will not look for security and personal guarantees for any loans (item A). They will normally invest (partly at least) in equity. It is unrealistic to expect that managers can invest as much as 50% of the finance for a buyout (item B) although a fairly substantial investment is desirable, as a sign of commitment. Venture capital schemes have often jointly financed a buyout (item C).

Venture capital organisations look for the promise of a good return and an acceptable level of risk, but they will also look for a way in which their investment can eventually be realised (cashed in) should they wish to sell it off. Plans for an eventual launch on to the USM will often feature in buyout proposals.

33 *Statement 1* is correct. Publicity material for the 3i group, the leading venture capital organisation, has stated: 'We are completely flexible in the type of finance we provide.... It could be either a loan, an equity subscription or a package combining the two.'

Statement 2 is incorrect. Venture capital is risk capital, and although *unsecured* bank lending can be thought of as a form of venture capital, *secured* loans cannot. When a bank asks for security for a loan, it is looking for a second basis of repayment in the event that the first basis - that the loan can be repaid out of the proceeds of the operations that it helps to finance - fails.

34 Business development schemes might be financed where a company needs a major capital injection. Business start-ups are high-risk ventures, but are occasionally supported: venture capital organisations might prefer several financial institutions to collaborate in the financing venture.

Circumstance 4 is rare, but a venture capital organisation such as 3i group might occasionally be prepared to purchase some of a company's equity from one of its owners who wants to 'get out' and the other owners cannot afford to buy his shares themselves.

35

Anticipated value of company in year 5 (£1,000,000 x 12)	£12,000,000
Value of investment required by venture capitalist (£300,000 x 8)	£2,400,000
Proportion of shares required by venture capitalist (2.4m ÷ 12m)	20%

The entrepreneur and the other investor will therefore each have 40% of the share capital, since they have an equal number of shares.

If 40% of the share capital is represented by 60,000 shares, the venture capitalist's 20% of the share capital will be represented by 30,000 shares.

3: MARKING SCHEDULE

Question	Correct answer	Marks for the correct answer	Question	Correct answer	Marks for the correct answer
1	C	1	11	A	1
2	A	1	12	D	1
3	B	1	13	B	1
4	A	1	14	C	1
5	C	1	15	B	1
6	D	2	16	D	1
7	D	1	17	A	1
8	A	1	18	B	2
9	C	1	19	D	2
10	B	2	20	A	2

YOUR MARKS

Total marks available　　| 25 |　　Your total mark　　| |

GUIDELINES - If your mark was:

| 0 - 8 | Not very good at all. Look carefully again at the questions and solutions, to check where you are going wrong.

| 9 - 14 | Not bad, but there are still quite a few things that you are getting wrong. Can you see what they are?

| 15 - 20 | Good. You are reaching a desirable standard. Check your mistakes, however, and see what you can learn from them.

| 21 - 25 | Very good. You can be well pleased with your mark.

COMMENTS

Question

1

Total earnings (300 + 60 + 20)   **£380,000**
Number of shares (400 x 2) + (200 ÷ 2)   **900,000**

EPS   42.2p

2

Earnings in the year after the merger (120 + 20 + 4)   **£144 million**
Number of shares (400 + ½ of 100)   **450 million**
EPS   **32 p**
Price per share   **180 p**
P/E ratio (180 ÷ 32)   **5.63**

3

Gross dividend $= 7.2 \times \dfrac{100}{75} = 9.6p$

Yield $= \dfrac{9.6p}{260} \times 100\% = 3.7\%$

4

EPS = Net dividend × dividend cover (since there are no extraordinary gains or losses)

$= 8.2p \times 3.1 = 25.42p$

P/E ratio $= \dfrac{Price}{EPS} = \dfrac{140}{25.42} = 5.5$ times

5

Dividend, gross in pence = 6.0% of 430p = 25.8p

Net dividend in pence $= 25.8 \times \dfrac{75}{100} = 19.35p$

EPS $= \dfrac{430}{15.0} = 28.67p$

Cover $= \dfrac{EPS}{Net\ dividend} = \dfrac{28.67}{19.35} = 1.5$ times

Question

6

EPS $= D_2 \times$ Cover $= 3D_2$

Since $\quad$ P/E $=$ MV $\div$ EPS, $\quad 7.0 =$ MV $\div 3D_2$

$\qquad$ MV $= 21D_2$ and $D_2 =$ MV $\div 21$

Gross dividend $= (D_2 \times \dfrac{100}{75}) \div$ MV $\times 100\%$

$$= \dfrac{MV}{21} \times \dfrac{100}{75} \times \dfrac{1}{MV} \times 100\%$$

$$= 6.3\%$$

7

	£
Profit after tax on ordinary activities	4,550,000
Number of shares in issue	18 million
EPS	25.28 pence

8

	£ million
Profit on ordinary activities after tax	126
Minority interests	(20)
Preference dividend	(15)
Earnings	91
EPS ($\div$ 250 million shares)	36.4p

9

The number of shares in issue in 19X2 needs to be weighted, to allow for the period of time during which they were in issue.

	million
Number of shares at 1 January	12.0
Shares issued on 1 May	
- 6 million, with a weighting $\times \frac{8}{12}$ months	4.0
Shares issued on 1 October	
- 2 million, with a weighting $\times \frac{3}{12}$ months	0.5
	16.5

EPS £9 million $\div$ 16,500,000 = 54.5p

Question

10

	£
Value of 4 shares cum rights (× £3)	12
Subscription price for 1 new share	2
Theoretical value ex rights of 5 shares	14

Theoretical ex rights price £14 ÷ 5 = £2.80

19X2 EPS. The number of shares before the rights issue must be adjusted by a factor of the cum rights price ÷ theoretical ex rights price, and shares in issue must also be weighted on a calendar basis for pre-issue and post-issue quantities.

8 million shares to 1 April: 8 million × $\dfrac{3}{12}$ × $\dfrac{£3}{£2.80}$ =   2,142,857

10 million shares from 1 April: 10 million × $\dfrac{9}{12}$ 7,500,000

Weighted number of shares   9,642,857

EPS in 19X2 = £4 million ÷ 9,642,857 = 41.5p

11

Actual EPS in 19X1 = £3.2 million ÷ 8 million = 40p

Corresponding EPS figure for 19X1   = 40p × $\dfrac{\text{Theoretical ex rights price}}{\text{Cum rights price}}$

= 40p × $\dfrac{£2.80}{£3}$ = 37.3p

12

	£000
Total profit after tax	2,900
Preference dividend	200
Profits available for distribution to ordinary shareholders	2,700
Actual dividend to ordinary shareholders	1,200

Dividend cover (2,700 ÷ 1,200) = 2.25 times.

13

		£	
Profit on ordinary activities after tax			£800,000
Number of shares			10 million
EPS			8p
Market price ex div:	Price cum div	0.80	
	less Dividend proposed/payable	0.03	
	Price ex div		0.77p

P/E ratio = 77p ÷ 8p = 9.625, say 9.6.

Question

14 Mid-market price ÷ EPS = 220p ÷ 15p = 14.7

15 A higher P/E ratio for listed companies is generally attributable to a lower perceived risk (the opposite of answer C) or higher EPS and dividend growth prospects (answer B).

The size of company (answer A) is *not* particularly related to P/E ratio for listed companies, because smaller listed companies will often have a higher P/E because of better growth prospects.

16 Items B and C will probably be reasons for the increase in the average P/E ratio.

Answer A is incorrect because if total corporate earnings double, say, but twice as many shares are in issue, the average price per share will be unchanged.

The correct answer is D, because P/E × EPS = Share price.

17

	£	£
Earnings		6,000,000
Add back interest savings if conversion took place	924,000	
Less tax on extra profits (35%)	323,400	
		600,600
		6,600,600

The maximum number of new shares that can be created is now (at a price of £2.10):

$$\frac{£9,240,000}{£2.10} = 4,400,000 \text{ shares.}$$

$$\text{FDEPS} = \frac{£6,600,600}{20 \text{ million} + 4.4 \text{ million}} = \frac{£6,600,600}{24.4 \text{ million}} = 27.1 \text{ pence.}$$

18 Yield on $2\frac{1}{2}$% Consols $= 2\frac{1}{2}\% \times \dfrac{100}{20} = 12\frac{1}{2}\%$.

Subscription monies receivable if the options are exercised in full.

	£
500,000 × £1.50	750,000
300,000 × £1.80	540,000
	1,290,000

Continued...

Question

	£	£
19X3 earnings		8,000,000
Yield on £1,290,000 at 12½%	161,250	
Less tax on these extra profits (30%)	48,375	
		112,875
		8,112,875
Number of shares if options exercised in full		20,800,000

FDEPS = 39.0p.

19

	£
19X1 profits	1,260,000
Add extra profits from 19X2	150,000
	1,410,000
Tax (35%)	493,500
Total earnings from 19X2	916,500
EPS from 19X2 (÷ 3 million shares)	30.55p

Number of shares on conversion:

Original number	3,000,000
New shares (£1,000,000 ÷ £3.33)	300,000
	3,300,000
EPS required from 19X6, to avoid a dilution in EPS	× 30.55p
Total earnings required per annum from 19X6	£1,008,150
Total pre-tax profits required (× 100/65)	£1,551,000

This is £291,000 above the 19X1 pre-tax profit level.

20

	£	£
Targeted earnings next year without the rights issue (9 million × 20p)		1,800,000
Savings in interest (12% of £8 million)	960,000	
Extra tax on savings (35%)	336,000	
		624,000
Targeted earnings next year with the rights issue		2,424,000
Targeted EPS		20p
Number of shares implied		12,120,000

This is an extra 3,120,000 shares, about ⅓ of the existing number of shares in issue.

With a 1 for 3 rights issue, 3,000,000 new shares would be issued and the price needed to raise £8 million would be £2.67.

4: MARKING SCHEDULE

Question	Correct answer	Marks for the correct answer	Question	Correct answer	Marks for the correct answer
1	A	1	14	D	1
2	C	1	15	B	1
3	C	1	16	A	1
4	D	1	17	B	1
5	D	1	18	D	1
6	B	1	19	A	1
7	C	1	20	A	1
8	D	1	21	B	1
9	B	1	22	B	1
10	B	1	23	C	1
11	D	1	24	C	1
12	D	1	25	D	1
13	A	1			

YOUR MARKS

Total marks available 25 Your total mark

GUIDELINES - If your mark was:

0 - 8 You don't really understand the theoretical concepts of cost of capital. Study this subject further.

15 - 19 Good. You understand most of what you ought to know, but make sure that you understand the reasons for the mistakes that you made.

9 - 14 Not quite there yet. This is a theoretical topic in financial management that you should try to learn a bit more.

20 - 25 Very good. You understand this important topic very well.

COMMENTS

Question

1

12% x (1 - 0.35) = 7.8%.

The market value of the loan stock will be $\frac{12}{14}$ x £100 = £85.71 per £100 nominal stock.

2

$$\text{Cost} = \frac{12}{95} \times (100 - 40)\%$$
$$= 7.6\% \text{ (after tax)}$$

3

The interest cost is allowable for tax purposes, but the redemption payment on maturity of the loan stock is not.

The cash flows for which an internal rate of return should be calculated are as follows. (It is assumed that tax is paid one year after profits arise).

Year	Item	Cash flow	Try 10% Discount factor	Present value	Try 8% Discount factor	Present value
		£		£		£
0	Current value	(97.2)	1.000	(97.20)	1.000	(97.20)
1-3	Interest	12.0 pa	2.487	29.84	2.577	30.92
2-4	Tax relief	(4.2)pa	*2.261	(9.50)	*2.386	(10.02)
3	Redemption	100.0	0.751	75.10	0.794	79.40
				(1.76)		3.10

* 3.170 - 0.909 = 2.261: 3.312 - 0.926 = 2.386

$$\text{Approximate IRR (cost of capital)} = 8\% + \left(\frac{3.10}{(1.76 + 3.10)} \times (10 - 8) \right)\%$$

$$= 9.3\%, \text{ say } 9\%.$$

Note. The company may decide to finance the redemption of the loan stock by raising funds from a new loan stock issue and using these to repay and 'replace' the old loan stock. In this way, the company will continue to obtain tax relief on loan interest payments, and so

(1) keep the cost of its debt capital down and
(2) leave its gearing unchanged

This is not an issue that was addressed by the question, however.

Question

4

Ex interest price = £92 - 5   = £87 per £100 nominal stock

Interest per £100 nominal stock   = £5 per half year

Cost of stock per half year $= \dfrac{5}{87} = 0.05747$

Cost of stock per year $= (1.05747)^2 - 1$
                                 $= 0.118 = 11.8\%$

5

The cost of equity, *including* retained profits, is based on expected dividend and market price ex div.

$$r = \frac{d}{MV \text{ ex div}} = \frac{10}{40} = 0.25 \text{ or } 25\%$$

Retained earnings are not 'free' with a zero cost of capital. They have a cost, which could be described as the opportunity cost of the dividends forgone by shareholders.

6

$$r = \frac{d_0(1 + g)}{MV \text{ ex div}} + g = \frac{5(1.20)}{200} + 0.20$$
$$= 0.23 \text{ or } 23\%$$

7

$$r = \frac{d_0(1 + g)}{MV \text{ ex div}} + g$$

$$= \frac{5(1.10)}{120} + 0.10 = 14.6\%$$

8

Dividend per share, 19X5 = £379,000 ÷ 2 million = 18.95p

The dividend growth in the four years 19X1-19X5 has been

$$\frac{379,000}{300,000} = 1.26333$$

The average annual growth rate is $\sqrt[4]{1.26333}$
             $= 0.06$ approx, or 6% per annum.

$$r = \frac{d_0(1 + g)}{MV} + g = \frac{18.95(1.06)}{118} + 0.06$$
$$= 0.23 \text{ or } 23\%.$$

Question

9

$$r = \frac{d_0(1+g)}{MVex\ div} + g$$

$$= \frac{35(1.10)}{250} + 0.10 = 0.254\ or\ 25.4\%$$

Notice that the growth rate in dividend should result in a comparable growth in the share price over time. Thus, the share price one year ago (227p) has risen by about 10% to 250p, which is consistent with the growth in dividends.

10

$$R_s = R_f + \beta(R_m - R_f)$$

$$= 13\% + 1.5(20 - 13)\%$$

$$= 23.5\%$$

11

A share's alpha value in CAPM analysis is a measure of its abnormal return, which is the amount by which the share's current returns are above or below what should be expected, given their systematic risk. If there were no unsystematic risk and so no abnormal returns, the CAPM and the dividend growth model should give the same cost of equity. CAPM is dealt with more fully in a later chapter.

12

The yield on equities consists of both dividend yield and capital gain, and so even when interest rates are high and well in excess of dividend yields, the expected capital gain on equities should make the expected total yield on equities higher than the yield on loan stock. Statement 1 is therefore incorrect. Statement 2, in contrast, is a correct explanation of differences in the cost of equity from one company to another.

13

When short term interest yields are higher than long term yields (inverted yield curve) market pressures will eventually force up longer term interest yields on gilts and corporate bonds, so that bond prices will fall.

If bond yields go up and bond prices fall, shareholders will want higher yields too, and so share prices will fall. Higher yields result in lower prices, for both bonds and shares.

Question

14 We are looking for a cost of capital that equates dividends of £1 pa in perpetuity from year 5 onwards with a current market price of £2.05 per share. The cost of capital is therefore the internal rate of return of the cash flows.

	£
Year 0	(2.05)
Year 5 →	1.00 pa

You will probably need to calculate the IRR by hit-and-miss methods.

Try 20%: PV of £1 per annum from year 5 in perpetuity

$$= \left(\frac{£1}{0.20} \right) \times \left(\frac{1}{1.20} \right)^4$$

$$= £2.41$$

Try 22%: PV of £1 per annum from year 5 in perpetuity

$$= \left(\frac{£1}{0.22} \right) \times \left(\frac{1}{1.22} \right)^4$$

$$= £2.05$$

This equates with the current market price per share, indicating a cost of equity of 22%.

15 *Per £100 of investment:*

	£
Shareholders require, post tax (18%)	18.00
Add tax (35% of pre-tax = 35/65 of post tax)	9.69
Shareholders require, pre tax (= 100/75 of actual dividend)	27.69
Imputed tax on dividends paid (= 25/75 of actual dividend)	6.92
Company must pay actual dividend of	20.77

Dividend must be 20.77% pa of value of investment cost of equity, to nearest 1% = 21% pa.

16 Cost of equity $= 9\% + 0.8(14 - 9)\%$
$= 13\%$

The Capital Asset Pricing Model takes into account the *actual* returns on a company's shares only to the extent that historical returns are used to estimate the share's beta factor.

Question

17

$$b = 12p \div 48p = 0.25$$

$$r = \frac{36(1 + 0.25r)}{250} + 0.25r$$

$$0.75r = \frac{36}{250} + \frac{9r}{250}$$

$$0.714r = 0.144$$
$$r = 20.168\% \text{ say } 20.2\%$$

The growth rate in dividends per year will be 0.25 x 20.168% = 5.0%.

18 The formula $r = \dfrac{d(1 + br)}{MV} + br$

can again be used, as in the previous question. We are told that br = 0.08.

$$d = 2/3 \text{ of } r, \text{ since dividend cover is } 1.5$$
$$= 0.6667r$$

$$r = \frac{0.6667r(1.08)}{4.5r} + 0.08 = 0.24 \text{ or } 24\%.$$

Alternatively, you can use hypothetical numbers. Suppose EPS in current year is 12p.

MV = 12p x 4.5 = 54p. Dividend = 8p. $r = \dfrac{8(1.08)}{54} + 0.08 = 0.24$

19 The statements are both correct, and should be self-explanatory. It is because the cost of capital is an opportunity cost that it ought to be taken into account in the investment decisions by firms, and depreciation is ignored in WACC calculations for the reason in Statement 2.

20 The after tax cost of debt capital will fall, because of the higher tax shield. However, the company's total earnings will fall, because of the higher rate of tax, and this will reduce the value of the company, having a much greater effect than the effect of the tax shield on the weighted average cost of capital.

Question

21

Cost of loan stock = 11% (1 - 0.40) = 6.6%

Item		Market value £m	Cost	MV x cost
Ordinary shares	(40m x 1.08)	43.2	0.180	7.7760
11% loan stock	(30m x 0.98)	29.4	0.066	1.9404
		72.6		9.7164

WACC = $\frac{9.7164}{72.6}$ = 13.4%

22

Cost of equity		18p ÷ 90p x 100% = 20%
Cost of 10% loan stock,	before tax	£10 ÷ £71.43 = 14%
	after tax	65% of 14% = 9.1%
Cost of variable rate loan, after tax		65% of 16% = 10.4%

The variable rate loan of £10 million ought to be included in the WACC calculation since it represents borrowing on a permanent basis.

Item	Market value £000	Cost	
Equity	36,000	0.200	7,200
10% loan stock	20,000	0.091	1,820
Variable rate loan	10,000	0.104	1,040
	66,000		10,060

WACC = $\frac{10,060}{66,000}$ x 100% = 15.2% approx.

23

The new cost of equity is 17p ÷ 85p x 100% = 20%
The market value of the equity will be 50 million shares x 85p = £42.5 million

Item	Market value £000	Cost	
Equity	42,500	0.200	8,500
10% loan stock	20,000	0.091	1,820
Variable rate loan	10,000	0.104	1,040
	72,500		11,360

WACC = $\frac{11,360}{72,500}$ x 100% = 15.7% approx.

Question

24 Cost of equity (using the capital asset pricing model) = 12% + 0.9(18 - 12)% = 17.4%.
Cost of preference shares = (£1 + £0.50p) x 7% = 14%.

Cost of loan stock after tax = 65% of $\left(\dfrac{£12}{£80} \times 100\% \right)$ = 9.75%.

Item	Market value	Cost	
	£000		
Equity	80,000	0.1740	13,920
Preference shares	10,000	0.1400	1,400
Loan stock	16,000	0.0975	1,560
	106,000		16,880

WACC = $\dfrac{16,880}{106,000}$ x 100% = 15.9% approx.

25 The current market value of the shares is (30m x £0.80) £24 million.

If the cost of equity rises to 25%, the annual dividend needed to sustain a MV of £24 million will be 25% of £24 million = £6 million

	£000
Dividend now required	6,000
Current dividend (30m x £0.16)	4,800
Interest in dividend required	1,200
Interest cost of loan (12% of £20m)	2,400
Required increase in profit before interest	3,600

Marginal cost of project capital = $\dfrac{£3.6 \text{ million}}{£20 \text{ million}}$ = 18%.

5: MARKING SCHEDULE

Question	Correct answer	Marks for correct answer	Question	Correct answer	Marks for correct answer	Question	Correct answer	Marks for correct answer
1	B	1	15	A	1	29	A	1
2	B	1	16	A	1	30	B	1
3	D	1	17	B	2	31	B	1
4	C	1	18	B	1	32	D	1
5	D	1	19	B	2	33	D	1
6	D	1	20	C	2	34	A	1
7	A	1	21	C	1	35	D	1
8	D	1	22	A	1	36	A	1
9	D	1	23	C	1	37	B	1
10	B	2	24	A	1	38	D	1
11	C	2	25	C	1	39	B	1
12	B	1	26	A	1	40	B	1
13	D	1	27	D	1	41	B	1
14	C	2	28	D	1	42	C	2

YOUR MARKS

Total marks available   **49**   Your total mark

GUIDELINES - If your mark was:

0 - 16	You still have a lot to sort out on this subject, and you need to go back to your study text.

30 - 40	Good. There are still one or two improvements that you could make, but you have achieved the basic understanding that you need.

17 - 29	Fair, but there are still quite a lot of things that you haven't learned properly yet. Can you see where you are going wrong?

41 - 49	Very good. You have a firm understanding of this important subject.

If you did not attempt the questions on share options (Qs 38-42) a score of 15-27 would be fair, 28-36 would be good and 37-42 would be very good.

COMMENTS

Question

1

	£ million
MV of zero coupon bonds $= \dfrac{£2 \text{ million}}{(1.10)^5} =$	1.2
MV of floating rate debentures - since issued at par and interest rates vary with market rates	2.0
MV of irredeemable loan stock $= \dfrac{£2 \text{ million} \times 9\%}{0.10} =$	1.8
Total MV	__5.0__

2

The dividend will be earned at the end of year 1 and so the current share price will be

$$\frac{8 + 80}{(1.18)^1} = 74.6p, \text{ say } 75p$$

This is an ex-div price, since the cum div price would be inclusive of any dividend *currently* payable on the share. Since we do not know whether there is any current dividend payable, and if there is, what it is, we cannot calculate a cum div price at all from the data given.

3

$$MV = \frac{d_0(1 + g)}{(r - g)}$$

Since $d_0(1 + g)$ is the dividend after one year, we have

$$74 = \frac{8}{(0.16 - g)}$$

$$74(0.16 - g) = 8$$
$$74g = 3.84$$
$$g = 0.052 \text{ or } 5.2\%.$$

4

At the end of the year

(1) the current dividend will be 22p ($+10\%$)
(2) the expected growth rate in dividends will still be 10%.

$$MV = \frac{22(1.10)}{(0.15 - 0.10)} = 484p$$

Question

5

The payment for redeeming the loan stock does not qualify for tax relief.

Year	Item	Cash flow £	Discount factor at 12%	Present value £
1-3	Interest net of tax relief = (0.65 x £8)	5.2	2.4019	12.49
3	Redemption of loan	105.0	0.7118	74.74
			MV of stock =	87.23

6

Let the redemption price per £100 of stock be £R.

Year	Item	Cash flow £	Discount factor at 11%	Present value £
0	Issue price	(100)	1.00	(100.00)
1-15	Annual interest	9	7.19	64.71
15	Redemption price	R	0.21	0.21 R
				(35.29) + 0.21 R

The minimum value of R must be where

$$
\begin{aligned}
(35.29) + 0.21R &= 0 \\
0.21R &= 35.29 \\
R &= £168.05
\end{aligned}
$$

Redemption premium (to nearest £) must be (£168 - £100) £68.

7

$$MV = \frac{d_0(1 + g)}{(r - g)}$$

$$40 = \frac{3(1 + g)}{(0.10 - g)}$$

$$
\begin{aligned}
40(0.10 - g) &= 3(1 + g) \\
4 - 40g &= 3 + 3g \\
43g &= 1 \\
g &= 0.0233 \text{ or } 2.33\%
\end{aligned}
$$

Question

8

The period 19X1 to 19X5 covers four years of growth, and the average growth rate g can be calculated as follows.

$$(1 + g)^4 = \frac{4.236}{2,200} = 1.9255$$

$$1 + g = 1.17796$$
$$g = 0.17796, \text{ say } 0.178$$

Inserting this into the dividend growth valuation model, we get

$$\text{MV (in £000)} = \frac{4.236(1.178)}{(0.25 - 0.178)} = \frac{4.990}{0.072} = 69,305.6$$

Price per share (40 million shares) = £1.73.

9

$$\text{MV before new information} = \frac{14(1.15)}{(0.22 - 0.15)} = 230p$$

$$\text{MV after new information} = \frac{14(1.13)}{(0.22 - 0.13)} = 176p$$

Fall in share price = 54p

10

$$\text{MV} = \frac{£1,000,000}{(1.15)} + \frac{£1,200,000}{(1.15)^2} + \frac{£1,440,000}{(1.15)^3} + \frac{(£1,440,000 \times 1.10)}{(1.15)^4}$$

$$+ \left[\frac{£1,440,000 \times (1.10)^2}{(0.15 - 0.10)} \times \frac{1}{(1.15)^4} \right]$$

Expected dividends in years 1, 2, 3 and 4 are simply discounted at 15%. Dividends from year 5 onwards can be valued at year 4 prices by the growth model formula

$$\frac{d(1 + g)}{(r - g),}$$

where $d(1 + g)$ is the end of year 5 expected dividend. This must then be discounted to present day values from its year 4 value.

MV = £(869,565 + 907,372 + 946,823 + 905,567 + 19,924,455) = £23,553,872.

Since there are 10 million shares, the price per share will be £2.355, say £2.36.

Question

11 $MV = \dfrac{11.5p \times 1.15}{(1.18)} + \dfrac{11.5p \times (1.15)^2}{(1.18)^2} + \dfrac{11.5p \times (1.15)^3}{(1.18)^3} + \dfrac{11.5p \times (1.15)^3 \times 1.08}{(1.18)^4}$

$+ \left[\dfrac{11.5p \times (1.15)^3 \times 1.08}{0.18} \times \dfrac{1}{(1.18)^4} \right]$

$= 11.21p + 10.92p + 10.64p + 9.74p + 54.13p$

$= 96.64p$, say 97p

12 PV of an annual final dividend of 25p in perpetuity $\dfrac{25p}{0.21}$ = 119.0p

PV of an annual interim dividend of 15p in perpetuity $\dfrac{15p}{0.21}$ = 71.4p

The PV of the interim dividend would apply at the end of month 6 in the current year and we need to convert this to a 'now' PV by discounting 71.4p from month 6 at 21% pa. An annual discount rate of 21% gives a 6-monthly rate of 10% ($1.10 \times 1.10 = 1.21$), and

$\dfrac{71.4}{1.10} = 64.9p$.

The price per share should be 119.0p + 64.9p = 183.9p, say 184p.

13 The growth rate in dividends, g, is assumed to be (a) the proportion of total earnings that are retained in the business for re-investing to produce higher profits and a dividend growth, multiplied by (b) the return on these re-investments, R. Thus $g = bR$.

Here $g = 0.60 \times 0.15 = 0.09$

$MV = \dfrac{180,000 (1.09)}{(0.20 - 0.09)} = £1,783,636$, say £1,784,000

14 Let the investor's share of the company's post-tax profits be P, and his marginal rate of income tax be t. Retained profits create a capital gain for the shareholder.

(a) Income if all profits are retained = P net of capital gains tax = $P(1 - 0.30) = 0.70P$

(b) Income if all profits are distributed

$= \dfrac{100P}{(100 - 25)} \times (1 - t)$

$= 1.333P (1 - t)$

$= 1.333P - 1.333Pt.$

Continued...

Question

(c)   The investor will be indifferent between dividends and capital gains when

$$0.70P = 1.333P - 1.333Pt$$
$$1.333Pt = 0.633P$$
$$t = \frac{0.633P}{1.333P} = 0.475$$

If the rate of income tax exceeds 0.475 (in effect, if it exceeds 47% and is 48% or higher) the investor should prefer capital gains to dividends.

15   Bond prices fall when investors require higher interest rates. The expectation of higher yields will make companies borrow less and since expected returns on share prices would also rise, share prices should fall.

16   The current MV of equity is $\frac{£490,000}{0.196} = £2,500,000 = £2.50$ per share.

If the project is financed by debt capital

	£
Profit before interest (+ £200,000)	1,200,000
Interest (£3,500,000 x 12%)	420,000
	780,000
Tax	234,000
Earnings and dividends pa in perpetuity	546,000
New cost of equity	22%
New MV of equity	£2,481,818
	= £2.48 per share

There would be a 2p fall in the share price.

17   *If the project is financed by equity*

	£
Profit before interest	1,200,000
Interest	300,000
	900,000
Tax	270,000
Earnings and dividends pa in perpetuity	630,000
New cost of equity	17%

Continued...

Question

	£
New MV of equity (£630,000 ÷ 0.17)	3,705,882
Old MV of equity	2,500,000
Gain in equity values	1,205,882
Less new funds raised as equity	1,000,000
Net gain	205,882

The new funds would be raised by issuing 400,000 shares at £2.50 each, and with a total MV of equity equal to £3,705,882, the share price will be (÷ 1,400,000 shares) £2.65, resulting in a gain of 15p per share.

18 *Option 1* Redeem: Investors will receive per £100 stock on 15 September

	£
Redemption value	100
Accrued interest ($\frac{4}{12}$ x 9% x £100)	3
	103

Option 2 Number of shares per £100 stock (÷ £12) 8.333
Minimum price to be as good as or better than Option 1

$\dfrac{£103}{8.333}$ = £12.36 per share

19 Current value of £100 of debentures as redeemable debentures.

	£
£8 interest pa x (3.79)	30.32
£105 redemption value x 0.62	65.10
	95.42

Current value of £100 of debentures as 25 ordinary shares:

Price per share	£3.70 (x25)	£92.5
Price per share	£4.40 (x25)	£110.0

(1) If the price per share is £3.70, the minimum value per £100 unit will be its value as redeemable debentures = £95.42, say £95.40

(2) If the price per share is £4.40, the minimum value will be their value as 25 shares, £110.

In reality, the market price per £100 unit would probably be higher than these figures, since investors would probably expect some increase in share prices from current levels over the next five years.

Question

20

Stockholders will not convert stock into equity unless the share price at the end of year 2 exceeds (£100 ÷ 40) £2.50 per share. The market value per share at the end of year 2 will be:

(1)

Growth rate in dividends		Option to convert stock into shares
5%	$MV = \dfrac{30(1.05)^3}{(0.20 - 0.05)} = 232p$	Do not convert
10%	$MV = \dfrac{30(1.10)^3}{(0.20 - 0.10)} = 399p$	Convert

(2) Present value of interest on £100 stock at the end of years 1 and 2

$$= \frac{£8}{(1.15)} + \frac{£8}{(1.15)^2} = £6.96 + £6.05 = £13.01$$

(3) Present value of £100 of loan stock if not converted = discounted value of interest in perpetuity = £8 ÷ 0.15 = £53.33.

(4) *Expected value of £100 convertible stock*

Outcome	Value of £100 stock		PV of value of 40 shares	PV of year 1&2 interest	Total PV	Proba-bility	EV
	£		£	£	£	P	£
1	53.33		-	-	53.33	0.3	16.0
2	-	$40 \times 399p \times \dfrac{1}{(1.15)^2}$	120.68	13.01	133.69	0.7	93.6
							109.6

21

This problem illustrates how the Capital Asset Pricing Model (CAPM) and the dividend growth valuation model can be combined.

The required return, using the CAPM, is 10% + 1.10(20 - 10)% = 21%.

$$MV = \frac{d_0 (1 + g)}{r - g} = \frac{d_1}{r - g}$$

Dividend at the end of year 1 will be 52.4% of £6 million = £3,144,000

$$MV = \frac{£3,144,000}{(0.21 - 0.10)} = £28.6 \text{ million}$$

Question

22

Expected return	$= 12\% + 1.15(20 - 12)\% = 21.2\%$
Actual return	$= 21.2\% - 6\% = 15.2\%$
Actual return in pence	$= 15.2\%$ of 250p $= 38$p

	pence
Actual return	38
Dividend	20
Share price increase	**18**

The share price at the end of the period was 250p + 18p = 268p.

23

$$\beta = \frac{0.0192}{0.0151} = 1.2715$$

Expected return from the share, given a 10% market return, is

$$6\% + 1.2715 (10 - 6)\% = 11.086\%.$$

The share price should rise by 11.086%, from £2.43 to £2.70.

Note. It is *incorrect* to say that the share price will rise by 10% x 1.2715 = 12.714%, which you might have been tempted to do. This is because the market return is expected to be 10% overall, and we are *not* saying that the *change* in market return is 10%. If the market return *changes* by x%, we *should* expect the return on the share to *change* by βx%.

25

Statement 1 is incorrect. The efficient markets hypothesis implies that share prices reflect all *available* information, *not* that they can predict all the information about companies that will *emerge in the future* and affect share prices.

Statement 2 is correct. The hypothesis is that current share prices are 'fair' because they reflect all available information, but the future is *uncertain*. New information continually emerges that surprises investors and alters their assessments, so that share prices will inevitably keep on rising and falling in a seemingly random way.

26

First proposition
Share price changes up or down from day to day are random because

(a)   share prices reflect currently available information;
(b)   investors behave rationally and competitively;
(c)   and so the market functions well and share prices are fair.

It is changes in available information, which are unforeseen and (randomly) favourable or unfavourable, that cause prices to change. Random walk theory is consistent with the efficient markets hypothesis.

Continued...

Question

Second proposition. Research (mainly in the USA) has confirmed the random walk proposition that share price changes from day to day are independent of each other, and there is no evidence of any tendency for share prices to rise on successive days, or to fall on successive days.

27 All three statements are correct, and you need to understand them in order to appreciate the efficient markets hypothesis.

Statement 1. The weak-form hypothesis states that share prices efficiently reflect all the information that has been made available and that is therefore contained in the record of past share prices. Since the *current* share price reflects all that is known about past share price changes, it is impossible to predict future price changes from the same information. Share price changes can only occur (*randomly* up or down) when new information becomes available.

Statement 2. The semi-strong form hypothesis states that share prices efficiently reflect all the information available from past share prices and other published information. Since all this information rapidly and accurately affects share prices when it becomes available, individual investors cannot study the same information to 'beat the market' and earn higher returns - except by luck or 'inside information'.

Statement 3. The strong form hypothesis states that share prices efficiently reflect *all* information that can be obtained through the most thorough fundamental analysis of companies and the economy. All share prices are fair, and so investors cannot earn consistently superior returns - except by luck.

28 The reduction in the volatility of the profits of Wharton Fingers plc will reduce the company's perceived business risk characteristics, and the cost of equity - the return required by equity shareholders - will fall. This should push up the price of the company's shares, provided of course that the stock market expects Wharton Fingers plc to make reasonable profits from its new product.

The reverse happens in the case of Saliva plc, because the reported incident will increase the uncertainty about the company's future profits. The cost of equity will rise and the share price will fall.

29 *Statement 1 is correct*. If MV is a constant multiple of earnings, and earnings are a constant multiple of dividends, MV will be a constant multiple of dividends.

Statement 2 is also correct. According to the strong form efficient markets hypothesis, share prices reflect all available information, including information about economic prospects, as soon as it becomes available. Changes in stock price indices (such as FT-SE or the All-Share Index) can therefore act as leading indicators of future economic change.

Question

30 The share price collapse on 'Black Monday' in October 1987 occurred without any change in the available information about prospects for companies or the economy, suggesting that the markets were witnessing the bursting of a speculative share price bubble. The simple efficient markets hypothesis implies that share prices cannot rise to artificially high levels in this way, and so the fact that share prices *did* collapse raises doubts about the validity of the hypothesis. Professor Myers suggested (in 1988) that 'the principle behind the simple form of the efficient market theory - that there is a single 'true' value for the level of share prices - has to be replaced with a view that there is a very wide range of plausible values.'

31 *Weak form efficiency.* The best estimate of the likely share price is the theoretical ex-rights price.

	£
Value of 4 shares (x £1.5)	6
Value of 1 new share	1
Theoretical value of 5 shares	7

Theoretical ex-rights price (£7 ÷ 5) £1.40 per share

Strong form efficiency. If investors believe that the project will earn an NPV of £3 million, the total value of equity will be

	£m
Total value prior to rights issue (8m x £1.50)	12
Funds raised from rights issue (2m x £1)	2
NPV of project	3
Total value of shares ÷ 10 million shares	17
Price per share	£1.70

32 *Semi-strong form efficiency*

Day 2. Coot's share price will rise to £3 because the bid price is public knowledge. The market will assume that Grays is paying £1 per share too much for Coot, and so £1 million too much in total, and so the Grays share price will fall by £1 million ÷ 4 million shares, 25p per share to £2.75.

Day 10. The present value of savings become public knowledge. These savings are a PV before deducting the cost of acquiring Coot.

	£m
Value of Grays, day 1	12
Value of Coot, day 1	2
	14
PV of savings	4
	18
less Purchase cost of Coot (1m x £3)	(3)
Value of Grays, day 10	15
÷ 4 million shares	£3.75

Question

33

With strong form efficiency, the value of the savings will be known immediately, even through they are not publicly announced until day 10, and so the share prices will change to £3 for Coot and £3.75 for Grays on day 2, and be unaffected by the eventual announcement on day 10.

34   *Lorn Cleggs*

(a)   If all profits are distributed as dividend, and taking his share of the net dividend as P, a shareholder would receive

$$\frac{100P}{70} (1 - 0.30) = P \text{ in dividends after tax}$$

(b)   If all profits are retained, the share price will rise by the amount of retained profit and the shareholder will benefit by this price increase (capital gain) net of tax. For Lorn Cleggs, this is P, since he pays no capital gains tax.

(c)   Both policies give him the same net benefit.

Shortbody Limited

(a)   With full distribution, income would be

$$\frac{100P}{70} (1 - 0.35) = 0.929P.$$

(b)   With retained earnings, net of tax capital gain would be $P(1 - 0.30) = 0.70P$

(c)   The full distribution policy gives a greater net benefit.

35

Option A: $MV = \frac{8}{0.16} = 50p$

Option B: $MV = \frac{6(1.06)}{(0.16 - 0.06)} = 63.6p$

Option C: $MV = \frac{4(1.08)}{(0.16 - 0.08)} = 54p$

Option D: $MV = \frac{2(1.125)}{(0.16 - 0.125)} = 64.3p$

D is marginally preferable to B.

Question

36 Modigliani and Miller argued that a company's value depends on the expected future earnings stream, and so one dividend policy is just as good as any other. Dividends do not appear in the equation and investment (I), profit (X), the price at time 1 (P_1) and the capitalisation rate (p) are all assumed to be independent of dividend.

The argument is based on several assumptions, such as perfect markets, no transaction costs and the absence of taxes. When the rates of income tax and capital gains tax differ, dividend policy could be relevant to investors - but when income tax and capital gains tax have the same marginal rate, the 'irrelevance of dividends' arguments become stronger.

37 Statements A, C and D all lend support to the argument that the pattern of dividend payout *is* relevant. Only statement D supports the argument of irrelevancy.

38 If the share price is 140p or 150p on the exercise date, the holder of the call option will not exercise his options, since the shares can be purchased either 10p cheaper or at the exercise price (140p or 150p) on the market.

Actual share price	Profit from exercising call option	Probability	EV
160p	10p	0.30	3p
170p	20p	0.25	5p
180p	30p	0.10	3p
			11p

39 This is simply a rearrangement of the Black-Scholes formula.

It applies to European call and put options, but cannot be applied exactly to American options, which can be exercised at any time before the given exercise date.

40 Suppose, for example, that the exercise price for a call option equals the current market price of the share, and there is a 50% probability that the share price will rise before the expiration date of the option and a 50% probability that it will fall.

The pay-offs for the holder of the call option will be as follows. (Let the share price at expiration = S and the exercise price of the option be E).

Outcome	Pay-off	Probability	EV of option
Share price rises: option is exercised	E - S	0.5	0.5(E - S)
Share price falls: option is worthless and *not* exercised	0	0.5	0
			0.5(E - S)

Continued...

Question

The greater the difference between E and S (that is to say, the greater the potential volatility of the share price) the greater will be the market value of the call option.

41   A put option is the right to sell shares at a fixed price, here £2,000 or £2 per share. The option has value for the investor at the expiration date provided that the actual market value is less than £2,000, giving the investor the ability to 'profit' by exercising the option. This is shown by Graph B.

Graph A shows how the value at expiration date of a *call* option for 1,000 shares at £2 each varies with the actual share price. Graph D shows the combined value of the option plus the 1,000 shares: the put option safeguards the investor against a fall in price of the shares below £2,000, which illustrates the advantage of put options to an investor seeking to hedge against share price falls.

For put options and call options *before* their expiration date, the lines in Graph B and Graph A respectively show the *minimum* values at which the options will be traded.

42   If investors are indifferent to risk, the EV of the return on the share will be the expected (risk-free) return of 10%.

Let the probability of a share price rise = p

The share price might rise by 40 pence (or 20%) or it may fall by 40 pence (or 20%).

$$
\begin{aligned}
\text{Expected return} &= 20p + (1 - p)(- 20) \\
10 \text{ per cent} &= 20p + (1 - p)(- 20) \\
10 &= 20p - 20 + 20p \\
30 &= 40p \\
p &= 0.75
\end{aligned}
$$

The *expected future value* of the call options at expiration date is:

	Value of option	Probability	EV
If share price rises to 240 pence	40 pence	0.75	30 pence
If share price falls to 160 pence	Nil	0.25	<u>0 pence</u>
			30 pence

The *current value* (PV) of the call option is

$$
\frac{\text{Expected future value}}{1 + \text{interest rate}} = \frac{30}{(1.10)^1} = 27 \text{ pence}
$$

6: MARKING SCHEDULE

Question	Correct answer	Marks for correct answer	Question	Correct answer	Marks for correct answer	Question	Correct answer	Marks for correct answer
1	B	1	11	B	1	21	D	1
2	A	1	12	C	1	22	A	2
3	D	1	13	D	2	23	B	2
4	C	2	14	C	2	24	C	1
5	C	1	15	D	1	25	D	1
6	D	1	16	A	1	26	C	1
7	A	1	17	A	1	27	C	1
8	B	1	18	D	1	28	D	2
9	B	1	19	C	1	29	D	1
10	A	1	20	D	1	30	B	2

YOUR MARKS

Total marks available **37** Your total mark [ ]

GUIDELINES - If your mark was:

0 - 10 You need to do quite a lot more studying to achieve a reasonable standard of knowledge on gearing.

20 - 29 Good. This is a difficult topic, but you understand much of it. Is there any particular subject area that is catching you out - MM theory, perhaps?

11 - 19 Fair, but there is at least one large part of this topic that you probably do not understand properly yet. If you don't need to know MM theory, however, this could be a very good score for the other questions on gearing.

30 - 37 Excellent mark for such a difficult topic. Very well done.

COMMENTS

Question

1 Operating gearing can be defined as the ratio of contribution (sales minus variable costs) to profit before interest and tax. In the original budget, this is £1,000,000 ÷ £200,000 = 5 times.

With the new machine:

	£000
Sales	1,600
Variable costs (30%)	480
Contribution	1,120
Fixed costs	870
PBIT	250

Operating gearing will now be £1,120,000 ÷ £250,000 = 4.48 times, and so in this example there will be a *reduction* in business risk, in spite of higher fixed costs, because of the higher contribution margin at existing sales levels.

2 Companies which are investing and operating in the early stages of a product's life cycle incur more risk than companies with a good portfolio of mature established products. Products in their early 'life' might fail to achieve hoped-for growth and profitability.

Companies with a high proportion of fixed costs have a higher operating gearing, are more vulnerable to a fall in sales, and so are more 'high risk' than companies with low fixed costs that need comparatively low sales to break even.

Financial gearing (factor 3) is a cause of *financial risk* rather than *business risk.*

3 Let the original PBIT $= X$
Let the interest charge $= Y$
Let profits before tax $= Z$

$$X - Y = Z \quad \text{..... (1)}$$
$$1.10X - Y = 1.30Z \quad \text{..... (2)(given)}$$
$$0.10X = 0.30Z \quad \text{..... (2) - (1)}$$
$$X = 3Z$$

Substituting in (1)
Since $\quad X - Y = Z$
$\quad\quad\quad 3Z - Y = Z$ and so $Y = 2Z$

Continued...

Question

	Original figures	Increase PBIT by 25%
PBIT	X = 3Z	1.25X = 3.75Z
Interest	Y = 2Z	Y = 2.00Z
Profit before tax	Z = 1Z	1.75Z

Profit before tax (and earnings, given a constant rate of tax) will go up by 75% from Z to 1.75Z.

4

Gearing can be measured as prior charge capital: equity or as prior charge capital: total company value.

(1) On market values $\dfrac{(10 \times 0.6) + (30 \times 0.95)}{(20 \times 1.8)} = 95.8\%$

(2) On balance sheet values, excluding bank overdraft

$\dfrac{30 + 10}{20 + 70} = 44.4\%$, or $\dfrac{30 + 10}{130} = 30.8\%$

(3) On balance sheet values, including bank overdraft in prior charge capital

$\dfrac{30 + 10 + 20}{20 + 70} = 66.7\%$

The other ratios in the question are all *invalid*, for various reasons, such as showing gearing as an equity: total value ratio, or including preference shares with equity.

5

Any proposed final dividends are to be included here as part of equity.

Tax charge for the year = Closing tax liability + Tax paid - Opening tax liability. This is (in £000) 350 + 300 - 250 = 400.

	Debt £000	Equity £000	
At 1 January	5,000	10,000	
Profits after tax		700	(1,100 - 400)
New issues	1,200	600	
Redemption of stock	(900)		
Dividend paid		(400)	
At 31 December	5,300	10,900	

Gearing $= \dfrac{5,300}{10,900} = 48.6\%$

Question

6

Interest cover = $\dfrac{\text{PBIT}}{\text{Interest}}$ = $\dfrac{200}{80}$ = 2.5

This is very low and potentially a very serious problem.

7

High interest rates might deter a company from borrowing, but will not limit how much it *is able* to borrow. In certain circumstances, items B, C and D might impose such a limit. Debentures might be issued with a covenant whereby the company agrees not to borrow beyond certain limits until the debentures have been redeemed (Item B). A bank might refuse to lend if security is insufficient (Item C). Some companies have an item in their Articles of Association (Item D) restricting the borrowing powers of its directors (for example, stating that without the sanction of ordinary shareholders, the directors cannot allow total borrowing to exceed the value of equity plus reserves).

8

Financial risk is the risk that operating profits might be insufficient to cover interest costs of debt capital and leave a reasonable return for equity shareholders. Financial risk therefore increases as gearing rises, and (as in this case) decreases when gearing falls.

Operating risk is the risk that contribution (sales minus variable costs of sales) will be insufficient to cover fixed costs and earn a profit, unless a sufficient volume of output and sales is achieved. Higher fixed costs, which are implied in this situation, cause operating risk to increase.

9

Statement 1 is correct. The ability of companies to increase their gearing to very high levels in order to finance takeovers was severely dented by the collapse of the junk bond market in late 1989/early 1990.

The first sentence of statement 2 is correct. However, the marginal cost of retained earnings is not zero, because (a) there is the opportunity cost to ordinary shareholders, who must forgo dividends when earnings are retained and (b) the change in gearing from either extra retained earnings or extra debt capital would probably alter the weighted average cost of capital, and the true marginal cost of the extra finance might be difficult to calculate. Companies would probably use their WACC (or any other 'established' method of establishing a cost of capital, such as project beta factors) to evaluate the investment project.

Question

10

	No loan stock	£1 million loan stock	£2 million loan stock	£3 million loan stock
	£000	£000	£000	£000
Profit before interest (X)	1,881	1,881	1,881	1,881
Interest at 12%	0	120	240	360
Profits = dividends	1,881	1,761	1,641	1,521
÷ Cost of equity	÷ 18%	÷ 20%	÷ 22%	÷ 24%
	£000	£000	£000	£000
MV of equity	10,450	8,805	7,459	6,337.5
MV of loan stock	0	1,000	2,000	3,000.0
Total MV of company (Y)	10,450	9,805	9,459	9,337.5
WACC (X ÷ Y)	0.18	0.192	0.199	0.201

The MV is at its highest, and so its WACC is at a minimum, when the company is all-equity financed.

11

	No loan stock	£1 million loan stock	£2 million loan stock	£3 million loan stock
	£000	£000	£000	£000
Profit before interest (X)	500	500	500	500
Interest	0	100	240	420
Profits = dividends	500	400	260	80
÷ Cost of equity	÷ 0.12	÷ 0.125	÷ 0.13	÷ 0.135
	£000	£000	£000	£000
MV of equity	4,167	3,200	2,000	593
MV of loan stock	0	1,000	2,000	3,000
Total MV of company (Y)	4,167	4,200	4,000	3,593
WACC (X ÷ Y)	12%	11.9%	12.5%	13.9%

The WACC is minimised at 11.9% (when the MV of the company is maximised) for the given annual profit, when there is £1 million of loan stock.

12

With higher gearing, shareholders' earnings become more variable.

This is a little bit difficult to illustrate, but suppose that we have a series of companies each £100,000 in total value (with market value = nominal value), each earning £15,000 pa before interest, but each differently geared. Debt interest, let's say, is 12%.

Continued...

Question

	Company X Nil geared £		Company Y 50% geared £		Company Z 80% geared £
PBIT	15,000		15,000		15,000
Interest	0	(50,000 x .12)	6,000	(80,000 x .12)	9,600
Profit before tax	15,000		9,000		5,400

Now suppose that PBIT fell by £1,000 (6.7%) in one year. Company X shareholders would suffer a 6.7% fall in EPS, company Y's shareholders would suffer a (1 ÷ 9) 11.1% fall, and company Z's shareholders would suffer a (1 ÷ 5.4) 18.5% fall in EPS. Total PBIT will vary from year to year, and the uncertainty in earnings will be greater for shareholders in highly geared companies. This, said Modigliani and Miller, is the reason that the cost of equity will *always* rise as gearing rises. The risk of *bankruptcy* (item A) isn't the issue!

13

Let the cost of equity in Gavin Waysign plc be K_e.
Since there are no taxes, MM argued that

$$WACC_g = WACC_u = 20\%$$

The market value of the ungeared company would be £6 million ÷ 20% = £30 million.

Also, since $MV_g = MV_u$
MV of debt + MV of equity in geared company $= MV_u$
£10m + MV_{eg} $= £30m$

The market value of Gavin Waysign plc's equity should therefore be £(30 - 10)m = £20 million.

$$WACC = 20\% = \frac{(20 \text{ million} \times K_e) + (10 \text{ million} \times 0.12)}{30 \text{ million}}$$

$$K_e = 0.24 \text{ or } 24\%$$

14

According to Modigliani and Miller's theory of gearing, ignoring taxation, the company's WACC will be the same at all levels of gearing.

This is currently $\frac{£4 \text{ million} + (14\% \text{ of } £10 \text{ million})}{£30 \text{ million}} \times 100\% = 0.18$ or 18%.

It will still be 18% at the new level of gearing, and the total market value of the company will still be £30 million, which means that the MV of equity will be £25 million (30 - 5 or 20 + 5). The dividends will be increased by the interest savings to £4 million + (14% of £5 million) = £4.7 million.

The cost of equity will be $\frac{4.7}{25} \times 100\% = 18.8\%$.

Question

15   As gearing rises, so too does the cost of equity, to compensate for the higher financial risk. However, because of the tax shield on loan interest, the weighted average cost of capital continues to fall as the gearing proportion is increased, up to 100% gearing. Modigliani and Miller's theory is in contrast to the 'traditional' view that the weighted average cost of capital (WACC) graph is saucer-shaped, with an optimal level of gearing below 100% where the WACC is minimised. The traditional view is shown in Graph A.

16   Statement 1 is correct, and is expressed in the formula $V_g = V_u + Dt$.

Statement 2 is not correct. Adapting the formula above,

$$V_{eg} + D = V_u + Dt$$
$$V_{eg} = V_u - D + Dt$$

Since t is a proportion, the value of equity in the geared company (V_{eg}) will always be *less* than the value of equity in the ungeared company (V_u).

Statement 3 is not correct, because the MV per share depends on how many shares have been issued by the geared and the ungeared company. This factor is irrelevant to Modigliani and Miller's arguments.

17   Value of geared company = Value of ungeared company
= (Debt capital x rate of tax relief on debt)

$$V_g = V_u + Dt$$
$$= £6,000,000 + (£3,000,000 \times 0.35)$$
$$= £7,050,000$$

Since the value of debt capital is £3,000,000, the value of equity in the geared company will be £4,050,000.

18   The formula $V_g = V_u + Dt$ applies.

The value of the company if it were all-equity, with the £20 million raised as equity finance, would be

Old value + Funds raised + NPV of project
£120m   + £20m   + £5m
=   £145m

However, since the company will become geared, and $V_g = V_u + Dt$

$$V_g = £145m + £(20 \text{ million} \times 35\%)$$
$$= £152 \text{ million.}$$

Question

19 We are back to Modigliani-Miller theory here, with

$$V_g = V_u + Dt$$

The market value of the loan stock will be £36m x 80% = £28.8m
The market value of an identical all-equity company = £7 million ÷ 0.18 = £38.9m

$$V_g = £38.9m + (£28.8m \times 25\%)$$
$$= £46.1m.$$

Since the debt capital has a value of £28.8m, the equity value of Otto Barnes plc will be £(46.1 - 28.8)m = £17.3 million.

20
$$K_g = K_u + \left[\frac{MV\ of\ debt}{MV\ of\ equity} \times (K_u - K_d) \right]$$

$$K_g = 18\% + [\tfrac{1}{3} \times (18 - 12)\%]$$
$$= 20\%$$

Note: the WACC = ($\tfrac{1}{4}$ x 12%) + ($\tfrac{3}{4}$ x 20%) = 18%, the same as in the ungeared company.

21
$$K_g = K_u + \left[\frac{MV\ of\ debt}{MV\ of\ equity}\ (1 - t)(K_u - K_d) \right]\%$$

$$= 18\% + [\tfrac{1}{3}\ (1 - 0.4)(18 - 12)]\%$$
$$= 19.8\%.$$

Note: the WACC = ($\tfrac{1}{4}$ x 12% x (1 - 0.4))% + ($\tfrac{3}{4}$ x 19.8)% = 16.65%, lower than in the all-geared company.

22 The first step in finding the answer is to calculate the weighted average cost of capital in an equivalent ungeared (100% equity) company.

$$WACC_g = WACC_u \left[1 - \frac{tD}{MV_g} \right]$$

$$18\% = WACC_u \left[1 - \frac{0.35 \times 1}{(1 + 2)} \right]$$

$$0.88333\ WACC_u = 18\%$$
$$WACC_u = 20.377\%.$$

Continued...

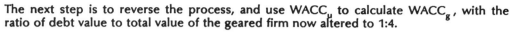

Question

The next step is to reverse the process, and use $WACC_u$ to calculate $WACC_g$, with the ratio of debt value to total value of the geared firm now altered to 1:4.

$$WACC_g = 20.377\% \left[1 - \frac{0.35 \times 1}{4} \right]$$
$$= 18.6\%.$$

23 We use the formula

$$K_g = K_u + Dt$$

K_u is the cost of equity in an identical ungeared company, which in this case is GHJ plc.

The value of DEF plc ought to be: £34 million + (£15 million x 0.35) = £39.25 million.

The value of DEF plc equity ought to be £39.25m - £15m = £24.25 million.

Since the equity has a current MV of £25 million, it is slightly over-valued.

The value of KLM plc ought to be: £34 million + (£20 million x 0.35) = £41 million.

The value of KLM plc equity ought to be £41m - £20m = £21 million.

Since the equity has a current MV of £19 million, it is under-valued.

24 Cost of equity = $\frac{£0.80}{£4}$ = 0.20

NPV of project $= -£10 \text{ million} + \frac{£1,950,000}{0.2}$
$$= -£10 \text{ million} + £9.75 \text{ million}$$
$$= -£250,000$$

25 If the project is undertaken and is all-equity financed, the total value of the company would be:

	£m
Existing value (10m x £4)	40.00
Present value of project benefits (see previous solution)	9.75
	49.75

We can use the formula $V_g = V_u + Dt$.

If the project is financed by £10 million of debt capital, the total value of the company will become:

$$V_g = £49.75 \text{ million} + (£10 \text{ million} \times 35\%)$$
$$= £53.25 \text{ million}$$

Continued...

Question

The value of equity will be

	£ million
Total value	53.25
MV of debt	10.00
Value of equity	43.25

Since the current MV of equity is £40 million, the new project and the change in gearing would increase the value of equity by £3.25 million.

26

$$\text{WACC} = \frac{\text{Total return}}{\text{Total MV}} = \frac{\text{Old return + New return}}{\text{Total MV}}$$

For the total MV, see the previous solution.

$$= \frac{(10 \text{ million} \times £0.80) + £1,950,000}{£53,250,000}$$

$$= 18.7\% \text{ approx.}$$

Alternatively

$$\text{WACC of geared company} = \text{WACC of ungeared company} \times \left[1 - \frac{tD}{V_g} \right]$$

$$= 20\% \times \left[1 - \frac{£10m \times 35\%}{£53.25m} \right]$$

$$= 18.7\% \text{ approx.}$$

27 Incremental cost of capital

$$= \frac{\text{Incremental reward (before interest)}}{\text{Incremental MV}}$$

$$= \frac{£1,950,000}{£(53.25m - £40m)} = 0.147 \text{ approx}$$

28 *Ignoring taxation.* The cost of Bonnitt plc's equity is

$$\frac{£11.7 \text{ million} - (£30m \times 12\%)}{15 \text{ million} \times £3} = 0.18$$

The WACC of Bonnitt plc is $\dfrac{£11.7 \text{ million}}{£45 \text{ million} + £30 \text{ million}} = 15.6\%$

Question

The WACC of Boot plc is $\dfrac{£11.7 \text{ million}}{£58.5 \text{ million}} = 20\%$

The cost of capital of Bonnitt plc is lower, and it will be worthwhile to carry out arbitrage.

	£
Sell 1% stake in Bonnitt plc for £3 x 150,000 shares =	450,000
Borrow personally an amount = 1% of the MV of Bonnitt plc's debt capital, to maintain same gearing	300,000
	750,000
Purchase 1% of shares in Boot plc for (300,000 x £1.95)	585,000
Capital gain	165,000

Note: Income will now be

	£
Dividends from 1% stake in Boot plc (1% of £11.7m)	117,000
Less personal loan interest (£300,000 x 12%)	(36,000)
Income will now be	81,000

Previously, it was 1% of dividends in Bonnitt plc = 1% of (£11.7m - £3.6m)
= £81,000, which is the same amount.

29 Arbitrage will cease when the WACC of the two companies is the same. Since Bonnitt plc's shares and loan stock are "correctly" valued, the equilibrium WACC is the WACC of Bonnitt plc, which is 15.6% (see previous solution).

The WACC of Boot plc must fall to 15.6%, and so the total MV of the company must be £11.7 million ÷ 15.6% = £75 million. This gives a price of (÷ 30,000 shares) £2.50 per share.

30

	£
Sell 1% of shares in Bonnitt plc for	450,000
Borrow personally an amount equal to 1% of Bonnitt's debt capital, adjusted to allow for Bonnitt's tax relief on debt (1% x £30 million x 65%)	195,000
	645,000
Buy 1% of shares in Boot plc for	585,000
Capital gain	60,000

Note: Income will now be

	£
1% of Boot plc dividends	117,000
Less interest on borrowing (12% of £195,000)	23,400
Net income	93,600

Continued...

Question

This compares with previous earnings from 1% of Bonnitt plc's equity:

	£	£
Bonnitt plc profits		11,700,000
Debt interest	3,600,000	
Tax relief on debt (35%)	1,260,000	
		2,340,000
		9,360,000

1% = £93,600 - the same amount.

7: MARKING SCHEDULE

Question	Correct answer	Marks for correct answer	Question	Correct answer	Marks for correct answer	Question	Correct answer	Marks for correct answer
1	D	1	15	B	1	29	D	1
2	A	1	16	D	1	30	C	1
3	A	1	17	C	1	31	B	1
4	C	1	18	B	1	32	B	1
5	A	1	19	C	1	33	D	2
6	B	1	20	A	2	34	A	2
7	A	1	21	C	1	35	B	1
8	A	1	22	D	1	36	A	1
9	B	1	23	A	1	37	A	1
10	D	1	24	B	1	38	C	1
11	D	1	25	B	1	39	B	1
12	C	2	26	A	2	40	D	1
13	B	1	27	C	1			
14	C	1	28	B	1			

YOUR MARKS

Total marks available   **45**   Your total mark

GUIDELINES - If your mark was:

0 - 14 This is a low score, and a lot of this tricky subject is obviously giving you difficulty.

15 - 25 Fair. You have some understanding of this subject, but there are still quite a lot of topic areas you might need to learn. If you don't need to know about geared and ungeared betas, a mark of 21 or more would be good for questions 1-34.

26 - 36 Good. There are still some aspects of portfolio theory and CAPM that you might need to learn, although some topic areas might be outside your subject syllabus.

37 - 45 Excellent mark for what is really quite a complex subject.

COMMENTS

Question

1

The efficient frontier of portfolios represents portfolios which are neither 'better' nor 'worse' than each other, because they have either a higher expected return but a lower risk, or a lower risk but a lower expected return, than other portfolios.

2

Covariance $= 0.6(0.1)(0.12)$
$= 0.0072$

3

Return $= 80\%$ of $0.16 + 20\%$ of 0.20
$= 0.168$ or 16.8%

Portfolio standard deviation (where p and q in the formula are the relative market values of the existing portfolio and the new investment)

$$= \sqrt{(0.8)^2 \ (0.10)^2 \ + \ (0.2)^2 \ (0.12)^2 \ + \ 2(0.8)(0.2)(0.0072)}$$

$$= \sqrt{0.0064 + 0.000576 + 0.002304}$$

$$= \sqrt{0.00928}$$
$$= 0.096$$

4

Risk averse investor
The return from P, Q and the PQ portfolio would all be 15%, and so the choice of the risk averse and risk seeking investors will depend on the standard deviation of expected returns.

Since the correlation coefficient between returns from P and Q is less than one (so returns are not perfectly positively correlated) diversifying into a portfolio consisting of P and Q will reduce the standard deviation of returns below 19%. The risk averse investor will choose the portfolio PQ.

Risk-seeking investor.
The risk seeking investor will choose the investment with the highest potential returns (although the lowest potential returns too) and this is offered by Q, which has the highest standard deviation of returns.

Question

5

$\bar{R}$ = mean portfolio return = 17%.

Probability	Security X: 40% of expected return	Security Y: 60% of expected return	Combined portfolio return		
P			R	R - $\bar{R}$	p(R - $\bar{R}$)²
0.3	10	10.8	20.8	3.8	4.332
0.4	8	9.0	17.0	0.0	0.000
0.3	6	7.2	13.2	(3.8)	4.332
				Variance	8.664

Standard deviation of return = $\sqrt{8.664}$ = 2.94%

6

Probability	Security X: 40% of expected return		Security Y: 60% of expected return		Combined portfolio return		
P					R	R - $\bar{R}$	p(R - $\bar{R}$)²
0.3	(40% of 25)	10	(60% of 12)	7.2	17.2	0.2	0.012
0.4	(40% of 20)	8	(60% of 15)	9.0	17.0	0.0	0.000
0.3	(40% of 15)	6	(60% of 18)	10.8	16.8	(0.2)	0.012
						Variance	0.024

Standard deviation of return = $\sqrt{0.024}$ = 0.15%.

Notice how by investing in securities whose returns are negatively correlated, an investor can reduce his investment risk significantly.

7

Probability	Return on X (60%)	Return on Y (40%)	Total return		
p			x	x - $\bar{x}$	p(x - $\bar{x}$)²
0.5 x 0.5 = 0.25	18	18	36	+ 11	30.25
0.5 x 0.5 = 0.25	18	2	20	- 5	6.25
0.5 x 0.5 = 0.25	12	18	30	+ 5	6.25
0.5 x 0.5 = 0.25	12	2	14	- 11	30.25
					73.00

Standard deviation = $\sqrt{73}$ = 8.54%.

Question

8 The expected return from each project is 14%, and so the pair of projects that will be selected is the one with the least risk for this return.

Projects	Variance of returns	
W and Y	$(0.5)^2$ 6 + $(0.5)^2$ 1.5 + 2(0.5)(0.5)(- 3.0)	= 0.375
W and Z	$(0.5)^2$ 6 + $(0.5)^2$ 54.0 + 2(0.5)(0.5)(- 18.0)	= 7.5
X and Y	$(0.5)^2$ 54 + $(0.5)^2$ 1.5 + 2(0.5)(0.5)(- 9.0)	= 9.375
X and Z	$(0.5)^2$ 54 + $(0.5)^2$ 54.0 + 2(0.5)(0.5)(- 46.8)	= 3.6

W and Y have a portfolio variance of 0.375 (and so a standard deviation of just 0.61%) which is the least-risk option.

9 The investor is indifferent between any portfolio on an indifference curve, and so he is indifferent between W and Z, W having a lower expected return but lower risk than Z and both lying on curve I_2. However, portfolio X lies on a 'better' indifference curve I_1, offering a better return for a lower risk or lower risk for a given return than portfolios on I_2. Portfolio X will be preferred to W and Z, and also to Y, which will be on an indifference curve somewhere between I_1 and I_2.

10 Don't mix up the columns for risk (standard deviation) and return. Portfolio D cannot lie on the efficient frontier because it has a lower return *and* higher risk than portfolio A. Portfolios A, B and C are not obviously 'better' or 'worse' than each other, since they offer a higher return or lower risk than the others (eg A offers a higher return than C but a higher risk, A offers a lower return than B but a lower risk).

11 Notice the similarities and differences between the Capital Market Line (CML) and Security Market Line (SML).

	Y axis (return)	X axis (risk)
CML	Return of portfolio	Standard deviation of portfolio returns
SML	Return of security	β of security

12 The expected return from a portfolio can be represented by the capital market line (CML) which has the formula

$$R_{rf} + \left[\frac{(R_m - R_{rf})}{\sigma_m} \sigma_p \right]$$

where R_{rf} is the risk free rate of return
R_m is the expected market return
σ_m is the standard deviation of the expected market return
σ_p is the standard deviation of a return for a portfolio on the CML   Cont...

Question

Here $\dfrac{R_m - R_f}{\sigma_m} = \dfrac{15 - 9}{4} = 1.5$

Portfolio	Standard deviation (σ_p)	Expected return of portfolio on CML		Expected return on actual portfolio	
X	5.4	(9 + 1.5 x 5.4)	17.1	16.5	Inefficient
Y	1.2	(9 + 1.5 x 1.2)	10.8	11.5	Efficient
Z	10.0	(9 + 1.5 x 10.0)	24.0	26.0	Efficient

Alternative method
You could draw the CML the CML as a straight line with two points.

	X axis Std deviation	Y axis Return
Risk free	0	4
Market portfolio	4	15

By plotting each portfolio X, Y and Z on the same graph, you would find that X and Z lie above the CML and so are efficient, whereas Y lies below the CML and so is inefficient.

13 A security whose expected return (%) is below the security market line (SML) is inefficient, indicating that it is overpriced. Security R is one of these. In contrast a security whose expected return is above the SML is efficient, and underpriced, because at the moment it is providing a high return for its perceived level of risk. P and Q are both efficient. A security will be correctly priced if it lies on the SML.

14

		Return
Original investment	100%	14%
Borrowed	+ 50%	7%
		21%
Less interest on loan	(50% of 8%)	4%
Portfolio return on original investment		17%

Standard deviation of return $= \sqrt{(150\%)^2 \ (16\%)^2}$
$= 150\%$ of 16%
$= 24\%$

15

	£
Return achievable net of interest (24% of £1,000,000)	240,000
Interest cost of borrowing (8% of £250,000)	20,000
Total return before interest on £1,250,000	260,000
	= 20.8%

Question

16 Factors A, B and C are all caused by unsystematic risk which an investor can avoid by diversifying his investments.

17 *Statement 1 is incorrect.* A share's measured beta is likely to change over time, partly because of changes in the share's risk characteristics but more because measurements of beta are based on limited data, and some statistical error is inevitable.

Statement 2 is correct. It might help to think of a share's alpha in terms of the formula (ignoring dividend payments).

Change in price of the share in the period = α + β (Change in market index).

18 The beta factor for a company's shares can be calculated as:

$$\beta = \frac{cov(s,m)}{var(m)}$$

Where   m   is the market rate of return
        cov(s,m)   is the covariance between the return on the company's shares (s) and the market rate of return
        var(m)   is the variance of the market return.

(Candidates for several examinations are expected to know this formula.)

19 Financial gearing and size influence the perceived risk of companies in such a way that their beta factors will be affected. Differences in risk suggested by items A and D should therefore both be reflected in existing betas. Some estimating errors will occur (item B) in the mathematical techniques for calculating betas, but these will influence the perceived risk of companies: a higher beta factor, even if inaccurately calculated, will indicate higher perceived risk.

Answer C is correct. Some companies might have a low systematic risk with share prices responding in only a relatively small way to changes in conditions affecting the rest of the market. However, their specific individual risk (unsystematic risk) might be very high, subjecting the company to sharp fluctuations in returns/share price. Firms of commodity dealers might be examples.

20

Actual return		pence
	Dividend	6
	Capital loss	5
	Total return	1
	As % of share price	1%

Continued...

Question

Market return   Increase in share index (408 - 400) 8

          As % of opening index (8 ÷ 400) 2%

Expectation on Lorn Mower plc shares

$$= R_f + \beta (R_m - R_f)$$

$$= \tfrac{1}{2} + 1.4 (2 - \tfrac{1}{2}) = 2.6\%$$

Returns due to unsystematic risk = 1% - 2.6% = <u>1.6% loss</u>

21 Since the CAPM estimates variations in returns on the company's shares given changes in the market return, market return data is represented by 'x' in the regression formula, and data for the shares by 'y'. There are 12 pairs of data (12 months).

$$b = \frac{12\,(184) - (15)(18)}{12\,(145) - (15)^2}$$

$$= \frac{2{,}208 - 270}{1{,}740 - 225} = \frac{1{,}938}{1{,}515} = 1.28$$

22

Shares	Market value	Beta value	MV x β
	£000		
W plc	200	1.20	240
X plc	140	1.40	196
Y plc	160	0.90	144
Z plc	<u>300</u>	1.10	<u>330</u>
	<u>700</u>		<u>910</u>

Portfolio beta = $\frac{910}{700}$ = 1.30

23

Project	Required return	PV of cash flow £000	
1	8% + 1.5 (13 - 8)% = 15.5%	86.58	(100 ÷ 1.155)
2	8% + 1.4 (13 - 8)% = 15.0%	86.96	(100 ÷ 1.15)
3	8% + 0.8 (13 - 8)% = 12.0%	<u>178.57</u>	(200 ÷ 1.12)
		<u>352.11</u>	

Question

24

Project	Present value £000	Beta	PV x β
1	86.58	1.5	129.87
2	86.96	1.4	121.74
3	<u>178.57</u>	0.8	<u>142.86</u>
	<u>352.11</u>		<u>394.47</u>

Portfolio β = $\dfrac{394.47}{352.11}$ = 1.12

25

State of economy		Net present value £	Probability	Expected NPV £
I	$\dfrac{£238,000}{1.18}$ - £200,000 =	1,695	0.3	509
II	$\dfrac{£242,000}{1.18}$ - £200,000 =	5,085	0.5	2,543
III	$\dfrac{£208,000}{1.18}$ - £200,000 =	(23,729)	0.2	<u>(4,746)</u> <u>(1,694)</u>

26

Variance of market returns

Average market return $\overline{m}$ = (0.3 x 30%) + (0.5 x 20%) + (0.2 x 5%) = 20% or 0.20

State of economy	Probability p	Market return m	$m - \overline{m}$	$p(m - \overline{m})^2$
I	0.3	0.30	0.10	0.0030
II	0.5	0.20	0.00	0.0000
III	0.2	0.05	-0.15	<u>0.0045</u> <u>0.0075</u>

Covariance of project returns and market returns

Average project return $\overline{x}$ = (0.3 x 19%) + (0.5 x 21%) + (0.2 x 4%) = 17% or 0.17

State of economy	Probability	Market return m	Project return x	$m - \overline{m}$	$x - \overline{x}$	$p(m - \overline{m})(x - \overline{x})$
I	0.3	0.30	0.19	0.10	0.02	0.0006
II	0.5	0.20	0.21	0.00	0.04	0.0000
III	0.2	0.05	0.04	- 0.15	- 0.13	<u>0.0039</u> <u>0.0045</u>

Project beta = $\dfrac{\text{Covariance}}{\text{Variance}}$ = $\dfrac{0.0045}{0.0075}$ = 0.6

Question

27

Project cost of capital, using the CAPM

$$= 10\% + 0.6 \, (20 - 10)\% = 16\%.$$

EV of project value in one year

Value £	Probability	EV £
238,000	0.3	71,400
242,000	0.5	121,000
208,000	0.2	41,600
		234,000

EV of project NPV $= \dfrac{£234,000}{1.16} - £200,000 = + £1,724$

28

The company's capital structure (using market values) is one-sixth debt and five sixths equity.

Required return on debt capital $\quad = \quad 8\% + 0.3 \, (20 - 8)\%$
$\qquad\qquad\qquad\qquad\qquad\qquad\quad = \quad 11.6\%$

Required return on equity capital $\quad = \quad 8\% + 1.20 \, (20 - 8)\%$
$\qquad\qquad\qquad\qquad\qquad\qquad\quad = \quad 22.4\%$

Required project returns $\qquad\qquad = \quad \dfrac{1}{6} \, (11.6)\% + \dfrac{5}{6} \, (22.4)\%$
$\qquad\qquad\qquad\qquad\qquad\qquad\quad = \quad 1.93\% + 18.67\% = 20.6\%$

29

The required return should be one which takes into consideration the β factor for the new investments.

New beta	= Current beta x proportion of funds	+	New investment beta x proportion of funds

$\quad 1.15 \qquad = 1.10 \, (90\%) \qquad\qquad + \qquad \beta_i \, (10\%)$
$\quad 10\% \; \beta_i \quad = 1.15 - 0.99$
$\qquad\;\; \beta_i \quad = 1.6$

Required return $= \; 7\% + 1.6 \, (17\% - 7\%) = 23\%$

Question

30

Current WACC = 6% + 0.9 (16 - 6)% = 15%
Revised WACC = 6% + 1.0 (16 - 6)% = 16%

31

The new beta factor of the company will be the weighted average of the betas of its existing operations and the new project. Let the beta of the new project be β_p.

New beta = 0.8 (old beta) + 0.2 (β_p)
1.0 = 0.8 (0.9) + 0.2 β_p
0.28 = 0.2 β_p
β_p = 1.4

32

1.26 = 60% x β for 'normal activities' + 40% x 1.80

1.26 = 0.60β + 0.72
β = 0.90

This β can be used to estimate a cost of capital for the financing of this 60% part of the company's operations, perhaps for using in DCF analysis of capital expenditure proposals.

33

The new project will add to market value by $\dfrac{£300,000}{0.205}$ = £1,463,415

	Market value (MV) £	β	β x MV
Current investments	4,000,000	0.9	3,600,000
New project	1,463,415	1.5	2,195,123
	5,463,415		5,795,123

New overall beta of the company = $\dfrac{5,795,123}{5,463,415}$ = 1.06

34

Project viability
The expected market return is (0.2 x 40) + (0.4 x 20) + (0.4 x 10) = 20%

The required return on the new project, using the CAPM, is
10% + 1.67 (20% - 10%) = 26.7%

The expected return on the project is (0.2 x 60) + (0.4 x 40) + (0.4 x 10) = 32%. This exceeds the required return and the project is viable.

Continued...

Question

Future cost of capital
The returns from existing projects match returns from the market portfolio exactly, and so their beta factor is 1.

The weighted average beta for the company will be $(0.25 \times 1.67) + (0.75 \times 1) = 1.1675$

Required return from future projects $= 10\% + 1.1675 (20\% - 10\%)$
$= 21.675\%.$

35 We can use the MM formula

$$MV_g = MV_u + Dt$$
$$MV_u = MV_g - Dt$$

If Q plc were all-equity financed, its value would be

$$£(60 + 30) \text{ million} - (30 \times 0.4) \text{ million} = £78 \text{ million}$$

	£m
Value of P plc	70
Value of Q plc if all-equity	78
Total value of merged company, if all-equity	148

36 If Q plc were all-equity financed, its equity beta β_u would be

$$\left[\frac{\beta_g}{1 + \dfrac{D(1-t)}{V_{eg}}} \right] = \left[\frac{1.4}{1 + \dfrac{30(1-0.3)}{60}} \right]$$

$$= \frac{1.4}{1.35} = 1.037$$

The equity beta of the merged company PQ plc will be the weighted average of the equity beta of (1) P plc and (2) Q plc, if Q were all-equity financed.

Company	Market value £m	Weighting	β	Weighting × β
P	70	47.3%	1.100	0.52
All-equity Q	78	52.7%	1.037	0.55
PQ	148	100.0%		1.07

Question

37 $\beta_u = \left[\dfrac{1.20}{1 + \frac{1}{4}(1-0.35)} \right] = \dfrac{1.20}{1.1625}$

= 1.032258, say 1.03

38 Following on from the previous solution

$\beta_g = \beta_u \left[1 + \dfrac{D(1-t)}{V_{eg}} \right]$

= 1.032258 [1 + ½(1-0.35)]

= 1.36774, say 1.37

39 $\beta_g = \beta_u \left[1 + \dfrac{D(1-t)}{V_{eg}} \right]$

= 0.90 $\left[1 + \dfrac{25}{75} \right]$

= 1.20

40 $\beta_g = \beta_u \left[1 + \dfrac{D(1-t)}{V_{eg}} \right]$

= 0.90 $\left[1 + \dfrac{25(1-0.30)}{75} \right]$

= 1.11

8: MARKING SCHEDULE

Question	Correct answer	Marks for the correct answer	Question	Correct answer	Marks for the correct answer
1	B	1	11	D	1
2	D	1	12	C	2
3	A	1	13	C	1
4	B	1	14	D	2
5	C	1	15	C	1
6	A	1	16	D	2
7	A	1	17	B	1
8	B	1	18	C	1
9	C	1	19	A	1
10	C	1			

YOUR MARKS

Total marks available | **22** | Your total mark |

GUIDELINES - If your mark was:

0 - 7 A disappointing mark. You need to understand working capital much better.

8 - 11 Fair, but there are some important aspects about working capital management that you still need to learn.

12 - 16 Good. You understand the key issues about working capital, but check your mistakes carefully.

17 - 22 Very good. You have reached a high standard of knowledge about working capital management.

237

COMMENTS

Question

1

Capital employed	£480,000
Fixed assets ($\frac{2}{3}$)	£320,000
Working capital ($\frac{1}{3}$)	£160,000

If current assets = CA and current liabilities = CL

$$CA - CL = 160,000 \quad ....(1)$$
$$CA = 3CL \quad ....(2) \quad \text{- current ratio}$$

Current assets = £240,000 and current liabilities = £80,000.

2

Net profit = 25% of £960,000 =	£240,000
ROCE = 10%	
Capital employed (x 100% ÷ 10%)	£2,400,000
Fixed assets (50%)	£1,200,000
Working capital (50%)	£1,200,000

If current assets = CA and current liabilities = CL

$$CA - CL = £1,200,000 \text{ and } CA = 1.5CL$$
$$CL = £2,400,000$$

3

	£
Debtors (90/360 x £2,000,000)	500,000
Stocks (72/360 x 50% x £2,000,000)	200,000
	700,000
Creditors (80% of £500,000)	400,000

The ratio of debtors plus stocks to creditors is 1.75, and since the current ratio is less than this, there must be a bank overdraft, B.

$$\frac{700,000}{400,000 + B} = 1.4, \text{ and so B = 100,000.}$$

$$\text{Liquid ratio} = \frac{\text{Debtors + Cash}}{\text{Current liabilities}} = \frac{500,000}{400,000 + 100,000} = 1.0.$$

4

Overtrading means trying to carry out an excessive volume of business for the size of the company's capital base (Answer B is a symptom of this). The current ratio (Answer A) is likely to be *low* with *long* periods of credit (Answer D) being taken from creditors.

Question

5

$$EOQ = \sqrt{\frac{2 \times 259 \times 3,000}{27}}$$

$$= 240 \text{ units}$$

Frequency of ordering $= \dfrac{240}{3,000} \times 50$ weeks $= 4$ weeks

6

Without the computer system, the EV of the invoicing delay is $(0.15 \times 3) + (0.35 \times 4) + (0.30 \times 5) + (0.20 \times 6) = 4.55$ days.

With the computer system, the expected delay is $(0.70 \times 1) + (0.10 \times 2) = 0.90$ days.

Annual interest cost of an average delay of

		£
(1)	4.55 days $= \dfrac{4.55}{250} \times £15,000,000 \times 20\% =$	54,600
(2)	0.90 days $= \dfrac{0.90}{250} \times £15,000,000 \times 20\% =$	10,800
	Interest saved pa	43,800
	Less net costs of operating the system	25,000
	Net profit	18,800

7

	Days
Raw material stock turnover (250 ÷ 1,070 x 365 days)	85.3
Less creditors: average payment period (162 ÷ 1,070 x 365)	(55.3)
	30.0
Production cycle (WIP turnover) (115 ÷ 1,458 x 365)	28.8
Finished goods stock turnover (186 ÷ 1,458 x 365)	46.6
Debt collection period (345 ÷ 1,636 x 365)	77.0
Full operating cycle	182.4

8

	£
Sales	1,636,000
Cost of sales	1,458,000
Gross profit	178,000
Reduction in gross profit from 25% fall in sales =	£44,500

Continued...

Question

	£
Working capital freed	
Reduction in stocks (25% of, in £000, (250 + 115 + 186))	137,750
Reduction in creditors (25% of £162,000)	(40,500)
	97,250

	£	
'Old' debtors	345,000	
'New' debtors (45 + 365 x 75% of £1,636,000)	151,300	
Reduction in debtors		193,700
		290,950

	£
Overdraft interest saved pa (x 14%) approx	40,700

Net loss from new policy = £(44,500 - 40,700) = £3,800, say £4,000

9 The company is offering to take £98 in 10 days instead of £100 in 30 days. The implied cost of capital is

$$\frac{2}{98} \times \frac{365}{(30 - 10)} = 0.372 \text{ or } 37.2\%.$$

10

	£
Before the campaign	
Annual discounts = 2% of (10% + 20%) of £10,000,000 =	60,000
After the campaign	
Annual discounts = 2% of (5% + 5%) of £12,000,000 =	24,000
Reduction in discounts allowed	36,000

11

	Before the campaign	*After the campaign*
Average collection period (days)	(20% x 10) + (40% x 30)	(5% of 10) + (20% of 30)
	+ (25% x 60) + (5% x 90)	+ (50% of 60) + (20% of 90)
	= 33.5 days	= 54.5 days
Average debtors	$\frac{33.5}{360}$ x £10,000,000	$\frac{54.5}{360}$ x £12,000,000
	= £930,600	= £1,816,700

Increase in debtors £886,100, say £886,000

240

Question

12

Payment pattern, ignoring discounts, when the policy is introduced.

	Old policy: income			Discount policy: income		
	Month 1	Month 2	Month 3	Month 1	Month 2	Month 3
	10%	10%	80%	70%	10%	20%
Sales in:	£000	£000	£000	£000	£000	£000
Month 1	100	100	800	700	100	200
Month 2		100	100		700	100
Month 3			100			700
	100	200	1,000	700	800	1,000

The change of policy would increase cash income by £600,000 in each of months 1 and 2. From month 3 onwards, there would be no difference in payment patterns (except for discounts allowed).

£

PV of extra cash received

Month 1 £600,000 x $\dfrac{1}{1.02}$ 588,235

Month 2 £600,000 x $\dfrac{1}{(1.02)^2}$ 576,701
                                                                              ————————
                                                                              1,164,936

PV of discounts allowed $2\frac{1}{2}$% of £700,000 per month =
£17,500 per month in perpetuity, discounted at 2% =
£17,500 ÷ 0.02   875,000
Net present value   289,936

13

		£
Debtors under current policy		140,000
Debtors under new policy (2 x £140,000 x 1.25)		350,000
Increase in debtors		210,000

	£	£
Annual financing cost of higher debtors	(£210,000 x 15%)	(31,500)
Bad debts:		
Current policy £1,400 x 12 months	16,800	
New policy (5% of £140,000 x 1.25 x 12 months)	105,000	
Increase in bad debts		(88,200)
Extra contribution from higher sales		
(12 months x 25% x £(140,000 - 75,000))		195,000
Increase in annual profits		75,300

Question

14

		£
(1)	Debtors will be ($\frac{1}{12}$ x 90% of £5,000,000)	375,000
	Debtors in original balance sheet	900,000
	Reduction in debtors	525,000
	Reduction in stocks (10% of £300,000)	30,000
	Reduction in creditors (10% of £250,000)	(25,000)
	Total reduction in working capital	530,000
	Interest benefits (20% cost of capital) = £106,000 pa	

		£
(2)	*Saving in bad debts*	
	Bad debts: old policy	210,000
	new policy (2% of £4,500,000)	90,000
		120,000

		£
(3)	*Summary*	
	Extra administrative costs	(45,000)
	Loss in gross profit (10% of £1,600,000)	(160,000)
	Interest benefits	106,000
	Bad debts savings	120,000
	Net profit increase	21,000

15

	£
Average debtors without the factor's services (90/360 x £14,400,000)	3,600,000
Average debtors with the factor's services (60/360 x £14,400,000)	2,400,000
	1,200,000

	£
Cost of factoring service (1$\frac{1}{2}$% of £14.4m)	216,000
Annual savings in admin costs	64,000
Effective annual cost	152,000

As a % of funds improvement (÷ £1,200,000)	12.7%

16

	£
Average funds advanced before commission (60/360 x 80% of £14,400,000)	1,920,000
Less commission (2$\frac{1}{2}$% of £1,920,000)	48,000
Average funds advanced	1,872,000

	£
Annual costs of Service 2	
Commission (2$\frac{1}{2}$% of 80% of £14,400,000)	288,000
Interest (15% of £1,872,000)	280,800
	568,800

Effective annual cost $\frac{£568,800}{£1,872,000}$ = 30.4%

Question

17 Credit cards are widely used and if retailers did not accept them, sales volume would almost certainly be much lower. The problem of bad debts is less with credit cards than with cheques. If the retailer uses the Cardnet service, cleared funds are available one day later - faster than with cheques. The cost of credit cards to retailers is higher than cheques - with retailers paying a commission of perhaps 2-3% (or even more) to the credit card company.

18

		£
Average debtors $\frac{80}{365}$ x £800,000 = £175,342		
Interest charge on debtors (x 15%)		26,301
Insurance premiums $\frac{55p}{£100}$ x £800,000		4,400
Bad debts 10% of 1% of £800,000 (90% covered by insurance policy)		800
		31,501

19

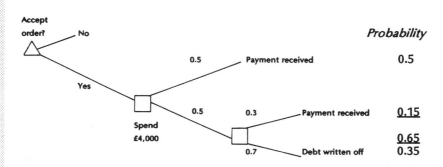

		Present value £
Year 0	Deposit (10%)	3,000
	Costs of making/despatching goods	(20,000)
		(17,000)
Year 1	*Probability*	
	0.65 Receive £27,000 ÷ 1.15	15,261
	0.5 Pay £(4,000) ÷ 1.15	(1,739)
Expected NPV		(3,478) say -£3,500

243

9: MARKING SCHEDULE

Question	Correct answer	Marks for correct answer	Question	Correct answer	Marks for correct answer	Question	Correct answer	Marks for correct answer
1	C	1	13	D	1	25	C	1
2	C	1	14	D	2	26	B	1
3	C	1	15	A	1	27	A	1
4	B	1	16	A	1	28	C	1
5	B	1	17	D	1	29	D	1
6	C	1	18	B	1	30	A	1
7	D	1	19	C	1	31	D	1
8	B	1	20	B	1	32	C	2
9	A	1	21	A	1	33	A	1
10	B	2	22	D	1	34	A	2
11	A	1	23	B	1	35	B	2
12	D	1	24	C	1			

YOUR MARKS

Total marks available   **40**   Your total mark   [ ]

GUIDELINES - If your mark was:

0 - 14   Disappointing. You do not understand this subject area yet.

24 - 31   Good. You have reached a competent standard of knowledge. Well done.

15 - 23   Not bad, but you still need to learn a bit more about this topic to understand it properly.

32 - 40   Excellent score. You have an impressive grasp of this topic.

COMMENTS

Question

1

In June, the payment will be for material purchases in March. These will relate to sales in September, which are expected to be £180,000.

Budgeted cash payment = 50% of £180,000 = £90,000.

2

Payment for materials in June is for May sales (purchased in April).

May sales	= £200,000 x $(1.02)^4$
Materials payments	= 30% of £200,000 x $(1.02)^4$
	= £65,000, to the nearest £000.

3

		£
Receipts in June		
20% of June sales	= 0.2 x £200,000 x $(1.02)^5$	44,163
40% x 97% of May sales	= 0.4 x 0.97 x £200,000 x $(1.02)^4$	83,997
35% of April sales	= 0.35 x £200,000 x $(1.02)^3$	74,285
		202,445

4

Holding	EPS		Dividend per share per year	Dividend per half year	Number of shares	Total dividend
	p.		pence	pence		£
Eggs Hibbit	15	(30%)	4.5	2.25	750,000	16,875
Watt Ness plc	19	(60%)	11.4	5.7	500,000	28,500
						45,375

$2\frac{1}{2}$% Consols: interest per half year = $\frac{1}{2}$ of $2\frac{1}{2}$% x 10,000 x £100 = 12,500

57,875

5

Statement 1 is correct. If a company treasurer knows what its usable cash balances are at any time, together with details of uncleared items that will be cleared the next day, he can increase profits by investing surplus cash overnight or for longer durations. This information can be provided by a computerised cash management service.

Statement 2 is incorrect. Usable cash balances are cash balances after payments and receipts have been cleared. Delays will occur between (1) recording a payment in the cash book and the cash leaving the bank account (postal delays, time for funds to clear etc) (2) recording a receipt in the cash book and the cash becoming available in the cash book.

Question

6

Cost of the facility £3

Benefit from speeding up clearance of funds $£(\frac{2}{365} \times 0.15)R$

where £R is the remittance value.

For the facility to be justified

$(\frac{2}{365} \times 0.15)\ R > 3$

$0.0008219R > 3$

$R > £3,650$

7

Exposure to interest rate movements (factor 1) will make treasury managers seek a *balance* between long term and short term borrowings in their debt portfolios.

Inaccurate cash flow forecasts, with the prospect of either (1) excessive cash holdings but 'locked-in' long term debt or (2) a short term cash deficit and the need to borrow, are likely to increase reliance on short term borrowings. Only factor 3, the risk that a company might be unable to renew its borrowing facilities, will give a clear preference for long term debt.

8

Treasury bills are issued by the Bank of England on behalf of the government, to raise short term cash (mostly for 90 days). They are traded 'second hand' on the discount market, and carry a low rate of interest because they are risk free.

Other money market instruments carry slightly higher rates of interest. A sterling CD is issued by a bank, acknowledging that a certain sum of money that has been deposited with it will become available on a given date to the certificate holder. CDs are also traded, on the CD market. Local authority deposits and finance house deposits are time deposits with local authorities and finance houses respectively. Local authorities raise money for short term cash needs and finance houses raise money for re-lending.

9

If £10,000 is deposited

	£
Cost of deposit £8 + (0.05% of £10,000)	(13.0)
If net cash flow is nil, a sum of £10,000 must be withdrawn in the week:	
EV of withdrawal cost = 0.2 x £13	(2.6)
Interest on £10,000 per week = (x 0.25%) £25	
EV of interest earned = 0.8 x £25	20.0
EV of net profit	4.4

Question

10   (1)   *If nothing is deposited:* net gain or loss = Nil

       (2)   *If £10,000 is deposited,* net gain = £4.4 (previous solution)

       (3)   *If £20,000 is deposited*

		£
Cost of deposit £8 + (0.05% of £20,000)		(18.0)
If net cash flow is nil, £20,000 must be withdrawn		
EV of withdrawal cost (0.2 x £18)		(3.6)
If net cash flow is + £10,000, £10,000 must be withdrawn		
EV of withdrawal cost (0.5 x £13)		(6.5)
Interest		
0.3 x (0.25% of £20,000)		15.0
0.5 x (0.25% of £10,000)		<u>12.5</u>
EV of loss		<u>(0.6)</u>

       (4)   *If £30,000 is deposited*

		£
Cost of deposit £8 + (0.05% of £30,000)		(23.0)
If net cash flow is nil, £30,000 must be withdrawn:		
EV of withdrawal cost (0.2 x £23)		(4.6)
If net cash flow is £10,000, £20,000 must be withdrawn		
EV of withdrawal cost (0.5 x £18)		(9.0)
Interest		
0.3 x (0.25% of £30,000)		22.5
0.5 x (0.25% of £10,000)		<u>12.5</u>
EV of loss		<u>(2.1)</u>

12   Futures are standardised contracts to buy or sell, at a future date, a quantity of a financial investment (gilts, bonds, shares), interest rates, foreign currency exchange rates, a commodity, and so on. They can be used by companies or investors to hedge against adverse movements in share prices, bond prices, interest rates, exchange rates, commodity prices, and so on.

13

Pays current bank	14%
Receives from swap counterparty	<u>13%</u>
Difference	1%
Pays swap counterparty	LIBOR + $\frac{1}{2}$%
Net interest cost to the company	<u>LIBOR + $1\frac{1}{2}$%</u>

If market rates *do* fall, as the treasurer expects, a loan at LIBOR + $1\frac{1}{2}$% could become cheaper than a fixed rate loan at 14%.

Note. LIBOR is the London Inter Bank Offer Rate, which is the rate which banks use for lending to each other on the money markets. Much variable rate lending is at a margin above LIBOR.

Question

14

Answer D is correct

Wigg plc gains $\frac{1}{2}$% pa by borrowing at 10% and re-lending at $10\frac{1}{2}$% fixed, and also $\frac{1}{4}$% pa by borrowing from Penn plc in the swap arrangement at $\frac{1}{4}$% below LIBOR.

Penn plc 'loses' $1\frac{1}{4}$% pa by borrowing at LIBOR + 1% and re-lending at LIBOR minus $\frac{1}{4}$%. However, because it borrows from Wigg plc in the swap arrangement at a fixed rate of $10\frac{1}{2}$%, which is $1\frac{1}{2}$% below the rate available from its bank, it 'gains' overall by a net $\frac{1}{4}$% pa.

Answer B is incorrect, because Penn plc does not benefit.

Answers A and C are incorrect because these arrangements do not enable the companies to exchange fixed interest rate for floating interest rate agreements, or vice versa, and so, simply, do not 'work' as a method of hedging against interest rate risk.

15

It is useful to illustrate how the trading in futures helps the investor to hedge against the risk of adverse price movements.

March	Cost of a future = £25 x 2,400 =		£60,000
	200 futures have a value of		£12 million
	Investor holds a portfolio of shares, value		£12,000,000
	Sells 200 FT-SE 100 Index futures		
	contracts at end-June value		£12,000,000
June	Suppose FT-SE 100 Index has fallen by 1/6 to		2,000
	Investor holds a portfolio of shares, value only		£10,000,000
	Buys 200 FT-SE 100 Index futures		
	at end-June spot value of 200 x 2,000 x £25		£10,000,000
	Loss on holding portfolio of shares		£2,000,000
	Profit on selling and buying futures		£2,000,000
	Net gain/(loss) on original £12 million		0

Since the investor sells 200 futures contracts to a LIFFE trader for delivery at the end of June, but does not own any, he must buy them back from the LIFFE trader at the end of June at the 'spot' rate. Answer A is therefore correct, not answer B.

16

The decline in the value of sterling will make the company's goods cheaper abroad, since exports will probably be priced in sterling. (For example, if a product sells for £100 and the exchange rate declines from $1.50 = £1 to $1.35 = £1, its cost to a US buyer would fall from $150 to $135). Lower prices to foreign buyers will increase overseas demand and exports.

Continued...

Question

The fall in sterling's value will also make imported goods more expensive to buy, because the company will need more sterling to pay for goods invoiced in a foreign currency. Unit variable costs will therefore rise and contribution/profit margins will be squeezed.

17

Received	$120,000 ÷ 1.50	=	£ 80,000
Paid	$132,000 ÷ 1.25	=	£105,600
	Cost of loan		£ 25,600

As a % of funds received 32%.

18 Leading with the payment eliminates the foreign currency exposure by removing the liability. Borrowing short term in francs to meet the payment obligation in 3 months' time matches assets and liabilities in francs, and so provides cover against the exposure. A forward exchange contract is a well-used method of hedging against transaction exposure.

19 According to purchasing power parity theory, the exchange rate will change according to the relative rates of inflation in each country next year.

Sterling's value against the yen will fall, as a percentage of its current level, to
$$100\% \times \left(\frac{1.03}{1.08} \right) = 95.4\%.$$

This is a fall of 4.6% in value. To prevent such a fall, the UK authorities might need to raise sterling interest rates, in order to attract more investors into buying sterling securities (investing in the UK).

20 $\$1.52 \times \dfrac{1.08}{1.14} = \$1.4400$

21 The increase in UK interest rates would strengthen sterling against the dollar at the spot rate, because sterling becomes a more attractive currency to buy and invest in.

The forward rate premium is measured approximately by

$$\frac{1 + \text{US dollar interest rate}}{1 + \text{sterling interest rate}}$$

Continued...

Question

So, for example, if US interest rates are 9%, and UK rates went up from 14% to 15%, the forward rate would change from 1.09/1.14 = 0.956 to 1.09/1.15 = 0.948 of the spot rate. The premium would increase from 0.044 (4.4% of the spot rate) to 0.052 (5.2% of the spot rate).

22 The company wants the currency $2\frac{1}{2}$ months from now, and the bank will quote a rate for the krona under a forward exchange option agreement. This will give the company the choice of when to obtain the currency at any time between 2 months and 3 months from the date of agreeing the contract - here, at any time between 1 June and 1 July.

The forward rate will be *either* the 2 month forward rate or the 3 month forward rate, whichever is more beneficial for the bank.

	2 month rate	3 month rate
Spot	9.90	9.90
Premium	$1\frac{1}{4}$	15
Forward rate	9.8875	9.8825

The bank is selling krona, and so the lower of these rates will be used.

Cost 200,000 ÷ 9.8825 = £20,237.79.

23 The company is buying francs (in order to pay the French supplier) and so the bank is selling. Forward rates are at a discount to spot rates, and discounts must be added.

	French francs
Spot	9.2225
1 month discount	0.0450
1 month forward rate	9.2675

Cost to the company = 35,000 francs ÷ 9.2675 = £3,776.64

24 The company is selling DM, and so the bank is buying. Forward rates are at a premium to spot rates, and premiums should be deducted.

	DM
Spot rate	2.74
2 months' forward premium	0.03
2 months' forward rate	2.71

Income to the company = DM 120,000 ÷ 2.71 = £44,280.44

Question

25

The expected receipts of $50,000 can be used to make some of the $80,000 payment, leaving the company exposed for a payment of $30,000. This exposure can be covered by means of a forward exchange contract to buy $30,000 from a bank in 3 months time. The cost will be

$$\frac{\$30,000}{\$(1.5640 - 0.0262)} = \frac{\$30,000}{\$1.5378} = £19,508.39$$

26

	£
Borrow $500,000 now	
Convert into sterling at $1.64 (bank buys $)	304,878.04
Forward cover needed for the interest	
of 7.5% of $500,000 = $37,500	
Forward rate $1.5790	(23,749.21)
Net proceeds	281,128.84

27

	£
Cost of $500,000, 1 year forward	
(÷ $1.5790) = £316,656.11	
Borrow now	316,656.11
Interest cost (11%)	(34,832.17)
Net proceeds	281,823.94

28

1 February
Forward contract to sell $40,000 (bank buys) at $1.6260 + 0.0155 = $1.6415

1 August
The bank will sell $10,000 to the company at $1.6630 to allow it to meet its forward exchange contract obligations. This is called a (partial) close out of the original contract.

	£
Received from forward contract ($40,000 ÷ 1.6415)	24,367.96
Cost of buying $10,000 (÷ 1.6630)	(6,013.23)
Net receipts	18,354.73

29

	$
Borrow now £500,000 x 1.5255	762,750
(These dollars can be sold to the bank for £500,000)	
Interest for 1 year (8%)	61,020
Dollars needed in 1 year's time	823,770
Forward rate in one year's time	$1.5235 - 0.095 = $1.4285
(Company buys $, bank sells)	
Sterling cost	£576,668

(*Note:* the total cost of interest + forward cover on the loan of £500,000 will be 15.3%).

Question

30

Policy 1
Paraguay's currency, the guarani, is closely tied to the US dollar, and so a manufacturing company can match its US dollar income against expenditures in guarani, and reduce foreign exchange exposure. As long as labour costs etc are cheaper in Paraguay than the USA, this could be a preferable policy to setting up a manufacturing facility in the USA itself. (Other currencies fixed against the US dollar are the Canadian dollar, the Saudi Arabian riyal, Bahraini dinar and (perhaps even beyond 1997) the Hong Kong dollar. Some other currencies such as the Singapore dollar and South Korean won are more loosely tied to the value of the US dollar).

Policy 2
The Deutschemark and the Italian lira are in another currency bloc - both are in the Exchange Rate Mechanism of the European Monetary System. Unless there is a major realignment of currencies within the EMS, the DM-lira rate will be fairly fixed over time, and so a company can benefit by borrowing in DM at a lower interest rate, converting lira receivables into DM to meet interest payments, and still enjoy good cover against exchange rate exposure.

31

Approximate cost of 3 months forward cover (annualised rate)

$$= \frac{0.0225 \times 12 \times 100}{3 \times (1.5425 - 0.0225)} = \frac{27}{4.56}$$

$$= 5.9\%$$

Total cost of borrowing in US dollars, as an approximate percentage, would be $8\frac{1}{2}\%$ + 5.9% = 14.4% pa. This is cheaper than borrowing in sterling at 15%.

32

Covered interest arbitrage activities refer to investing in a foreign currency and *covering* forward the eventual proceeds, in order to make more money than by investing in domestic currency.

Here, suppose an investor in Germany has DM1,000 and decides to invest in US dollars to earn a higher interest rate.

	In Germany		In USA
Now	DM 1,000	at 2DM - $1 →	US $500
Interest earned in 3 months	(1.25%) 12.5		(1.75%) 8.75
Earned by investing in DM	1,012.5		$508.75
Convert back to DM at forward rate of (2DM - 0.005 =)			1.995 DM
Earned by investing in US dollars			DM 1,014.960

Continued...

Question

The German investor can make profits by investing in US dollars and covering his exposure in the forward exchange market. For equilibrium to be restored, (1) German interest rates must increase or US interest rates fall, *reducing the interest rate differential* and/or (2) the forward premium for the DM must *increase* so that the forward rate for the DM against the $ declines.

33 The option premium makes foreign currency options quite expensive, and could therefore be unsuitable for any company trading on narrow profit margins. Options are often used by companies faced with (1) a currency exposure that might not arise at all or (2) where the amount of the total receipt or payment is uncertain.

Option premium = 240 x 1.2% = 2.88 yen
Worst case   = 240 - 2.88 = 237.12 yen

If the spot rate in 6 months time is 245, the company will allow the option to lapse, and buy yen at the spot rate; its all-in cost would be 245-2.88 option premium = 242.12 yen to £1.

34 (1) Forward exchange rate to buy $450,000 (bank sells) = $1.6764
Cost to the company of forward exchange cover = $450,000 ÷ 1.6764 = £268,432

(2) Using the money markets, the company would need to invest ($450,000 ÷ 1.05) $428,571.42 now to obtain $450,000 in six months time to make the payment.

To buy $428,571.42 now would cost (÷ 1.7000) £252,100.83 at the spot rate. The cost of borrowing this amount in sterling to buy and invest US dollars would be (£252,100.83 x 1.075) - £271,008.

	£
Cost of forward exchange cover	262,432
Cost of cover through money markets	271,008
Difference in cost	8,576

35 (a) Each option is for £12,500 x 1.80 = $22,500
The company would need $450,000 and so would have to buy ($450,000 ÷ $22,500) = 20 currency options.

(b) Put options on sterling are required, because sterling is to be sold in exchange for dollars.
The cost of the options is 20 x 12,500 x 9.3 cents = $23,250

(c) In June, since the spot rate is $1.67, the company would exercise the options at $1.80. The $450,000 would cost (÷ 1.80) £250,000.

The cost of the options, £23,250 would cost (÷ 1.67) £13,922 in sterling.

Total cost £250,000 + £13,922 = £263,922.

10: MARKING SCHEDULE

Question	Correct answer	Marks for the correct answer	Question	Correct answer	Marks for the correct answer
1	D	1	11	D	1
2	D	1	12	A	1
3	B	1	13	C	2
4	B	1	14	B	1
5	C	1	15	A	1
6	D	1	16	D	1
7	C	1	17	D	1
8	D	1	18	A	1
9	C	1	19	D	1
10	A	1			

YOUR MARKS

Total marks available   **20**   Your total mark   [   ]

GUIDELINES - If your mark was:

0 - 7   Disappointing. You should be able to do better than this.

8 - 11   Fair. Check your errors and assess what you are getting wrong.

12 - 16   Good, especially if you do not need to know Stock Exchange rules or the City Code.

16 - 20   Very good mark. You know enough to tackle the more subjective aspects of mergers, takeovers and reconstructions with confidence.

COMMENTS

Question

1

Combined earnings post merger £7.2 million x 110% = £7.92 million

Total value of enlarged company (£7.92m x 11)	£87.12m
Value per share (÷ 32 million shares)	£2.7225

	£ million
Value of shares held by former Y shareholders (x 12 million shares)	32.67
Value of Y shares pre-merger (£2.2m x P/E of 12)	26.40
Gain for former Y shareholders	6.27

2

	£
Profits after tax of RS Ltd	200,000
Tax (50%)	200,000
Profits before tax	400,000
Depreciation	50,000
Savings	80,000
Profits before depreciation, after the takeover	530,000
Less tax (£200,000 + (50% of £80,000))	240,000
Cash flows: cash profits less tax	290,000
Discount factor at 20% of £1 pa, years 1-10	4.19

Valuation of RS Ltd's shares £1,215,100 minus PV of capital expenditures (£150,000) = £1,065,100, say £1,065,000.

3

Asset valuations for the balance sheet do not affect EPS. Selling off parts of the acquired business (answer C) is a fairly common method of achieving EPS growth in spite of a high purchase price. Buying the target company's shares for cash (answer D) will improve the buying company's EPS provided that the increase in profits before interest as a result of the takeover exceeds the interest cost of a loan used to raise the cash for buying the Gumm shares.

4

The owners could obtain £4.5 million by selling off the assets individually, and since this is the most they can get other than from selling the company to the potential buyer, it is the *minimum* price they should demand. The *maximum* the *buyer* should pay is £5 million, which is what it would cost him to set up a similar business from scratch.

Question

5

Combined earnings	£1,100,000
P/E ratio of new company	20

	£
Total MV of new company's equity	22,000,000
Current MV of Polo (800,000 x 21)	16,800,000
Maximum price to pay for Marco	5,200,000

A price of £5.2 million would leave Polo's shareholders no better and no worse off as a result of the takeover.

6

Let the volume of extra sales be X

(1) *Rights issue* at 75% of (20p x 16) = £2.40 per share. To raise £6,000,000, an extra 2,500,000 shares must be issued, giving 12.5 million shares in total.

$$\text{EPS would be } \frac{\text{£2,000,000 - £400,000 + 0.4X}}{12.5 \text{ million}}$$

(2) *Issue of £6 million of 10% debt*

$$\text{EPS would be } \frac{\text{£2,000,000 - £400,000 - £600,000 + 0.4X}}{10.0 \text{ million}}$$

These will give the same EPS (and given the same P/E ratio, the same share price too) when they are equal. This is where:

$$\frac{\text{£1,600,000 + 0.4X}}{12.5} = \frac{\text{£1,000,000 + 0.4X}}{10.0}$$

$$X = \text{£3,500,000}$$

7

	£
Expected profits in year 1, Nara plc	
Previous year's profits	750,000
10% growth in year 1	75,000
Saving in MD's salary, less tax (65% of £50,000)	32,500
	857,500

We can use the growth model for a DCF valuation since growth in profits is expected to be 10% pa.

$$MV = \frac{\text{£857,500}}{(r - g)}$$

$$= \frac{\text{£857,500}}{(0.20 - 0.10)} = \text{£8,575,000}$$

Question

8	Earnings in year 1 (as in previous solution)	£857,500
	P/E ratio - maximum	12
	Purchase price - maximum	£10,290,000

9		£
	Fixed assets	600,000
	Stocks and WIP	580,000
	Debtors, 98% of £396,000 x (100 ÷ 99)	392,000
	Bank balances	20,000
	Bank overdraft and trade creditors	(540,000)
		1,052,000

10 On the basis of the data, the minimum price acceptable to Dickson Ltd's shareholders is the opportunity cost of not realising the assets piecemeal - its net realisable value.

The price that Mace plc might be willing to pay is up to £200,000 ÷ 15% = £1,333,333, but this is not the question. The value to Dickson Ltd's shareholders of an annual earnings stream of £200,000 cannot be evaluated unless we can estimate their opportunity cost of capital (or 'marginal rate of time preference') which we do not know, but which is likely to exceed 15% because of Dickson Ltd's private company status.

11 Takeover bids are referred to the Monopolies and Mergers commission by the Office of Fair Trading and/or the Department of Trade and Industry, not by companies themselves.

From September 1990, new merger control regulations for the European Community as a whole come into effect, with the EC taking on some of the responsibilities that were previously with the MMC.

| **12** | Profits of merged company (£3m + £1m + £400,000) | £4,400,000 |
| | Number of shares (6 million + ½ of 8 million) | 10,000,000 |

	£
EPS in merged company	0.44
Existing EPS for Scratch plc	0.50
Dilution in EPS	0.06

257

Question

13

Let the number of new shares in Scratch issued to shareholders of Tickel be x and let the amount of loan capital issued be y. For the EPS in Scratch to remain at £0.50:

Earnings $\dfrac{£4,400,000 - (70\% \text{ of } 10\% \text{ of } y)}{(6,000,000 + x)} = 0.50$

	£1,400,000	$= 0.5x + 0.07y$.... (1)
Purchase price	£18,500,000	$= 5x + y$.... (2)
Multiply (1) by 10	£14,000,000	$= 5x + 0.7y$.... (3)
Subtract (3) from (2)	£4,500,000	$= 0.3y$
	y	$= £15,000,000$

(*Note:* $5x + y = £18,500,000$ and so $x = 700,000$. Shareholders in Tickel would receive £15,000,000 in 10% loan stock and 700,000 shares in Scratch.

Annual earnings	£4,400,000 - 70% of 10% of £15 million)	£3,350,000
Shares in issue		6,700,000
EPS		50p).

14

This obligation to extend comparable offers to all the other shareholders is called the 'mandatory offer'.

A formal offer cannot be made *unconditional*, however, without the offeror acquiring or agreeing to acquire shares carrying more than 50% of the voting rights.

15

An acquisition is a Class 1 transaction where a comparison on *any one* of the following bases amounts to 15% or more.

		In this case
(1)	Value of assets acquired as % of assets of acquiring company	$15 \div 120 = 12.5\%$
(2)	Net profits, as % of net profits of acquiring company	$3 \div 10 = 30\%$
(3)	Consideration given, as % of assets of acquiring company	$25 \div 120 = 20.8\%$
(4)	Equity capital issued as consideration, as % of equity previously in issue	$5 \div 50 = 10\%$

For Class 1 transactions, an announcement must be made to the Company Announcements Office and the press, *and also* either listing particulars must be published or a circular must be sent to shareholders.

Question

16 Pension funds, insurance companies and unit trusts are all institutional shareholders, who are known to hold 52.9% of the shares. Nominees could hold shares on behalf of institutional investors, commercial companies or individuals and so an exact calculation is not possible. Under Section 212 of the Companies Act 1985, the company can write to nominee shareholders and ask them to reveal on whose behalf they hold shares. This is a course of action - to obtain information - that the directors will probably take in their defence against the takeover bid.

17 Cost of repurchases 10 million x 300p = £30,000,000

	£	£
Earnings if no share repurchases		25,000,000
Interest forgone (£30 million x 11%)	3,300,000	
less tax (35%)	1,155,000	
		2,145,000
Earnings after share repurchases		22,855,000
Number of shares		70,000,000
EPS		32.65p
New P/E ratio		9.4
Share price		307p

18

	£000
On liquidation	
1. Proceeds from freehold	120
less 1st charge - debenture holders	100
	20
less 2nd charge - bank	100
Bank is unsecured creditor for	(80)
2. Proceeds from plant, stocks and debtors	125
less liquidation costs	15
	110
less preferential debts	10
Available for unsecured creditors	100

Unsecured creditors would get $\dfrac{100}{80 + 120}$ = 50p in the £1

The bank would get £20,000 + (50p/£1 x £80,000) = £60,000.

Question

19 The loan stock holders at the end of year 3 would opt to realise the company's assets by putting it into liquidation *unless* their share of the equity (5 + 15 = $\frac{1}{3}$) exceeds £3 million on a going concern basis.

Probability	Realisable value	Going concern value	On conversion, stockholders share of going concern value	Liquidate or convert?	Value to stock holders	EV
	£m	£m	£m		£m	£m
0.2	2	2	($\frac{1}{3}$) 1	Liquidate	2	0.4
0.4	4	6	($\frac{1}{3}$) 2	Liquidate	3	1.2
0.4	10	15	($\frac{1}{3}$) 5	Convert	5	2.0
						3.6

EV of convertible loan stock = £3.6 million

Further information

The Password series includes the following titles:

Order code

Economics	P01X	EC
Basic accounting	P028	BA
Financial accounting	P036	FA
Costing	P044	CO
Foundation business mathematics	P052	FB
Business law	P060	BL
Auditing	P079	AU
Organisation and management	P087	OM
Advanced business mathematics	P095	AB
Taxation	P109	TX
Management accounting	P117	MA
Interpretation of accounts	P125	IA
Financial management	P133	FM
Company law	P141	CL
Information technology	P15X	IT

Password is available from most major bookshops. If you have any difficulty obtaining them, please contact BPP directly, quoting the above order codes.

BPP Publishing Limited
Aldine House
Aldine Place
London W12 8AW

Tel: 081-740 1111
Fax: 081-740 1184
Telex: 265871 (MONREF G) - quoting '76:SJJ098'

261

CONTENTS

iii

iv